The book presents an edition of seventeen *ad status* model sermons for the preaching of the crusades from the thirteenth and early fourteenth centuries, by James of Vitry, Eudes of Châteauroux, Gilbert of Tournai, Humbert of Romans and Bertrand de la Tour.

Most of these texts have never been printed before. They are unique sources for the content of crusade propaganda in the later middle ages, giving a rare insight into the way in which propaganda shaped the public's view of crusading during that period. Accompanying the Latin texts is an English translation which is aimed at making these sources accessible to a wider circle of students and scholars.

The first part of the book consists of a study of the sermons which focuses on their place in the pastoral reform movement of the thirteenth century, their specific character as models for the use of crusade propagandists, their internal structure and the image of the crusade conveyed in the texts.

CHRISTOPH T. MAIER teaches medieval history at the University of Zurich. His book *Preaching the Crusades: Mendicant Friars and the Cross in the Thirteenth Century* was published by Cambridge University Press in 1994 (paperback edition 1998).

CRUSADE
PROPAGANDA
AND
IDEOLOGY

MODEL SERMONS
FOR THE
PREACHING OF THE CROSS

CHRISTOPH T. MAIER

CAMBRIDGE
UNIVERSITY PRESS

PUBLISHED BY THE PRESS SYNDICATE OF THE UNIVERSITY OF CAMBRIDGE
The Pitt Building, Trumpington Street, Cambridge CB2 1RP, United Kingdom

CAMBRIDGE UNIVERSITY PRESS
The Edinburgh Building, Cambridge CB2 2RU, UK   http://www.cup.cam.ac.uk
40 West 20th Street, New York, NY 10011–4211, USA   http://www.cup.org
10 Stamford Road, Oakleigh, Melbourne 3166, Australia

First published 2000

Printed in the United Kingdom at the University Press, Cambridge

Typeset in 10/12pt Stempel Garamond . [CE]

A catalogue record for this book is available from the British Library

Library of Congress cataloguing in publication data

Maier, Christoph T.
Crusade propaganda and ideology: model sermons for the preaching of the cross /
Christoph T. Maier.
p. cm.
Includes bibliographical references and index.
ISBN 0 521 59061 2
1. Crusades – propaganda.   2. Crusades Sermons.   I. Title.
D159.M35   2000
909.07–dc21   99–24432   CIP

ISBN 0 521 59061 2 hardback

CONTENTS

v

ACKNOWLEDGEMENTS

During my PhD viva in 1990, one of the examiners expressed his hope for an edition and study of the manuscript crusade sermons listed at the back of my thesis, and subsequently also in its published version which appeared with Cambridge University Press in 1994 as *Preaching the Crusades: Mendicant Friars and the Cross in the Thirteenth Century*. I am grateful to the Press, and in particular to William Davies, for having offered me the chance to follow up this examiner's suggestion, and my own wish, to make these largely unknown sermon texts available in print. I decided to include an English translation alongside the Latin text, so as to avoid the frustrating experience reported to me by a French scholar, who once was told that it was all very well editing Latin sermons, but that it was somewhat futile because so few people made the effort to read such texts in the original. I am convinced that publishing these sermons in Latin with an English translation corresponds to the needs of students and scholars alike, who will find in these texts important sources for the history of the crusades and medieval preaching.

There are a number of people who have assisted me with various aspects of this publication, each in their own way. In particular, I should like to thank Nicole Bériou, Jessalynn Bird, Alexis Charansonnet, David d'Avray, Michele Ferrari, Jean Longère and Simon Tugwell. All of them took time to discuss different points of my work and helped me out in moments when I was stuck. Many of them also gave me more than generous access to their unpublished material or wrote long informative letters to answer my queries, offering assistance far beyond the call of duty. I should also like to thank Jean Field for having performed such a thorough and thoughtful job in copy-editing this book. My greatest thanks, however, once more go to Cathy Aitken, whose critical mind and strict sense of style, exercised in many patient hours of reading and discussing my text, allowed me to bring this project to fruition.

ABBREVIATIONS

CCCM   *Corpus Christianorum Continuatio Mediaevalis* [in progress] (Turnhout, 1970ff).

CCSL   *Corpus Christianorum Series Latina* [in progress] (Turnhout, 1954ff).

CGBP   *Catalogue général des manuscrits des bibliothèques publiques de France (B. Départements)* [in progress] (Paris, 1886ff).

Crane   *The Exempla or Illustrative Stories from the Sermones Vulgares of Jacques de Vitry*, ed. T. F. Crane (London, 1890).

CSEL   *Corpus Scriptorum Ecclesiasticorum Latinorum* [in progress] (Vienna, 1866ff).

Hesbert   *Corpus Antiphonalium Officii*, ed. R.-J. Hesbert, 6 vols. (Rerum Ecclesiasticarum Documenta, series maior 7–12; Rome, 1963–79).

MGHSS   *Monumenta Germaniae Historica. Scriptores* [in progress] (Hanover, 1826ff).

PG   *Patrologiae Cursus Completus. Series Graeca,* 161 vols. (Paris, 1857–1945).

PL   *Patrologiae Cursus Completus. Series Latina,* 221 vols. (Paris, 1844–1963).

Schneyer   J. B. Schneyer, *Repertorium der lateinischen Sermones des Mittelalters für die Zeit von 1150–1350*, 11 vols. (Beiträge zur Geschichte der Philosophie und Theologie des Mittelalters 43; Munich, 1969–90).

Tubach   F. C. Tubach, *Index Exemplorum. A Handbook of Medieval Religious Tales* (FF Communications 204; Helsinki, 1969).

Walther   *Proverbia, Sententiaeque Latinitatis Medii Aevi,* ed. H. Walther, 9 vols. (Carmina medii aevi posterioris Latina 2; Göttingen, 1963–86).

Part I

I

THE AUTHORS, THE SERMONS
AND THEIR CONTEXT

ROM THE TWELFTH CENTURY onwards, sermons concerning the crusade were preached on many different occasions. In the thirteenth century alone, crusades were fought against Muslims in Spain, Africa, the Holy Land and Apulia, the Mongols, non-Christian peoples in the Baltic, heretics in Languedoc, Germany, Italy and the Balkans, Orthodox Christians in Greece and the Hohenstaufen rulers and their supporters in Italy and Germany. These crusades were usually announced by sermons. Propagandists preached in order to recruit participants and collect money for the crusade. Sermons also marked the departure of a crusader or a crusade army. During the campaigns, the clergy accompanying the crusade armies regularly preached sermons in order to sustain the participants' enthusiasm or to give them courage on the eve of a battle or in moments of crisis. Last but not least, sermons concerning the crusade were also preached to those at home in the context of penitentiary processions and prayers in support of crusaders in the field. Indeed, the number of different types of crusade sermons preached at various times in late medieval Europe must have been immense.[1]

Despite this, we are not particularly well informed about what exactly crusade preachers said in their sermons. As with sermons generally, crusade sermons were not the stuff of medieval chronicles or of other narrative accounts of the period. Although these sometimes mention that crusade sermons were preached, they seldom give details about their

---

[1] For a general survey of post-1200 crusading see J. Riley-Smith, *The Crusades. A Short History* (London, 1987), 119–78, 221–54. For crusade propaganda see P. J. Cole, *The Preaching of the Crusades to the Holy Land, 1095–1270* (Medieval Academy Books 98; Cambridge, Mass., 1991). Also C. T. Maier *Preaching the Crusades. Mendicant Friars and the Cross in the Thirteenth Century* (Cambridge Studies in Medieval Life and Thought 28; Cambridge, 1994 and 1998).

content. Most of our evidence for crusade preaching comes from manuscript sermon texts preserved in some of the many surviving sermon collections of the middle ages. But even here crusade sermons are few and far between. The main reason for this is that the majority of collections were arranged by liturgical dates to suit the requirements of clerics who had to preach regularly on Sundays and feastdays throughout the year. Even if there were preferred times for preaching the crusade, such as Lent or the feastdays of the cross, crusade sermons did not belong to specific liturgical dates. On the contrary, preachers had to be prepared to preach crusade sermons at any time of the year.[2]

The sermon collections which include most crusade sermons are those (few) in which the sermon texts were not arranged by liturgical themes or the dates of the church year. These are collections of memorable sermons by individual preachers and the so-called *ad status* sermon collections which presented model sermons addressing specific social groups. The large majority of crusade sermon texts in fact come from the *ad status* collections and it is with these that this book is concerned. All in all, there are only a handful of medieval *ad status* sermon collections.[3] The first rudimentary collections of this type, written in the late twelfth century by Honorius of Autun and Alain of Lille, do not contain any crusade sermon texts. In the first half of the thirteenth century, James of Vitry for the first time prepared a comprehensive collection of *ad status* model sermons addressing a great variety of social groups, which included two models written for preaching to 'those who are or will become crusaders' (*ad crucesignatos vel crucesignandos*). The other two great *ad status* collections of the thirteenth century by Gilbert of Tournai and Humbert of Romans also feature several crusade sermon texts, as does the little known *ad status* collection by Bertrand de la Tour written at the beginning of the fourteenth century. Also included in this book are some of the crusade sermon texts by Eudes of Châteauroux which are presented as *ad status* model sermons in a mixed collection of sermon texts composed for feastdays and other special occasions.

The five authors whose *ad status* crusade model sermons are presented here all occupied a prominent place in the pastoral reform movement which originated at the University of Paris in the circle of Peter the Chanter around the year 1200 and which, in the course of the following

---

[2] Maier, *Preaching the Crusades*, 111–22.

[3] D. d'Avray and M. Tausche, 'Marriage Sermons in *ad status* Collections of the Central Middle Ages', *Archives d'histoire doctrinale et littéraire du moyen âge*, 55 (1981), 71–119, here pp. 71–5.

century, swept through many of the schools and universities in France and elsewhere.[4] The pastoral reform movement was born out of a desire to reform the religious life of the laity by making the word of God more directly relevant to people generally, and to apply moral theology as it was studied in the academic circles of the schools to society at large. The issues that were addressed extended from matters concerning large sections of society, such as basic religious instruction, the teaching of penance or canon law regulations concerning marriage, to topics of concern to particular groups, such as war, government, the execution of justice or money lending. Although academic in origin, the reform movement aimed primarily to disseminate the teachings of moral theology outside the schools. Since the Church, as the guardian of orthodoxy, considered itself responsible for spreading the word of God, it was the clergy that was expected to communicate the ideas of the reformers to wider circles of society. This was a formidable task for which large sections of the clergy were unprepared, falling far short of the educational and moral standards expected by the reformers. As a consequence, the initial thrust of the reforms was directed towards improving the theological training and pastoral work of the clergy. This triggered the production in the schools and universities of didactic writings, usually called *pastoralia*, which were aimed at instructing the clergy in the basic elements of theology, doctrine and pastoral duties.[5]

For communicating with society at large, the main medium of the pastoral reform movement were sermons. Thus, the preaching reforms of the thirteenth century formed an integral part of the more general pastoral reform movement.[6] In Paris, many in the circle of Peter the

[4] J. W. Baldwin, *Masters, Princes and Merchants. The Social Views of Peter the Chanter and his Circle*, 2 vols. (Princeton, 1970). F. Morenzoni, *Des écoles aux paroisses. Thomas de Chobham et la promotion de la prédication au début du XIIIe siècle* (Collection des Etudes Augustiniennes. Série moyen-âge et temps modernes 30; Paris, 1995), 67–95.

[5] L. E. Boyle, 'The Inter-Conciliar Period 1179–1215 and the Beginnings of Pastoral Manuals', *Miscellanea Rolando Bandinelli Papa Alessandro III*, ed. F. Liotta (Siena, 1986), 43–56. Boyle, 'Robert Grosseteste and the Pastoral Care', *Proceedings of the Southeastern Institute of Medieval and Renaissance Studies, Summer 1976*, ed. D. B. J. Randall (Medieval and Renaissance Series 8; Durham, N.C., 1979), 3–51. Morenzoni, *Des écoles aux paroisses*, 172–87.

[6] For the preaching reform see J. Longère, *La prédication médiévale* (Paris, 1983), 78–126. D. L. d'Avray, *The Preaching of the Friars. Sermons Diffused from Paris before 1300* (Oxford, 1985). Morenzoni, *Des écoles aux paroisses*, 25–66. A. Forni, 'La "nouvelle prédication" des disciples de Foulques de Neuilly: intentions, techniques et réactions', *Faire croire: modalités de la diffusion et de la réception des messages religieux du XIIe au XVe siècle* (Collection de l'Ecole Française de Rome 51; Rome, 1981), 19–37. R. Rusconi, 'De la prédication à la confession: transmission et contrôle de modèles de comportement au XIIIe siècle', *Faire croire: modalités de*

Chanter were famous preachers and prolific writers of preaching aids. Accompanying the efforts at the university, diocesan synods, from the beginning of the thirteenth century, promoted regular preaching throughout the bishoprics on Sundays and the main feastdays of the liturgical calendar.[7] In 1215, the Fourth Lateran Council demanded that initiatives be taken throughout Christendom to appoint preachers in each diocese to support the bishop in spreading the word of God.[8] These preachers were to be carefully chosen for their ability to preach well and to instruct people by word and deed.

In order to achieve the establishment of regular preaching throughout Christendom, it was necessary to educate and train a sufficient number of preachers. One of the principal means of doing so was the systematic production and dissemination of preaching aids for the instruction of preachers and as reference material for trained preachers. Throughout the thirteenth century, more and more preaching aids appeared: from handbooks of theology, such as *distinctiones* and *florilegia* and various types of *summae*, to treatises of preaching, the *artes praedicandi*, and collections of model sermons and *exempla*.[9] These all provided inspiration and material for the large number of sermons that preachers were expected to address to the laity throughout the liturgical year.

In many ways the most useful of these preaching aids were the collections of ready-made model sermons. The vast majority of model collections were, for practical reasons, arranged by liturgical dates: collections of *sermones de tempore* or *dominicales* listed models for sermons to be preached on Sundays; *sermones de sanctis* or *de communi sanctorum* offered examples for sermons on saint's days. Judging by the number written between 1150 and 1350, such collections must have been

---

la diffusion et de la réception des messages religieux du XIIe au XVe siècle (Collection de l'Ecole Française de Rome 51; Rome, 1981), 67–85. L.-J. Bataillon, 'Early Scholastic and Mendicant Preaching as Exegesis of Scripture', *Ad Litteram. Authoritative Texts and their Medieval Readers*, ed. M. D. Jordan and K. Emery, Jr. (Notre Dame Conferences in Medieval Studies 3; Notre Dame, 1992), 165–98.

[7] J. Longère, 'La prédication et l'instruction des fidèles selon les conciles et les status synodaux depuis l'antiquité tardive et jusqu'au Concile de Trente', *Colloque sur l'histoire de la Sécurité Sociale. Actes du 109e Congrès Nationale des Sociétés Savantes, Dijon 1984*, vol. I (Paris, 1985), 390–418, here pp. 401. Morenzoni, *Des écoles aux paroisse*, 163–71.

[8] *Conciliorum oecumenicorum decreta*, ed. J. Alberigo, P.-P. Ioannou, C. Leonardi et al. (Basle, 1962), 215–16.

[9] D'Avray, *The Preaching of the Friars*, 64–90. L.-J. Bataillon, 'Les instruments de travail des prédicateurs au XIIIe siècle', *Culture et travail intellectuel dans l'Occident médiévale* (Paris, 1981), 197–209. M. G. Briscoe and B. H. Jaye, *Artes Praedicandi, Artes Orandi* (Typologie des sources du moyen âge occidental 64; Turnhout, 1992), 9–76. Morenzoni, *Des écoles aux paroisses*, 189–240.

the mainstay of many preachers in the late middle ages.[10] The *ad status* sermon collections, from which the majority of our crusade model sermons come, are rare in comparison.[11] This is because an *ad status* collection was, in practical terms, not so useful to most preachers since most preaching addressed mixed church communities rather than homogenous social groups. Nevertheless, the *ad status* collections were a typical product of the pastoral reform movement. These systematic collections of model sermons to different social groups reflected the concern of the reformists to tailor moral theology to various different kinds of people and to all aspects of human behaviour.

Although the instigators, and also many later supporters, of the preaching movement of the thirteenth century were secular clerics, the arrival of the two big mendicant orders of the Franciscans and Dominicans accounted for the reform movement's strength and success.[12] These two orders of mendicant friars came into existence at about the time when the reform movement began to gather momentum. Both orders made preaching to the laity their principal business and they founded schools, trained preachers and encouraged the production of preaching aids.[13] Early on the two orders prominently established themselves at the University of Paris and developed close links with the secular reformist circles. In a certain sense, the Franciscan and Dominican orders were as much a product of the reformist tendencies of the thirteenth century as they were the main motors of pastoral reform.

The spectacular success and the rapid growth of the mendicant orders throughout Europe enabled them to build up an infrastructure which provided the medium of the sermon with channels for effective broadcasting and wide dissemination. It was ultimately because of the activities of the Franciscan and Dominican friars that preaching came to be the nearest that the middle ages had to a mass medium.[14] This was also one of the main reasons why the mendicant orders became so heavily involved in the organisation of the crusades. One of the major problems affecting the crusade movement at the beginning of the thirteenth

---

[10] J. B. Schneyer, *Repertorium der lateinischen Sermones des Mittelalters für die Zeit von 1150–1350*, 11 vols. (Beiträge zur Geschichte der Philosophie und Theologie des Mittelalters 43; Munich, 1969–90).

[11] D'Avray and Tausche, 'Marriage Sermons', 71–5.

[12] D'Avray, *The Preaching of the Friars*.

[13] D. Berg, *Armut und Wissenschaft. Beiträge zur Geschichte des Studienwesens der Bettelorden im 13. Jahrhundert* (Bochumer Historische Studien 15; Düsseldorf, 1977). J.-P. Renard, *La formation et la désignation des Predicateurs au début de l'ordre de Prêcheurs 1215–1237* (Fribourg, 1977).

[14] G. Steier, 'Bettelorden-Predigt als Massenmedium', *Literarische Interessensbildung im Mittelalter. DFG-Symposion 1991*, ed. J. Heinzle (Germanistische-Symposien-Berichtsbände 14; Stuttgart, 1993), 314–36.

century was the lack of an effective propaganda structure. With the movement growing and moving into new theatres of war against heretics, non-Christian peoples in the Baltic and political enemies of the papacy, crusade propaganda undertaken by individually commissioned preachers and the resident secular clergy had become desperately inadequate. The building up of an effective propaganda machinery for the crusades was only possible with the help of the many well-trained Franciscan and Dominican preachers and thanks to the hierarchic structure of the two orders which allowed them to spread information quickly and effectively over large geographical areas. Their efforts made it possible for the papacy to control crusade propaganda and carefully allocate the resources of people and money for the many crusades organised in Europe throughout the thirteenth century.[15]

The universities and the pastoral reform movement of the thirteenth century, the propagation of preaching and the mendicant orders, the propaganda for the crusades – this was the world from which our five authors came and it was the world for which they wrote. With the exception of Bertrand de la Tour, whose academic career was divided between Paris and Toulouse, all the authors spent a considerable time in the reformist climate of the University of Paris, first as students and later as teachers; Eudes of Châteauroux even served as the university's chancellor for six years. All the authors were prolific writers of preaching aids and their sermon collections ranked among the most popular ones of their time and, indeed, of the entire later middle ages. Three of the five authors were mendicant friars, with two of them serving as heads of their respective orders. And finally, all but one of our authors can be shown to have played an important active role in propagating the crusades.

James of Vitry, the oldest of the five authors, was born sometime between 1160 and 1170.[16] As a young man, he studied and later became a master at the University of Paris, which he left shortly before 1210. During this time, James came under the direct influence of Peter the Chanter and was thus closely connected with the beginnings of the Paris reform movement.[17] In 1213, by then a canon of St Nicolas at Oignies, James preached the crusade against the Albigensian heretics in France and Lotharingia; after that he became a propagandist for the Fifth

---

[15] Maier, *Preaching the Crusades*.

[16] For James's biography see the brief sketch with further references in Hinnebusch's introduction to Iacobus de Vitriaco *Historia Occidentalis* (Spicilegium Friburgense 17; Fribourg, 1972), 3–7. See also J. Longère, *Oeuvres oratoires des maitres parisiens au XIIe siècle*, 2 vols. (Paris, 1975), I, 31–3. A. Paravicini-Bagliani, *Cardinali di Curia e 'familiae' cardinalizie dal 1227 al 1254*, 2 vols. (Italia Sacra 18, 19; Padua, 1972), I, 99–109.

[17] Baldwin, *Masters, Princes and Merchants*, 36–9.

Crusade. Having been elected bishop of Acre, James accompanied the army of the Fifth Crusade to Damietta. He returned to Europe in 1225 and was made cardinal bishop of Tusculum in 1229.

During this last period of his life, between his return from the East and his death in 1240, James of Vitry spent a good part of his time writing sermon literature and a number of historical works.[18] He composed a comprehensive series of sermon collections comprising the four classical types: *sermones de tempore, sermones de sanctis, sermones de communi sanctorum*, and *sermones vulgares* or *ad status*.[19] As mentioned above, it is the *sermones vulgares*, the first full-scale *ad status* collection, which contain James's two crusade model sermons.

Like James of Vitry, **Eudes of Châteauroux** was a particularly gifted and successful preacher. Throughout his career, first as an academic at the University of Paris and then as a cardinal, preaching was one of the focal points of Eudes's activities. Born probably around 1190, he was a student at Paris from around 1210. He became a master there at some time before 1229 and his academic career was crowned by his election as chancellor of the university, a post which he held between 1238 and 1244.[20] As the successor to James of Vitry, Eudes was appointed cardinal bishop of Tusculum in 1244, a position which he held until his death in 1273.

Eudes of Châteauroux personally preached the crusades against the Albigensian heretics in 1226 and later also against the Mongols and the Muslims in the Holy Land; as cardinal, he masterminded the propaganda campaign for Louis IX's first crusade in France and later accompanied the French king on crusade to the East as papal legate.[21]

---

[18] Longère, *La prédication médiévale*, 88–9. J. Longère, 'Quatres sermons *ad religiosas* de Jacques de Vitry', *Les religieuses en France au XIIIe siècle*, ed. M. Parisse (Nancy, 1985), 215–300, here p. 217.

[19] Schneyer, III, 179–221. See also James's introduction to the *sermones vulgares* printed in *Analecta Novissima Spicilegii Solesmensis Altera Continuatio*, ed. J. B. Pitra, 2 vols. ([Paris], 1885, 1888), II, 193.

[20] For Eudes's career see F. Iozzelli, *Odo da Châteauroux. Politica e religione nei sermoni inediti* (Studi e Testi 14; Padua, 1994), 23–42. M.-M. Lebreton, 'Eudes de Châteauroux', *Dictionnaire de spiritualité*, IV, cols. 1675–78. Paravicini-Bagliani, *Cardinali di Curia*, I, 198–209. A. Charansonnet, 'Du Berry en Curie: la carrière du Cardinal Eudes de Châteauroux (1190?-1273) et son reflet dans sa prédication', *Territoires et spiritualité dans le bas-Berry au Moyen Age* (Châteauroux, 1999), [forthcoming].

[21] For the Albigensian crusade see N. Bériou, 'La prédication de croisade de Philippe le Chancelier et d'Eudes de Châteauroux en 1226', *La prédication en Pays d'Oc (XIIe-début XVe siècle)* (Cahiers de Fanjeaux 32; Toulouse 1997), 85–109, here pp. 91–2. Also C. T. Maier, 'Crisis, Liturgy and the Crusade in the Twelfth and Thirteenth Centuries', *Journal of Ecclesiastical History*, 48 (1997), 628–57, here pp. 640–54. The only evidence for Eudes's involvement in the preaching of the Mongol crusade is the references in his second model sermon, see Eudes II, 3, 4, 6.

After his return from the Levant, Eudes spent the majority of his time at the papal curia, where he pursued an active preaching career. Eudes edited and recorded many of the sermons preached in those years, including a series in which he commented on the progress of the Angevin crusade to southern Italy in the 1260s.[22] He was thus much more deeply involved in the crusade movement than any of the other authors of *ad status* crusade sermons.

Although Eudes of Châteauroux wrote a number of theological works, his main literary activity consisted in writing sermons. Indeed, Eudes was one of the most prolific sermon writers of the thirteenth century, having left some 1,100 manuscript sermons to posterity.[23] Drawing much of the material for his model sermons from his own preaching, he produced a full series of *de tempore* and *de sanctis* sermons and a mixed collection of *sermones de diversis casibus* and *de communi sanctorum*. It is his mixed collection that contains the five *ad status* crusade sermons. Eudes was also a meticulous editor of his own sermons. After the first compilation, which he finished some time before 1261, Eudes re-edited all his collections in the later 1260s, changing some and adding new sermons. It was only his death that prevented Eudes from completing a third edition in the early 1270s.[24]

Gilbert of Tournai, the most scholarly of our five authors, was born around 1200 and came to the University of Paris at an early age, where he was first a student and then became a master.[25] Around 1240 Gilbert resigned his academic duties in order to became a friar and he seems to have enjoyed a relatively quiet life as a member of the Franciscan house at Paris. There is a possibility that he joined Louis IX's first crusade to the Holy Land.[26] Whether or not he really did, as a member of the

For the Holy Land crusade see Maier, *Preaching the Crusades*, 61–4. P. Cole, D. L. d'Avray and J. Riley-Smith, 'Application of Theology to Current Affairs: Memorial Sermons for the Dead of Mansurah and on Innocent IV', *Historical Research*, 63 (1990), 227–47, here pp. 229–39.

[22] Iozzelli, *Odo da Châteauroux*. See also C. T. Maier, 'Crusade and Rhetoric against the Muslim Colony of Lucera: Eudes of Châteauroux's *Sermones de Rebellione Sarracenorum Lucherie in Apulia*', *Journal of Medieval History*, 21 (1995), 343–85.

[23] Schneyer, IV, 394–483. See also A. Charansonnet, 'L'évolution de la prédication du Cardinal Eudes de Châteauroux (1190?-1273): une approche statistique', *De l'homélie au sermon. Histoire de la prédication médiévale*, ed. J. Hamesse and X. Hermand (Publications de l'Institut d'Etudes Médiévales. Textes, Etudes, Congrès 14; Louvain, 1993), 103–42, here p. 104. Longère, *La prédication médiévale*, 92.

[24] Charansonnet, 'L'évolution', 114–16.

[25] For Gilbert's life and works see B. d'Amsterdam, 'Guibert de Tournai', *Dictionnaire de spiritualité*, VI, cols. 1139–46. L. Baudry, 'Wibert de Tournai', *Revue d'histoire franciscaine*, 5 (1928), 29–61.

[26] This is unclear and will probably remain an unsolved question. If Gilbert was indeed the author of the crusade chronicle *Hodoeporicon primae profectionis*

northern French province of the Franciscans it is likely that Gilbert would have been involved in the preaching of the cross for this crusade.[27] Around 1260 he again taught at the University of Paris for a short period, before once more resigning his chair in favour of a life which gave him more time for his literary activities.

Gilbert left a vast corpus of writings including treatises on education, historical and hagiographic works, theological and devotional literature, sermons and reformist tracts. Gilbert was a well-known and highly esteemed author in his time both inside and outside the Franciscan order; he wrote for King Louis IX and his family and for Popes Alexander IV and Gregory X, and he was a very close associate of St Bonaventure, the Franciscan master general. Gilbert of Tournai's *ad status* sermons, which contain his three crusade model sermons, form part of one of the most comprehensive and also most popular corpora of model sermons by any individual author of the later middle ages.[28]

While Gilbert probably wrote with a view to training Franciscan preachers, **Humbert of Romans** did the same for the Dominican friars. He, too, left a large corpus of writings, most of which were meant for the instruction of his fellow friars. Born around 1200, Humbert also went to the University of Paris as a young man, finishing his studies before becoming a friar in 1224.[29] He had a successful career within the Dominican order, making rapid progress. In 1226 Humbert became a *lector* at the order's house in Lyons and was its prior by 1237. In 1240 he was appointed provincial prior of the Roman province and four years later he succeeded Hugh of St Cher as the head of the northern French province of Francia. He finally served as master general of the Domini-

---

S. Ludovici regis ad partes transmarinas, as some scholars have claimed, he would have been on Louis IX's first crusade. But as the only known manuscript of this chronicle has been lost for some time, the question of its authorship must, for the time being, remain a moot point. For this discussion see E. Longpré in the introduction to his edition of Gilbert's *Tractatus de Pace* (Bibliotheca franciscana ascetica medii aevi 6; Ad Claras Aquas [Quarracchi], 1925), xii-xiii. G. Golubovich, *Biblioteca Bio-bibliographica della Terra Santa e dell'Oriente Francescano,* 16 vols. (Ad Claras Aquas [Quarracchi], 1906–27), I, 219; II, 362–6. F. Cardini, 'Gilberto di Tournai. Un francescano predicatore della crociata', *Studi Francescani,* 72 (1975), 31–48, here p. 38.

[27] For the involvement of the French Franciscans in the propaganda for Louis's crusade see Maier, *Preaching the Crusades,* 62–9.

[28] Schneyer, II, 282–318.

[29] For Humbert's life and works see E. T. Brett, *Humbert of Romans. His Life and Views of Thirteenth-Century Society* (Studies and Texts 67; Toronto, 1984). M.-H. Vicaire, 'Humbert de Romans', *Dictionnaire de spiritualité,* VII, cols. 1108–16. T. Kaeppeli, *Scriptores Ordinis Praedicatorum Medii Aevi* [in progress] (Rome, 1970ff), II, 283–95.

cans from 1254 to 1263, before retiring to the convent at Lyons, where he stayed until his death in 1277.

Like Gilbert of Tournai, Humbert made use of his retirement to produce a number of writings, amongst which were his principal works on preaching. His *ad status* model sermons were part of his *De Eruditione Predicatorum*, a large didactic treatise on preaching, which he wrote between 1266 and 1277.[30] Although we have no direct evidence that Humbert preached the cross, he was certainly engaged in organising and conducting crusade propaganda. As provincial prior of the northern French province in the late 1240s and early 1250s, Humbert would have been responsible for organising the Dominican crusade preaching force in one of the most important recruitment areas for Louis IX's first crusade.[31] Probably arising from his duties as master general and the growing importance of the Dominicans' role as crusade propagandists, Humbert later spent much effort in promoting the crusades to the Holy Land. Towards the end of the 1260s he put together a preaching handbook for crusade preachers, the *De Predicatione Sancte Crucis*, while one part of his *Opus Tripartitum*, written as a deposition for the Second Council of Lyons, is entirely devoted to the question of the recovery of the Holy Land.[32]

Like Humbert, **Bertrand de la Tour** served as head of one of the two big mendicant orders. Like Gilbert of Tournai, he was a Franciscan and like James de Vitry and Eudes of Châteauroux he ended his life as cardinal bishop of Tusculum. By far the youngest of the five authors, Bertrand was born around 1265.[33] He became a friar early in life, studied at the University of Toulouse, but took his degree at Paris. Later on, Bertrand probably taught at both Paris and Toulouse universities. In 1312 he was elected provincial minister of the Franciscans' southern French province

---

[30] See S. Tugwell, 'Humbert of Romans's Material for Preachers', *De Ore Domini. Preacher and Word in the Middle Ages*, ed. T. L. Amos, E. A. Green and B. M. Kienzle (Studies in Medieval Culture 27; Kalamazoo, 1989), 105–17. S. Tugwell, '*De huiusmodi sermonibus texitur omnis recta predicatio:* Changing Attitudes towards the Word of God', *De l'homélie au sermon. Histoire de la prédication médiévale*, ed. J. Hamesse and X. Hermand (Publications de l'Institut d'Etudes Médiévales. Textes, Etudes, Congrès 14; Louvain, 1993), 159–68.

[31] Maier, *Preaching the Crusades*, 62–3, 70–2.

[32] Humbertus de Romanis, *De Predicatione Sancte Crucis* (Nuremberg, 1495) and 'Opus Tripartitum', *Appendix ad Fasciculum Rerum Expetendarum et Fugiendum*, ed. E. Brown (London, 1690), 185–229.

[33] For Bertrand's life see J. Goyens, 'Bertrand de la Tour', *Dictionnaire d'histoire et de géographie écclesiastiques*,VIII, col. 1084. P. Gauchat, *Cardinal Bertrand de Turre. His Participation in the Theological Controversy concerning the Poverty of Christ and the Apostles under Pope John XXII* (Rome, 1930), 31–55. B. Smalley, *English Friars and Antiquity in the Early Fourteenth Century* (Oxford, 1960), 242–4.

of Aquitania. While holding this office, Pope John XXII sent him on several important diplomatic missions. As it turned out, these were the first steps of a successful career within the church hierarchy. Bertrand de la Tour became titular archbishop of Salerno in 1320, only to be promoted to cardinal presbyter of S. Vitale that same year. Three years later he was appointed cardinal bishop of Tusculum. Bertrand, however, did not lose touch with the Franciscan order. He took part in several of the order's chapters and in 1328–9 the pope made him administrator general of the Franciscans after the deposition of their general minister, Michael of Cesena.[34] Despite his closeness to the papal court and the Franciscan order, there is no evidence as to whether Bertrand was involved in any aspect of the crusade movement at any stage of his life.

Bertrand's vast corpus of over 1,000 model sermons dwarfs his other theological writings and bears witness to his Franciscan background and interests. In addition to a *de tempore et de quadragesima* and a *de sanctis et communi sanctorum* sermon series, Bertrand wrote a collection of *collationes abbreviate*, short model sermons, which includes his *ad status* sermons and in particular the three models for the preaching to crusaders.[35] Like Gilbert of Tournai's sermons, some of Bertrand's collections seem to have been among the most popular sermon materials of the later middle ages.[36]

Generally speaking, it is difficult to say how widely known and used the crusade model sermons collected here were. The collections in which they appear enjoyed various degrees of popularity, to judge from the number of surviving manuscripts.[37] By far the most manuscripts, between sixty and seventy, have survived for Gilbert of Tournai's *ad status* sermons. In part this must be due to the fact that they were easily available from the University of Paris stationers, on whose *pecia* list of 1304 they featured.[38] Next comes the collection by Humbert of Romans

---

[34] J. H. R. Moorman, *A History of the Franciscan Order from its Origins to the Year 1517* (Oxford, 1968), 321.

[35] Contrary to what I claimed in my *Preaching the Crusades* (p. 170, n. 1) there are only three crusade model sermons in Bertrand's *ad status* collection. At the time, I was misled by Schneyer, who identified the sermons as anonymous crusade sermons only in his listing of the Barcelona manuscript (for this see below, pp. 78–9) but not among Bertrand de la Tour's sermons. Schneyer was also mistaken when he listed as many as five crusade sermons. When I had finally seen all the manuscripts of Bertrand's *ad status* collection, it became clear from the rubrics that only three of the five models were designated for crusade preaching.

[36] Schneyer, I, 505–91. Longère, *La prédication médiévale*, 103–4.

[37] About the manuscripts see below pp. 74–9.

[38] *Chartularium Universitatis Parisiensis*, ed. H. Denifle and A. Châtelain, 4 vols. (Paris, 1889–97), II/1, 109, no. 642. See also d'Avray, *The Preaching of the Friars*, 278.

which survived in just under twenty manuscript copies. It seems safe to assume that both these collections were widely used, presumably by fellow Franciscan or Dominican friars. This supposition is moreover supported by the fact that they found their way into print in the late fifteenth and the early sixteenth centuries.[39] James of Vitry's *sermones vulgares* exist in at least fourteen manuscripts which indicates that they, too, must have been fairly well known. The *ad status* models by Eudes of Châteauroux and Bertrand de la Tour, on the other hand, probably never enjoyed a large readership, because only a few manuscripts of them are known today. For Bertrand's *ad status* model this is surprising since some of his other collections have survived in a great number of manuscripts. One must, however, be cautious not to read too much into the number of surviving manuscripts. On the one hand, we are dealing with chance survival and we do not really know why individual manuscripts have or have not been preserved through the ages.[40] On the other hand, it is difficult to postulate the popularity of individual sermons on the basis of the popularity of a whole collection. Even notes in the margins are no safe guideline for the use of individual sermons,[41] because texts could have been used without obvious traces being left in the manuscript. However, while it is virtually impossible to prove whether these crusade model sermons – as opposed to the collections in which they appear – were read and used widely, crusade preaching aids such as these must have played a significant role in shaping a common approach to crusade propaganda amongst preachers of the cross.

Crusade model sermons have been studied before. Scholarly research started at the end of the nineteenth century with the first short studies by Röhricht, Lecoy de la March and Wolfram.[42] These three authors,

---

[39] Gilbert of Tournai's *ad status* sermons were printed at Louvain in 1473 and 1484, Paris in 1508 and 1513 and Lyon in 1511 (see Schneyer, II, 307), those by Humbert of Romans at Hagenau in 1508, Venice in 1603, Barcelona in 1607 and Lyon in 1677 in volume XXV of the *Maxima Bibliotheca Veterum Patrum* (see Kaeppeli, *Scriptores Ordinis Praedicatorum*, II, 288).

[40] In a personal communication, Simon Tugwell, for example, suggested that the reason why so few thirteenth-century copies of Humbert of Romans's *ad status* sermons survived might be that they were already damaged at the time because of overuse.

[41] See for example the marginal notes on Gilbert of Tournai's first crusade model sermon in the M manuscript, fol. 98v.

[42] R. Röhricht, 'Die Kreuzpredigten gegen den Islam. Ein Beitrag zur Geschichte der christlichen Predigt im 12. und 13. Jahrhundert', *Zeitschrift für Kirchengeschichte*, 6 (1884), 550–72. A. Lecoy de la Marche, 'La prédication de la croisade au treizième siècle', *Revue des questions historiques*, 48 (1890), 5–28. G. Wolfram, 'Kreuzpredigt und Kreuzlied', *Zeitschrift für deutsches Altertum*, 30 (1886), 89–132.

however, only knew James of Vitry's models and were unaware that, around the same time, Cardinal Pitra published the full texts of the second model by James of Vitry and the first, second and third by Eudes of Châteauroux, as well as extracts from James's first and Eudes's fourth and fifth models.[43] But despite Pitra's edition, the study of crusade sermons was not revived until forty years later, when Valmar Cramer published the first full-scale study of crusade preaching.[44] Cramer's work did not create much interest in these texts; except for the occasional mention, the study of crusade sermons was not taken up again until quite recently.[45] In 1991, Penny Cole published a study of preaching in the context of the Holy Land crusade between 1095 and 1270.[46] In this overview study, Cole discussed the general development of crusade preaching over almost 200 years in the context of the history of the crusade movement. Alongside chronicle reports, preaching tracts and a number of texts from sermon collections, Cole included some of the *ad status* crusade model sermons in her study. Since then more manuscript crusade sermons have come to light.[47] Some recent articles have treated individual crusade sermons, including some which were preached in the context of crusades other than to the Holy Land.[48] There are now also modern editions of several manuscript crusade sermons from various types of sermon collections.[49]

The *ad status* model sermons for the preaching of the crusade form a

---

[43] *Analecta Novissima*, II, 310–15, 328–33.

[44] V. Cramer, 'Kreuzzugspredigt und Kreuzzugsgedanken von Bernhard von Clair-vaux bis Humbert von Romans', *Das Heilige Land in Vergangenheit und Gegen-wart*, 1 (1939) [= *Palästinahefte des Deutschen Vereins vom Heiligen Land*, 17], 43–204.

[45] See, for example, Cardini, 'Gilberto di Tournai'.

[46] Cole, *The Preaching of the Crusades*.

[47] See the list in Maier, *Preaching the Crusades*, 170–2 and p. 174 of the paperback edition (1998). N. Bériou, *L'avènement des maîtres de la parole. La prédication à Paris au XIIIe siècle*, 2 vols. (Paris, 1998), 58–70. Bériou, 'La prédication de croisade'.

[48] See Cole, D'Avray and Riley-Smith, 'Application of Theology'. Maier, 'Crusade and Rhetoric'. Bériou, 'La prédication de croisade'. Maier, 'Crisis, Liturgy and the Crusade'.

[49] Cole edited one sermon each by John of Abbéville, Roger of Salisbury and an anonymous author and two by Eudes of Châteauroux (*The Preaching of the Crusades*, 222–43). I myself published Eudes's three sermons about the Lucera crusade ('Crusade and Rhetoric', 376–85). The sermon collection by Frederick Visconti, including two crusade sermon texts, is about to be published by a team of French and Italian scholars. Nicole Bériou and I are in the process of publishing six sermons from the Albigensian crusade of 1226 by Philip the Chancellor and Eudes of Châteauroux to appear in the series Les Classique de l'histoire de France au moyen âge. References to all these sermons can be found in Maier, *Preaching the Crusades*, 170–2.

distinct group among crusade sermons. Most of them have never been studied or edited before. This book makes them available to students and scholars in the hope of stimulating new research. Like most model sermons, the *ad status* crusade sermons were primarily written as didactic texts and cannot simply be understood as records of sermons preached. Even though, when composing their models, the authors might well have drawn on the crusade sermons that they themselves had preached, they arranged their materials so as to make it easy for other preachers to use their models. To elucidate this point, chapter 2 explores the relationship between 'live' crusade preaching and the model sermons from the *ad status* collections. This concerns both the question of how 'live' preaching might have influenced the writing of crusade model sermons and the question of how preachers might have made use of the models in their own 'live' preaching. In many ways the conclusions drawn are tentative because they are necessarily based on circumstantial evidence. But the questions are well worth exploring as a way of better understanding the nature of the crusade model sermons as historical sources, counteracting the widespread assumption that they are straight-forward records of sermons that were actually preached.

Chapter 3 on the structure of the *ad status* crusade model sermons contributes towards an understanding of how the authors worked when composing their models and how the structure of the models determined the way in which other preachers could use them. This area of research is primarily concerned with the formal aspects of the sermon models and has as yet been little explored in sermon studies. Whether in this respect crusade model sermons are representative of model sermons generally remains to be seen. Chapter 4 is concerned with the way in which the crusade model sermons portray the activity of crusading. Although all the authors of *ad status* crusade model sermons came from a clerical and academic background, their views on crusading as they appear in their sermon texts clearly were of more than marginal importance. Their models no doubt reflected, as well as to some extent shaped, the prevailing public image of the crusade at the time. The three essays, as well as the appendix on the relationship between the models of James of Vitry and Gilbert of Tournai, are not meant to be the final word on the subjects treated. They are rather first inroads into as yet little explored areas of research.

2

CRUSADE SERMONS AND CRUSADE MODEL SERMONS

I N THE PREFACE to the second edition of his sermons, Eudes of Châteauroux wrote the following:

> I, Eudes, [cardinal] bishop of Tusculum, having before my mind's eyes this [passage] of Ecclesiastes: *In the morning, sow your seed, and in the evening your hand shall not rest*, refuse to disgrace the evening of my old age by idleness and wish to offer to the Lord *an evening sacrifice*, which consists of a fattened lamb; after the [earlier] sermons which I composed not by my own means but by a gift of God, from whom all wisdom, understanding and knowledge [come], I composed some more sermons and had them written down; those who are not so well trained in sacred writings may consult these, as may those who, because they are prevented by other business or pressed by time, cannot find free time to think about and arrange that which they have to preach to others.[1]

Eudes worked on the revised edition of his sermons while staying with the papal court in Italy in the late 1260s.[2] He was then probably already into his seventies and anxious to pass on his rich experience as a preacher to other clerics. From what Eudes tells us, his motive for recording his

---

[1] The preface is transcribed from MS Pisa, Biblioteca Cateriniana del Seminario, 21, ff. 2va: 'Ego Odo episcopus Tusculanus habens pre oculis mentis mee illud Ecclesiastes [xi, 6]: *Mane semina semen tuum et vespere non cesset manus tua*, renuens fedare otio mee vesperam senectutis et desiderans offerre Domino *sacrificium vespertinum* [Ps. cxl, 2] quod de agno pinguiori fiebat, post sermones quos non ex meo ingenio composueram sed ex dono Dei, a quo omnis sapientia et intellectus atque prudentia, iam in senio constitutus quosdam alios sermones composui et scribi feci, ad quos haberent recursum minus exercitati in sacris voluminibus et etiam qui, negociis prepediti vel tempore artati, vacare non possunt ad excogitandum et ordinandum ea que habent aliis predicare.' Also in Iozzelli, *Odo da Châteauroux*, 173 and Charansonnet, 'L'évolution', 141.

[2] For the chronology of the manuscripts and the three different editions of Eudes's sermons see Charansonnet, 'L'évolution', 107–22.

sermons was primarily didactic and not historiographic. His main aim was not to preserve a record for posterity of the sermons that he had preached throughout his life, but to write down his sermons in such a way that they might serve as models for other preachers.

When describing the process of writing his sermons, Eudes used the term *componere*. It is not quite clear what *componere* meant in this particular context.[3] However, since we know that Eudes was drawing on his own 'live' preaching when putting together his sermon collections, *componere* presumably refers to the process at play when he turned the sermons he had preached into model sermons for the use of other preachers. Research into Eudes's manuscript sermons has shown that he was a meticulous editor, who wrote and rewrote his sermons, and in the process revised the entire corpus of his sermon collections. The degree to which he changed his sermons from one edition to the next could vary greatly. Sometimes he only added single words and short phrases, at other times he merged two or more sermons to make up an entirely new one. *Componere* is thus an essentially creative process by which Eudes turned his own preaching into written sermons for the use of other preachers.

Like the vast majority of medieval manuscript sermons, Eudes's sermons were no word-by-word record of his own preaching. But since we do not know what Eudes actually said in his 'live' sermons, it is difficult to say what the exact relationship was between the sermons Eudes preached and the recorded version of his sermons. Generally speaking, however, the relationship between 'live' sermons and manu-script sermons is of profound interest for the study of medieval preaching. For the historian trying to assess what impact preaching had on specific audiences or on society as a whole, it is important to know, firstly, to what extent manuscript sermons reflect actual preaching and, secondly, how preachers might have used the material from manuscript sermons in their own preaching. The main difficulty in addressing these issues is that there is hardly any direct evidence to document the exact relationship between 'live' preaching and written model sermons. Even when sermons were recorded by *reportatio*, that is, by listeners present at the sermon, the manuscripts provide no entirely reliable record of the exact words pronounced during the live sermon.[4] All we usually have to

---

[3] Here and in the following see A. Charansonnet, 'La tradition manuscrite des collections de sermons du Cardinal Eudes de Châteauroux (1190?-1273): étude et application', *Revue d'histoire des textes* [forthcoming].

[4] For *reportationes* in general see the articles published in *Medioevo e Rinascimento*, 3 (1989), in particular the contributions by L.-J. Bataillon ('Sermons rédigés, sermons réportés [XIIIᵉ siècle]', 69–86), J. Hamesse ('La méthode de travail des reporta-teurs', 51–61) and N. Bériou ('La reportation des sermons parisiens à la fin du XIIIᵉ siécle', 87–124). See also Bériou, *L'avènement des maîtres*.

go by is internal evidence found in the manuscript texts themselves and circumstantial evidence that helps us to understand how sermons were recorded and how model sermons were used.

'LIVE' SERMONS INTO MANUSCRIPTS

Are the *ad crucesignatos* sermons collected here records of sermons as they were actually preached? Were they based on sermons that the authors themselves preached when recruiting crusaders or addressing those who had already taken the vow and were about to leave home or go into battle? These seem legitimate questions to ask, considering that most of our authors were themselves involved in preaching the crusades, but they are also virtually impossible to answer because we have next to no information about what exactly crusade preachers said during crusade recruitment events or when preaching to crusaders en route.[5] There is little doubt that the authors' own experience as crusade preachers had a bearing on how they composed crusade sermons for other preachers. Some of the authors seem to have relied heavily on the sermons that they themselves had preached. But even if there are indications that a written sermon went back to a sermon once preached, there is normally no clear-cut answer to the question about the relationship between the 'live' sermon and its recorded version.

In order to get to grips with the question of the relationship of 'live' crusade sermons and their recorded versions, it is worth looking at a number of manuscript crusade sermons of the thirteenth century, not included in this edition, which according to their rubrics had once been preached to a specific audience on a particular occasion. The aim is to show the different types of crusade sermon texts which we encounter in manuscript sermon collections and explain how they relate to 'live' preaching.

Two of these sermon texts seem at first sight to be straightforward records of actual sermons, since they appear in a collection of sermons compiled primarily to provide a historical record of the author's preaching. They are two sermons by Archbishop Frederick Visconti of Pisa, one concerning the crusade against the Mongols and the other the Holy Land crusade: Frederick addressed them to the Pisan clergy in 1260 and 1261 respectively to announce these crusades officially.[6] The two

---

[5] This is discussed in Maier, *Preaching the Crusades*, 111–22.
[6] MS Florence, Biblioteca Medicea-Laurenziana, Plut. 33 sin. 1, ff. 39vb–41rb ('Quando idem dominus predicavit crucem litteraliter clero Pisano de mandato domini pape'), 41va–42ra ('Quando idem dominus predicavit [here follows the sign of the cross] respondendo nuntiis Tartarorum in clero Pisano'). Schneyer, II, 83, nos. 26, 27. Maier, *Preaching the Crusades*, 171–2.

sermons appear in a collection of 114 sermons preached by Frederick between the early 1240s and his death in 1277.[7] Contrary to most thirteenth-century sermon collections, this compilation was not an attempt to gather a series of sermons for a particular selection of liturgical dates. It was quite simply a record of memorable sermons preached by Frederick Visconti and they were presented as such with the rubrics supplying the time and place of the original sermons, saying who the audience was and adding in most cases whether the sermon had been delivered in Latin or the vernacular. It therefore seems safe to assume that the compiler of this particular collection made an attempt to produce texts which were close to the original 'live' sermons. But even if these texts were written down to serve as a historical record, there are some indications of editing which obscure the original sermons. They were certainly not reproduced exactly, that is, word by word, as they had been preached. In the first crusade sermon, for example, two entire passages, including the protheme, have been left out and replaced by cross-references to other sermons.[8] How much editing was done is, of course, difficult to say but this indicates that Frederick Visconti's sermons were not only written down in order to keep a historical record. His sermons were clearly presented with a readership in mind that would want to use the texts as models or inspiration for their own sermons. In several cases, the rubrics even point out that a sermon might be used for preaching on occasions other than the one for which they were originally preached.[9] In fact, there seems to have been a dual intention in recording these sermons: firstly, to bear witness to Frederick Visconti's preaching, and secondly, to provide model sermons for other preachers.

The same is, in a sense, also true for a series of six crusade sermons preached in Paris between 1210 and 1220, which have survived in the form of *reportationes*.[10] Although the anonymous *reporteur* was clearly recording sermons he had heard himself, the idea of producing a historical record was probably not his primary aim. The compiler only

[7] J. B. Schneyer, 'Das Predigtwerk des Erzbischofs Friedrich Visconti von Pisa (1254–77) auf Grund der Rubriken des Cod. Florenz, Laur. Plut. 33 sin. 1', *Recherches de théologie ancienne et médiévale*, 32 (1965), 307–32. A. Murray, 'Archbishop and Mendicants in Thirteenth-Century Pisa', *Stellung und Wirksamkeit der Bettelorden in der städtischen Gesellschaft*, ed. K. Elm (Berliner Historische Studien 3, Ordensstudien 2; Berlin, 1981), 19–75, here pp. 20–2.

[8] MS Florence, Biblioteca Medicea-Laurenziana, Plut. 33 sin. 1, ff. 39vb, 40ra.

[9] MS Florence, Biblioteca Medicea-Laurenziana, Plut. 33 sin. 1, ff. 13va, 16vb, 24ra, 98va, 103ra, 109va, 112rb. From Murray, 'Archbishop and Mendicants', 22.

[10] MS Paris, Bibliothèque Nationale de France, nouv. ac. lat. 999, ff., 169va- 70ra, 188ra-89ra, 199ra-va, 233ra-vb, 240ra-va, 240va-241ra. See Bériou, *L'avènement des maîtres*, 58–60, 681. The first sermon is by John of Abbéville and there is a transcription of it in Cole, *The Preaching of the Crusades*, 222–6.

once named the author of a crusade sermon, John of Abbéville, and in none of the cases recorded the time and the place or the exact circumstances of the original sermon. This suggests that here, too, the idea of producing a historical record of the sermons as they were preached was not the *reporteur's* primary aim.[11] As is the case with most *reportationes* of sermons, the *reporteur* most likely wrote down other people's sermons so that he could use them as models for sermons that he might one day have to preach.[12] How close these *reportationes* were to the original sermons is ultimately difficult to say, especially as there are no other copies or autographs of these sermons with which to make comparisons.

There exists, however, a particularly interesting series of crusade sermons that allows us to observe some further points about the process of recording and presenting sermons that were originally preached at specific occasions. They are five sermons by Philip the Chancellor which he delivered in the context of the crusade of 1226 against the Albigensian heretics.[13] Four of the five sermons have survived in three different manuscripts, one at Avranches, one at Troyes and one at Vitry-le-François; the fifth sermon only appears in the Avranches manuscript.[14] The extant copies of the sermons only differ slightly from one manuscript to another.[15] The principal difference lies in the way in which the sermons were presented in the various manuscripts.

For the first three sermons, and the fifth, the Avranches manuscript gives the clearest information concerning the occasion at which the sermon was originally preached, indicating the audience, the time and the circumstances. For the first three sermons the rubrics state that they were preached 'to scholars between Epiphany and Purification at the time when King Louis took the cross against the Albigensians' and each rubric then further describes exactly when in the run up to the crusade the sermon had been delivered.[16]

---

[11] It is only by inference that the author of one of the other sermons, Peter of Capua, could be established; see Bériou, *L'avènement des maîtres*, 59.

[12] For this see the articles mentioned above, p. 18, note 4.

[13] Bériou, 'La prédication de croisade'. Maier, 'Crisis, Liturgy and the Crusade', 641–53.

[14] Bériou, 'La prédication de croisade', 101–2.

[15] The Vitry-le-François manuscript has been destroyed, but there exists a record of the rubrics and incipits; see Bériou, 'La prédication de croisade', 87.

[16] MS Avranches, Bibliothèque Municipale, 132, f. 248va: 'Sermo scolaribus inter Epiphaniam et Purificationem tempore quo rex Ludovicus assumpsit crucem in Albigenses, de dolore et signis doloris ecclesie sancte matris nostre et infirmitate et causis doloris et remediis contra dolorem et quid sit clipeum levare'; f. 250ra: 'Sermo de eodem, quomodo apparuit potentia Dei et sapientia et bonitas in eo quod mutavit voluntatem regis et principum prius contradicentium ad assumendum crucem, quod factum est per tria suffragia supradicta, scilicet elemosinam, ieiunium

In the Troyes manuscript the first three sermons appear in an only very slightly altered version compared with the Avranches manuscript, with just a few words and short phrases added. In this manuscript the rubrics provided in the margins merely state that they were sermons 'about the signing of the cross against the Albigensians'.[17] The sermons are further described in the contents list of this collection. Here, the circumstances in which the sermons were originally preached are explained in much more general terms. Rather than giving the exact historical event, the description in the contents list merely informs the reader about the type of occasion at which the original sermon was preached and about its general theme.[18] The aim of giving this information must have been to suggest that the texts might be used as models for preaching at such occasions. This is borne out by the fact that the contents lists each sermon under a thematic key word and a suggestion as to when the sermon might be used. The first two sermons were listed under the key words of *adversitas* and *auxilium* respectively and both were suggested for use on the feast of the Conversion of St Paul; the third one was indexed under *beneficium* and as a model for preaching at a council of prelates and princes.[19] Thus, the three sermons that are presented as a historical record in the Avranches manuscript are here offered as preaching materials to be used for occasions quite different from the ones at which their 'live' versions were delivered. Whoever compiled the Troyes manuscript was not primarily interested in these sermons because of their historical context, but because of their usefulness as models for other preachers and other occasions.

In the now lost manuscript of Vitry-le-François, as far as we can tell today, the three sermons were presented without any clear indication of their historical setting at all. The headings merely indicate the theme and

---

et orationem, et nota quinque psalmos qui intitulantur ab oratione'; f. 251ra; 'Sermo de eodem, de gaudio quod rex et principes assumpserunt crucem, quod sic altare et que oblationes, et quomodo concordant que facta sunt in Purificatione.' For the exact circumstances of the original sermons see Maier, 'Crisis, Liturgy and the Crusade', 642–5.

[17] MS Troyes, Bibliothèque Municipale, 1099, f. 15va: 'Sermo de crucesignatione contra Albigenses', f. 250ra: 'Sermo de eodem', f. 251ra: 'Sermo de eodem'.

[18] MS Troyes, Bibliothèque Municipale, 1099, f. 1r: 'De multiplici adversitate ecclesie inter principibus et prelatis sibi adversantibus, scimaticis hereticis et ceteris infidelibus matris ecclesie scindentibus unitatem' (first sermon); 'Quod in tribulatione ecclesie non est cessandum ab oratione et bonis operibus donec omnium adiutorium impetretur' (second sermon); 'De agendis gratiarum actionibus post reconciliationem prelatorum et principum cum assument cruces contra Albigense se offerentes Deo, sicut et de principibus legimus sermo vii in unctione altaris' (third sermon).

[19] MS Troyes, Bibliothèque Municipale, 1099, f. 1r.

the occasion in most general terms, without betraying any of the original historical context.[20] If the Vitry-le-François manuscript were the only one to have survived, it would indeed be very difficult for us now to know that these texts derived from sermons preached at particular historical occasions. The compiler of the Vitry-le-François manuscript thus seems to have been even less interested in these sermons as historical records than the compiler of the Troyes manuscript. This example shows well that the same sermon texts could be presented in different ways in different manuscripts: here as a record of sermons preached at specific historical occasions, there as model sermons for preaching at various occasions, with no indication that they derived from sermons preached at particular historical events.

The fourth sermon by Philip the Chancellor is an example of how a sermon originally delivered at a specific occasion was altered very considerably in the process of recording. If it were not for the rubric in the now lost manuscript of Vitry-le-François, we would probably not know that the sermon as it survives in the Avranches and Troyes manuscripts went back to a sermon preached at Bourges on 17 May 1226 in front of King Louis VIII and the assembled crusaders who were about to set out for Languedoc.[21] Indeed, the extant versions of this sermon were presented in both manuscripts as model sermons for preaching on the feast of the Exaltation of the Cross (4 September).[22] The references to the theme of crusading in the extant versions are also very tenuous and we cannot even be sure whether all of them went back to the original 'live' version of the sermon. At the beginning, for example, it is mentioned that the feast of the Exaltation of the Cross marked the beginning of preaching about the business of the cross.[23] We know that crusade propaganda campaigns sometimes started on this date,[24] but this remark makes no sense for the crusade of 1226, which was only preached during spring and early summer of that same year. This remark was, therefore, almost certainly added when the sermon was edited.

There are also no direct references at all either to the conflict with the Albigensians or to the theme of heresy in general. The theme of

---

[20] Bériou, 'La prédication de croisade', 101–2: 'Sermo in dissensione clericorum parisiensium' (first sermon), 'Sermo in dissensione de spe pacis' (second sermon), 'Sermo in actione gratiarum pro pace reddita in Purificatione beate Marie' (third sermon).

[21] For the rubric see Bériou, 'La prédication de croisade', 102: 'In concilio Bituricense ad crucesignatos presente rege'. See also Maier, 'Crisis, Liturgy and the Crusade', 650–2.

[22] MS Avranches, Bibliothèque Municipale, 132, f. 272rb; MS Troyes, Bibliothèque Municipale, 1099, f. 110vb.

[23] MS Avranches, Bibliothèque Municipale, 132, f. 272rb.

[24] Maier, *Preaching the Crusades*, 108.

crusading is mentioned at several points in the sermon, but it is never elaborated. In an apposition which forms part of a discussion on the theme of 'taking the cross', it is mentioned that King Louis also took the cross, but no further explanation or detail is added.[25] In another passage on the significance of the feast of the Invention of the Cross, the sermon develops the theme of 'loosing the cross' by mentioning the loss of the True Cross at the battle of Hattin 1187, and adds that since that time Psalm 78 was regularly sung in church.[26] Neither the crusading theme nor the historical context is developed further. Thus, in this model sermon for the Exaltation of the Cross, there is no coherent argument about the crusade left. It is only by knowing the original historical context that we can assume that there are also traces of the original sermon in the overall argumentative structure.[27] It appears that the original sermon, which Philip preached at Bourges on 17 May 1226, was thoroughly reworked in the process of recording. In its extant forms the sermon presents an argument about the significance of the feast days of the Exaltation and the Invention of the Cross in terms of the need to do penance, metaphorically speaking to take the cross. Philip the Chancellor's fourth sermon thus shows us that a sermon that was actually preached could be included in a sermon collection in an altered version that almost totally obscured the fact that it was derived from a sermon preached for a specific occasion.

The examples referred to so far illustrate the different ways of turning a 'live' crusade sermon into a manuscript sermon. The author, compiler or *reporteur* had various options as to how to record and present a 'live' sermon. These ranged from what appears to be a fairly accurate representation of the 'live' original, as in the case of Frederick Visconti's sermons, to a more or less total reworking in order to produce a model for a feastday sermon, as in the case of Philip the Chancellor's fourth sermon. Not only the degree of editing and altering could vary, there were also different ways of presenting the manuscript sermon, depending on whether or not the author or compiler wanted to acknowledge the 'live' sermon from which the recorded sermon was derived. Some sermons were presented without clear reference to their original historical setting. Non-regarding the exact degree of editing, altering or elaborating which occurred when these sermons were written down, the extant sermon texts were usually recorded to serve as preaching aids. They thus form part of a primarily didactic discourse between the author

[25] MS Avranches, Bibliothèque Municipale, 132, f. 273ra.

[26] MS Avranches, Bibliothèque Municipale, 132, f. 273va. For the singing of Psalm 78 after Hattin see Maier, 'Crisis, Liturgy and the Crusade', 631–3.

[27] Maier, 'Crisis, Liturgy and the Crusade', 651–2.

or compiler and the reader or user. In most cases, the manuscript sermons cannot be read as straightforward historigraphical records. Much rather, they are historical voices, 'live' sermons once preached in front of a specific audience, which were filtered through the process of recording according to the conventions and characteristics of a written didactic discourse.

'LIVE' PREACHING AND THE *AD STATUS* CRUSADE MODEL SERMONS

Even though none of the *ad status* crusade model sermons gathered in this book are presented in their manuscripts as sermons that were originally preached at specific occasions, they share many of the characteristics of the sermon texts just mentioned. Some of them are clearly derived from 'live' sermons. Thus, for example, Eudes of Châteauroux's second sermon model must have gone back to a sermon originally preached during a recruitment campaign for the crusade against the Mongols, probably in 1241, since in the first part the text refers to the Mongols as the crusade's objective.[28] But none of the three manuscripts of the sermon presents it as a crusade sermon against the Mongols; rather, it is designated in general terms as a 'sermon for the invitation to the cross'. In its extant form, the sermon has only a few references to the crusade against the Mongols, but half way through the sermon these stop altogether. They are in the text because they were part of the original sermon which the author was editing for recording, but they were apparently not considered to be an essential element of the new text. Eudes could simply lose these references in the second part of the recorded text. In fact, what we are left with is a sermon text which would read just the same had the references to the Mongols been left out. One must presume that the reader would have been expected to read 'Tartari', the word used for the Mongols, as just an example of an enemy of the 'Lord's people'.[29] A preacher using this model could easily have adapted the arguments to any occasion at which he wanted to preach, no matter which crusade he was preaching for. It is impossible to say to what extent the extant version of this sermon was altered from the sermon originally preached in 1241, but it seems clear that in the process of recording Eudes consciously, though also somewhat haphazardly, edited this sermon to serve as a model for all kinds of crusade preaching, while

---

[28] See Eudes II, 2, 3, 6. The chronology of Eudes's sermon collection suggests the sermon to belong to the 1240 crusade against the Mongols, see below p. 76. For crusade preaching against the Mongols see Maier, *Preaching the Crusades*, 59–60.
[29] Eudes II, 2.

leaving out most references to the historical situation which must have formed part of the original sermon.

Research has shown that most of Eudes of Châteauroux's model sermons derived from sermons that he actually preached on one or possibly several occasions.[30] Nevertheless, with the exception of the model just mentioned, none of his crusade model sermons holds any clear references to the historical circumstances of the original 'live' sermons. The first and third sermons only once mention the crusade against the Muslims, a reminder that Eudes, when composing these models, was probably using sermons he himself preached in support of the Holy Land crusade in the 1230s, 1240s and 1260s.[31] But these references are tenuous and none of the sermon texts makes a case against any particular enemy of the cross nor does any of them mention the historical circumstances of any particular crusade. In fact, one gets the impression that, as with the model based on the sermon against the Mongols, any references to a specific crusade were edited out on purpose during the process of recording because they were not considered useful in a model.

Unless there are indications in a rubric or appropriate circumstantial evidence, it is often virtually impossible to determine if a manuscript sermon text was, in fact, derived from a 'live' sermon. And even if we know that it was, it is often uncertain which passages of the model were part of the 'live' sermon that served as the point of departure. This is certainly true for the remainder of the crusade model sermons presented in this book. None of them claims to represent a crusade sermon that was ever preached. Like Eudes of Châteauroux, their authors may well have drawn on their own crusade preaching experience when composing their model sermons, as they were probably all involved in some aspect of crusade propaganda. But clear references to actual sermons and historical situations are virtually non-existent.

Direct speech, in which an imaginary audience is addressed, might be considered as an indication that an extant sermon text includes passages of 'live' sermons. Such direct speech appears in ten of the seventeen model sermons and is usually phrased as an invitation to take the cross or pray for the crusaders in the field, occurring towards the end of the sermons.[32] We must be cautious, however, about interpreting these passages as left-over fragments of spoken language deriving from actual sermons. One of these invitations forms part of one of the very abridged

---

[30] Charansonnet, 'L'évolution', 109–10, 124–38.
[31] Eudes I, 25; Eudes III, 3.
[32] James I, 4, 20, 23. James II, 5, 6, 7, 9, 47. Eudes II, 13. Eudes III, 12. Eudes IV, 1, 15. Eudes V, 11, 14. Gilbert, I, 22, 23. Gilbert II, 7, 8. Humbert II, 10. Bertrand III, 4.

and formalised model sermons by Humbert of Romans, which make no attempt at all to represent actual sermons. This suggests that direct speech might just as well be freely invented text, included as an example of how to issue a formal invitation to members of an audience to come forward to take the cross. Indeed, in his *De Predicatione Sancte Crucis* Humbert listed a great number of such formulaic 'invitationes' for the use of 'crusade preachers who were not yet trained in this kind of preaching'.[33] There is, therefore, no reason to believe that the short invitations rendered in direct speech in our crusade model sermons are necessarily left-over passages of 'live' sermons.

Whereas it is virtually impossible clearly to identify passages of 'live' preaching in the sermon texts collected here, to do the opposite is much easier. There are passages in these sermons that were certainly never preached in the way in which they appear in the recorded texts. This is certainly true for those passages of Gilbert of Tournai's texts which were directly lifted from model sermons by James of Vitry.[34] However, this does not mean that the remainder of Gilbert's models might not include passages that went back to his own preaching, but it is only with the passages copied from James of Vitry that we can be sure that they did not. Another indicator for sections of sermons that are unlikely to have been preached as they appear in the written texts is the listing of biblical references concerning one particular point. A good example of this can be found in James of Vitry's first sermon. Under the heading 'About the destruction and desolation of the Holy Land', James listed an abundance of biblical authorities concerning this point.[35] A similar list of references to various Bible verses appears in James's second sermon in a discussion of the 'virtue of the cross'.[36] These are clearly meant to give the user of the model a choice of different references to the biblical authorities and narratives. Taken together, such a mass of references would be far too unwieldy to include in a 'live' sermon.

It is ultimately impossible to distinguish in the sermons presented here between remnant passages taken from 'live' preaching and passages 'added' in the process of composing a sermon model. Even for Eudes of Châteauroux's models, which may be closer to 'live' sermons than the others, the texts as we have them now offer no clear and safe indicators to tell such different types of passages apart. However, the value of these model sermons does not really depend on their exact relationship with 'live' preaching because they were not meant to be historiographical

---

[33] Humbert, *De Predicatione Sancte Crucis*, chs. 2–26. The treatise as a whole was addressed to 'predicatores crucis nondum in tali predicatione exercitati' (ibid., ch. 1).
[34] See Appendix.   [35] James I, 15–18.   [36] James II, 12.

records. They were composed as models to give examples and materials, possible themes, arguments and authoritative references to other preachers. What applies to the recorded 'live' crusade sermons discussed above is even more true for the crusade model sermons from *ad status* collections: their character was above all didactic as the texts seem to have been composed and arranged in the way their authors believed to be most useful for other preachers who were seeking inspiration for their own crusade sermons.

CRUSADE MODEL SERMONS FOR PARTICULAR OCCASIONS AND 'OPEN' MODELS

The authors sometimes indicated for what occasions their crusade model sermons might be most useful by the way in which they presented them. This is most obvious with Humbert of Romans's models. Two of them were written for the preaching of specific crusades: the third for crusades against heretics and the fourth for the crusade to the Holy Land. In contrast, the other two models were designated for all kinds of crusades: the first one was addressed 'to pilgrims signed with the cross' and the second one, entitled 'about the preaching of the cross of whatever kind', was meant to be used for all types of crusades. In addition, the first model was probably geared towards preaching to those who had already taken the cross rather than to potential recruits, even though some of its themes could, theoretically, be used for preaching a recruitment sermon. In contrast, the other three sermons were composed with a recruitment situation in mind, since the themes presented in them were most appropriate for convincing people to join a crusade army.

James of Vitry's first sermon model was clearly written for the preaching of the cross to the Holy Land. Here, most of the general crusade themes were developed with reference to Jerusalem and the Holy Land and many specific points directly addressed crusaders going to the Holy Land.[37] In contrast, James seems to have carefully avoided references to any particular crusade in his second crusade model sermon. He only once mentioned the Holy Land when he made a general point about the salutary aspect of the crusade for the individual.[38] It seems that James of Vitry made a conscious distinction between his two models. While addressing the specific needs of preachers for the Holy Land crusade in his first model, he intended his second model to supply materials for preaching a variety of different crusades.

Similarly, Gilbert of Tournai's models do not seem to have been written with any particular crusade in mind. Of his three models only

---

[37] James I, 2, 7, 8, 9, 15, 16, 17, 18, 19, 20.   [38] James II, 26–9.

the first one has one reference only to a specific crusade. In a passage explaining what it meant for a crusader to be 'a friend of God', Gilbert used the example of the Holy Land crusade to illustrate that God tested his followers' friendship by their willingness to help him recover Jerusalem from the Muslims.[39] Since this is the only reference of this kind in all three of his sermons, it seems very likely that Gilbert, too, made a conscious effort not to aim the model sermons at the preaching of any particular crusade. Just as Gilbert of Tournai, like James of Vitry, suggested that his models might be used for the preaching to potential as well as actual crusaders, he also seems to have wanted his models to be adaptable for the preaching of various different crusades.

What is true for James and Gilbert also applies to Eudes of Château-roux's crusade model sermons. Although they seem closer to the author's own crusade sermons as he preached them and were, therefore, possibly less 'constructed' than some of the other model sermons, there were very few references to any specific type of crusade. There is only one mention of the Holy Land crusade in his first sermon model and a few inconsistent references to the crusade against Mongols in the second.[40] By the same token, Eudes only once explicitly mentioned the crusade to the Holy Land in the third model when he compared the tasks expected of crusaders with the deeds of the participants of the First Crusade.[41] In his fourth and fifth model sermons there is not even a single reference to any specific crusade. This suggests that, despite the fact that his sermon texts were probably based on sermons preached on specific occasions, Eudes of Châteauroux was concerned about presenting them as 'open' models for easy adaptation to all kinds of preaching situations in the context of various types of crusade.

Bertrand's model sermons stand apart from all the other models collected here. They were written not only for the purpose of preachers accompanying crusade armies but also for the preaching to the members of any other army in the field. Because of this, there are no direct references to crusading in these models, let alone to any specific type of crusade. By the same token, Bertrand de la Tour's models were also not designated for any particular crusade. Nevertheless, the main theme of all four sermon sketches, which could be described as 'divine guidance in war', could easily have served as a useful theme for various different kinds of crusade sermons.

Whether or not a crusade sermon model was aimed at preaching a particular type of crusade, the author's objective probably was to create an 'open' sermon model which presented other preachers with a basic set

[39] Gilbert I, 17–18.
[40] Eudes I, 25. See also above pp. 25–6.   [41] Eudes III, 3.

of themes and arguments for preaching, but without the focus and elaboration necessary for addressing a specific audience about a particular crusade. A preacher using the model could adapt it by developing the themes, arguments and particular rhetoric that he personally deemed appropriate for a specific occasion. He would also draw on supplementary information about the crusade and the occasion at which he was to preach. For propaganda purposes prior to a crusade, for example, preachers would have turned to the information given in the papal bulls with which they were issued. There, the popes usually explained the circumstances of a particular crusade and gave a set of arguments to justify it.[42] When preaching during a crusade, a preacher would probably consider the progress of the crusade so far and the specific conditions facing the crusaders, etc. Preachers using the sermon models when composing their own sermons would weave this type of information into the flow of themes and arguments that they obtained from the models.

It becomes even more plausible that in principle the authors wanted to provide 'open' models when we consider that most of the texts were presented as 'multi-purpose' sermons. All the sermon models of James of Vitry and Gilbert of Tournai were designated for the preaching *ad crucesignatos et crucesignandos*, meaning for recruiting crusaders as well as for preaching to those who had already taken the cross. Sermons would have to have been constructed differently depending on the intended audience. In the first case, people had to be convinced to join a crusade; in the second, preachers had to give encouragement and comfort to those who, for example, were leaving on crusade or were about to go into battle. Different themes would have to be chosen and different tones adopted for each type of occasion. By presenting 'open' models of crusade sermons, the authors seem to have tried to cater for all these different preaching situations.

Some of the sermons were intended for an even broader range of uses than the preaching of the cross. One of Eudes's sermons, for example, was designated as a sermon to be preached 'for the [feastday of the] Conversion of St. Paul or an exhortation to take the cross'.[43] Regarding his first crusade sermon model, Gilbert of Tournai pointed out that it was also suitable for preaching on any saint's day.[44] Finally, Bertrand de la Tour's models were aimed at 'those going to war or battle, or those taking the cross against infidels'.[45] In all these models many themes and arguments were not directly connected to the crusade, but rather to the

---

[42] See Maier, *Preaching the Crusades*, 100–3, 117–18.
[43] Eudes I: 'Sermo in conversione sancti Pauli, et exhortatio ad assumendam crucem.'
[44] Gilbert I, 1: 'Verbum hoc competit cuilibet sancto et crucis negoitio.'
[45] Bertrand I–IV: 'Euntibus ad bellum vel pugnam, vel accipientibus crucem contra infideles.'

other suggested occasion. A crusade preacher using these texts for the preaching of the cross would indeed have had to do a fair amount of selecting and adapting.

There is little doubt that the crusade sermon models gathered here were primarily part of a didactic discourse in which authors instructed preachers by offering them material which they could use when composing their own crusade sermons. Even though the authors sometimes drew on their own preaching experience, a faithful rendering of spoken sermons was not what they intended. On the contrary, they presented their material in such a way that it might easily be adapted by preachers who wanted to address a specific audience for a particular purpose. These sermon models do not transport the immediacy of the spoken word nor do they communicate the rhetorical elaboration and the dramatic quality of 'live' preaching. These texts are rather the sober products of scholarly work aimed at giving an idea about the themes and arguments that might be employed in the preaching of the cross.

3

THE TEXTS AND THEIR STRUCTURE

THE CRUSADE sermon texts collected here represent different types of models. Some are very long and elaborate, showing fairly detailed argumentative structures. Others are short and succinct, giving only basic points and mere hints as to how the themes presented might be developed in an actual sermon. In principle, we can establish three categories: the 'extended model sermon' (James of Vitry), the 'simple model sermon' (Gilbert of Tournai, Eudes of Châteauroux), and the 'abridged model sermon' (Humbert of Romans, Bertrand de la Tour).

James of Vitry's extended model sermons are considerably longer than any of the other ones and supply more preaching material than a preacher would probably use for one sermon. The texts were certainly much longer than the average crusade sermon, which was expected to be short and to the point.[1] Not only do they include a protheme, which none of the others do, but they are also the only models that supply a variety of different *exempla*. The other model sermons only ever include one *exemplum*, if indeed they include any at all.[2] The two model sermons by James of Vitry also differ from the others in that the material presented is only roughly arranged in the form of a sermon. They have a composite structure with both models falling into three parts: a protheme, the main section in which an exposition of the initial Bible passage is developed and a final part which lists a choice of subthemes and *exempla* which are not directly related to the main section.[3] Even more than the other model sermons, James of Vitry's extended models must be regarded as carefully

---

[1] This point was made by Salimbene de Adam, 'Cronica', *MGHSS* , XXXII, 394–5. See also Maier, *Preaching the Crusades*, 115.
[2] Gilbert I, 24. Bertrand I, 5; II, 5; III, 5; IV, 5.
[3] For a detailed discussion of the structure of these sermons see below pp. 35–8.

arranged stores of themes, arguments and stories from which a crusade preacher was expected to select specific items.

The simple model sermon is represented by Eudes of Châteauroux's and Gilbert of Tournai's texts. In essence, their models reproduce the structure of a whole sermon with the exposition of the chosen biblical passage, its themes and arguments presented in detail. A preacher using one of these model sermons could, if he wished, follow the text step by step, memorise the argument and reproduce it for a specific preaching situation. All he had to do was to make suitable adaptations depending on whether he was preaching to potential recruits, crusaders or supporters on the home front, translate the argument into the vernacular and adopt the appropriate language register for the audience he wanted to address. In this sense, the simple model sermons by Eudes and Gilbert were probably the easiest ones to use. But they were also the least flexible. The themes and arguments were much more closely connected to the exegesis of one particular Bible verse than in the other two types of models. It must, therefore, have been more difficult to use this type of model for a sermon based on a different passage of the Bible.

The models by Humbert of Romans and Bertrand de la Tour are the shortest ones and can be described as abridged versions of the simple model sermon. Instead of presenting themes in a detailed argumentative framework, the sermon sketches offer a list of themes with only a rough outline of how they might be developed. Often the language passes from whole sentences to a telegram-like enumeration of different aspects of a theme, sometimes presented in the form of a scholastic distinction. Humbert did not even supply a specific Bible passage at the beginning of his models, as if to encourage preachers to tailor the arguments presented to their own choice of biblical theme or to the reading required by a specific liturgical date. However, he suggested a text on which to preach at the end of the model sermon, as though as a last resort for those who could not find one themselves.[4] Humbert also provided 'fill-in formulae', where the preacher was supposed to name the specific enemies of the cross against whom he was preaching.[5] All in all, the aim of both authors seems to have been to create maximum flexibility for adapting their models to all kinds of preaching situations. Their models required a great deal of elaboration in order to turn them into proper sermons, but provided useful material for the experienced preacher to do so.

---

[4] For this see also Tugwell, 'Humbert', 109–11. Tugwell, '*De Huiusmodi Sermonibus*', 161.

[5] Humbert II, 10: 'ecclesia . . . movet bellum contra tales propter tales et tales causas fidei'. Humbert III, 13: 'Sed contra tales et tales nichil ista potuerunt proficere . . . et ideo sancta mater ecclesia . . . contra eos convocat exercitum Christianum.'

THE SERMONS AND THEIR STRUCTURE

For their sermons to be successful, medieval preachers were expected to structure their discourse well and choose appropriate rhetorical means for presenting their arguments. There were three main reasons why structure and rhetoric mattered so much. Firstly, a clear structure and apt rhetorical packaging facilitated understanding on the part of the audience. Secondly, they allowed the listeners to remember the sermon in order to reflect on its message. Thirdly, they made it easier for the preacher to memorise a sermon for free delivery. Medieval treatises on preaching, the *artes praedicandi*, explained at some length how to construct sermons, pointing out the necessity of dividing a sermon into set sections, structuring its argument logically, for example by using distinctions, and elucidating specific points with the help of stories, images, metaphors and similitudes.[6] Even though model sermons rarely adopted the exact precepts found in the medieval *artes praedicandi*, the models often feature distinctions, similitudes, metaphors, explanatory narratives and all kinds of comparisons which helped to arrange the themes and made the arguments easier to grasp.

Investigating the structure and rhetoric of model sermons helps us to understand how they were composed and how they might have been used by preachers preparing their own sermons. Crusade model sermons not only presented preaching material, they also gave examples of techniques for structuring sermons preached on the basis of the models. One can distinguish three principal, though sometimes overlapping, ways of arranging the overall argument. The main structuring tool is either a *theme* that is followed throughout the sermon, a *comparison* in the form of a metaphor, similitude or allegory which is exploited from different angles throughout the sermon, or a *distinction* on a particular term which provided the structural backbone of the sermon.

One important reason for choosing a clear and coherent overall structure for model sermons was to offer preachers a basic mnemonic framework for their own sermons. With the exception of James of Vitry's models, which have no overall unifying structure, each model follows a clear organisational principle which made it easy to remember. By memorising the initial Bible verse together with the theme, comparison

---

[6] For the theory of how to construct sermons in the medieval *artes praedicandi* see the seminal study by E. Gilson, 'Michel Menot et la technique du sermon médiéval', *Revue d'histoire franciscaine*, 2 (1925), 299–350 [repr. in E. Gilson, *Les idées et les lettres* (Paris, 1932), 93–154]; M. G. Briscoe and B. H. Jaye, *Artes Praedicandi and Artes Orandi*, 1–76 and in particular the survey of thirteenth-century *artes* in Morenzoni, *Des écoles aux paroisses*, 189–240. For further comments on preaching and the *artes praedicandi* see d'Avray, *The Preaching of the Friars*, 204–59.

or distinction on which the model was fashioned, a preacher acquired the prompts needed to recall the principal argument of the sermon. Further rhetorical devices helped to guide him through the successive stages of the argument. The types of devices and their frequency varied from model to model and might depend on its length and intricacy. Thus, authors used distinctions to structure individual themes and sections of a model or they employed images and metaphors to highlight specific points. These, of course, also made sermons more entertaining and often easier to understand for audiences who were not used to academic modes of structuring thoughts.

STRUCTURING BY THEME

One way of organising the overall argument of a model sermon was by developing a main theme or topic throughout the entire sermon. All the model sermons by James of Vitry and Bertrand de la Tour and one each by Eudes of Châteauroux and Humbert of Romans belong to this type. Normally, the main theme was taken directly from the initial Bible verse or indirectly from an interpretation of it. In most model sermons of this type, the theme was explained at the beginning with reference to the exegesis of the initial Bible passage. In the subsequent sections of the model sermon, certain aspects of the main theme were discussed alongside a varying number of subthemes and suitable *exempla*. Other rhetorical devices, such as distinctions or comparisons, were often used to structure individual parts of the argument, but it was the strict thematic unity which gave these models their structural coherence.

James of Vitry's first model sermon starts off with a protheme on Isaiah 62: 1 ('For Zion's sake I will not be silent, for Jerusalem's sake I shall not rest', etc.). This first part explains to the preacher why it is necessary to preach the cross and suggests that the materials presented in the model might be used against 'those who despise the word of God'.[7] What James meant by this becomes clear in the second and third part of the model, where he provided specific material for addressing 'those who do not care about the Holy Land', 'the lazy and slack', 'those who do not want to avenge the Lord's honour', and 'those who put off being signed [with the cross] and are slow coming to the aid of the Holy Land'.[8] The protheme itself finishes with a suggestion for a short prayer-like invocation in which Christ is asked for the success of the sermon about to be preached.

The principal theme, which is developed in the second, main part of James's first model sermon, is 'the signing with the cross'.[9] James derived

---

[7] James I, 2–4.   [8] James I, 8, 10, 13, 19.   [9] James I, 5–13.

this principal theme from his reading of the initial Bible verse, Revelation 7: 2–3 ('I saw an angel rising from the sunrise, carrying the sign of the living God', etc.), interpreting 'the angel . . . carrying the sign of the living God' as '[Christ] signing his followers with the cross'.[10] Following on from there, James chose different parts of the initial Bible verse and interpreted them with reference to the principal theme.

He divided this main part into two sections. In the first section, James expounded the significance of 'the sign of the cross' for the crusaders: the sign of the cross distinguishes them from 'the unfaithful and reprobate' and 'arms them for defence, so they may not be hurt by the enemies';[11] it is in fact Christ who signs the crusaders as 'his soldiers', just as 'God the Father signed him';[12] the crusader's cross stands 'for the love and devotion of Christ' which draw them to Jerusalem to see the tomb of Christ, 'to serve [it], come to its aid and liberate it from the enemies'.[13] In the second section of the main part, James turned his attention to those who refused to be signed with the cross.[14] With reference to the initial Bible verse, he explained that 'those who do not care about taking the cross' would fall under the spell of 'the four angels, to whom it is given to harm land and sea';[15] instead of enjoying the benefits of the cross of Christ, those who are not signed with the cross are said to have to suffer the onslaughts of the devil and the pains of hell.[16] James went on to elaborate this interpretation with regard to 'the lazy and the slack', 'those who refuse to be signed with the cross' and 'those who do not want to avenge the Lord's honour'.[17] Here the main part of the model sermon with the interpretation of the initial Bible verse ends.

In the remainder of the text, James of Vitry included three sections of additional themes and two *exempla*, before finishing with an example of a formal invitation to take the cross.[18] These additional themes and *exempla* are no longer directly connected to the interpretation of the initial Bible verse. The first section of this third and final part of the model consists of a list of biblical references to the 'destruction and desolation' of the Holy Land, which are explained in terms of biblical parallels to the crusades.[19] The second section suggests a Bible verse for the preaching 'against those who delay being signed [with the cross] and are slow coming to the aid of the Holy Land'.[20] The third section is an explanation of why the Lord called upon 'his friends' to liberate the Holy Land, which includes a short discussion of the value of the crusader's indulgence.[21] This final part of the sermon provided supple-

---

[10] James I, 5–6.   [11] James I, 6.   [12] James I, 7.
[13] James I, 7–8.   [14] James I, 9–14.   [15] James I, 9.
[16] James I, 11.   [17] James I, 10–14. [18] James I, 15–23.
[19] James I, 15–18.   [20] James I, 19.   [21] James I, 20.

mentary material, some of which a preacher could combine with the main, second part of the model to form his own sermon based on the initial Bible verse. Alternatively, he could use it for a new sermon based on a different passage of the Bible.

James of Vitry's second model shows the same tripartite structure as his first. The protheme at the beginning explains that the task of the crusade preacher is to lure sinners away from their evil deeds and lead them 'towards Christ' by appropriate words and good examples.[22] As in the first model, the protheme finishes with a suggestion for a short prayer.[23] In the second, main part of the model, James put forward an interpretation of the initial Bible verse, Jeremiah 4: 6 ('Raise a sign in Zion, be strong and do not delay!'). Again James drew his principal theme from an interpretation of this passage. He read the biblical precept 'to raise a sign in Zion' as the Lord's command to his preachers 'to raise the banner of the cross . . . in the church of God by preaching the virtue of the cross, singing the praise of the cross with the voice of the herald and inviting the people to [take] the cross'.[24] From this, James derived his principal theme, 'the preaching of the cross'.

The main part of the model sermon, in which this theme is discussed, is relatively short.[25] Unlike the main part of James's first model, the principal theme is not discussed in the form of an interpretation of the initial Bible verse. Instead, James chose four additional Bible passages in which the Lord commanded a sign to be raised, Isaiah 11: 12, 13: 2 and 18: 3 and Jeremiah 51: 27, in order to explain further aspects of 'the preaching of the cross'.[26] In terms of the theme and the implied addressee, the main part is an extension of the protheme rather than the presentation of material for a sermon to crusaders or potential recruits. Like the protheme, the main part is addressed to other crusade preachers who might be using the model sermon. It was probably not primarily meant to supply material for preaching the cross to the laity, but could very well have been used for preaching to other crusade propagandists.

The remainder of this second model sermon has no formal connection to the main part. The only other reference to the initial Bible verse comes in the formulaic invitation to take the cross at the very end of the text. As in the first model, James added to the main part a number of sections in which he presented different themes for preaching to crusaders and potential recruits, interspersed with *exempla*.[27] This third part of the second model is much longer than its equivalent in the first, including twelve additional themes and three *exempla* which are presented in a somewhat haphazard order. There are short sections such as 'About the

[22] James II, 2–4.   [23] James II, 5.   [24] James II, 6.
[25] James II, 6–9.   [26] James II, 7–9.   [27] James II, 10–46.

standard-bearers and the key-bearers, the treasurers and the chancellors of the highest king' or 'About the altar of the cross and the sign-post', in which individual themes based on one or two Bible verses are briefly discussed.[28] Then there are longer sections that present additional themes in much greater detail, sometimes offering a choice of biblical passages in connection with these themes or *exempla* to elucidate particular points.[29] At the end of the model, James added a number of further sections and *exempla* on various aspects of crusading, mostly presented without any references to biblical or other authorities.[30]

Preachers using James's second model would primarily have turned to this third section. There were many biblical themes which could have served as points of departure for a sermon, and there was a wealth of different themes and arguments for showing the devotional aspects of the crusade, convincing individuals of the merits of joining, or exhorting those reluctant to support the crusade. In addition, there were several sections discussing the indulgence and explaining its value.[31] There was enough material for preachers to design different types of sermons for various occasions and audiences. But the material presented in the third part of James's second model was not structured in the form of a sermon. It was a list of themes, arguments, *exempla* and similitudes without a clear formal or logical connection between the individual sections. It would have been the preacher's task to select the parts he found suitable and arrange them in the shape of a formal sermon.

Eudes of Châteauroux's first model sermon is also built around one main theme, but it has a more straightforward structure than James of Vitry's models. It was meant both for the preaching on the feastday of the Conversion of St Paul and for recruiting crusaders. Eudes constructed it around the theme of 'conversion'. This was derived from the feastday in question, but it was also considered to be a suitable theme for preaching to potential crusaders: Eudes described the taking of the cross as an act of conversion from a worldly life of sin to one of 'following the Lord'. He introduced the theme of 'conversion' at the beginning of the text, explaining it in terms of an interpretation of the initial Bible verse, Matthew 19: 28 ('In truth I tell you who have left everything and followed me' etc.).[32] He divided it into three parts: 'In truth I tell you who have left everything' stood for the act of 'conversion to God'; 'and you followed me' described the 'life after conversion'; the remainder of the verse indicated 'the reward' of a life after conversion. Eudes thus derived three aspects of the main theme of 'conversion' from the initial Bible verse. He then discussed these three aspects in the three main

---

[28] James II, 10, 21.   [29] James II, 11–12, 13–16, 17–20, 22–5, 26–9, 30–2.
[30] James II, 33–46.   [31] James II, 18–20, 35, 40.   [32] Eudes I, 1.

sections of the model.[33] In this way, Eudes presented an interpretation of the initial Bible verse, divided into three parts, with the main theme of 'conversion' providing the structural framework of the overall argument.

The first section about the act of conversion is much longer than the other two. This may be because the model was written for two different purposes. A sermon preached on the feastday of the Conversion of St Paul would most likely have concentrated on the act of conversion. For this, the first section of the model would have provided ample material. A preacher using the model for the preaching of the cross might, however, have been more selective and chosen only some of the material offered in the first section in order to combine it with material from the second and third sections. Even though a number of different aspects of the theme of crusading are touched upon in the model, the text establishes no coherent argument concerning the crusade.[34] Because of this, a crusade preacher would have had to adapt the material considerably in order to use it for the preaching of the cross.

Like Eudes of Châteauroux, Bertrand de la Tour constructed his model sermons on a theme which he discussed in close relation with an interpretation of the initial Bible verse. The three models were fashioned around the same general theme of 'divine guidance in war'. In each model, an aspect of this theme is developed on the basis of a close, word-by-word reading of the initial Bible passage. The formal structure of all three models is the same. In the first part, Bertrand gave a short interpretation of the initial Bible verse in terms of the overall theme. This he ended with a three-part distinction in which he subdivided the interpretation into three aspects. In parts 2 to 4 he then explained each of these three aspects with reference to a section of the initial Bible verse. At the end of each model one or two *exempla* were added.

In the first model, Bertrand presented material for preaching to participants of a war campaign or a crusade. At the beginning, he explained that the proposed Bible passage, Deuteronomy 20: 1 ('You will not be afraid of them, because the Lord your God is with you'), could be used for dispelling 'the timid spirit of the fighter' because it drives away 'the timidity caused by cowardice', scorns 'the fear caused by pride' and shows 'the giver of victory'.[35] These three subthemes are then discussed separately with reference to the following three sections of Deuteronomy 20: 1 respectively: 'You will not be afraid', 'of them', 'because the Lord your God is with you'.[36] In the second model, Bertrand proposed material suitable for preaching a sermon with the aim of reminding

[33] Eudes I, 2–19, 20–5, 26–7.
[34] Eudes I, 7, 18, 19, 22, 24–6 mention the crusade.
[35] Bertrand I, 1.   [36] Bertrand I, 2, 3, 4.

people of their obligations in fighting a 'war of God' in situations where the Church and 'divine worship' were threatened.[37] Again the initial Bible verse, 2 Chronicles 20: 15 ('It is not your war but the Lord's'), is divided up into three sections, to each of which a subtheme is linked: 'war' is connected to appropriate behaviour on the 'battlefield'; 'the Lord's' is to remind people to attack with a trusting 'hand' because God's concerns are at stake; 'it is not our' indicates the 'manner' in which to approach a war of which the progress and outcome are in God's hand.[38] In his third model, Bertrand de la Tour again discussed three aspects of a war fought by God's command.[39] This time, he selected as the initial Bible verse Joshua 8: 18 ('Raise the shield against Ai'). Bertrand again chose three subthemes, elaborating on 'the leader's encouragement' in connection with 'raise', explaining the importance of the sign of the 'cross' in an interpretation of 'shield' and interpreting 'Ai' as God's 'threat' to the enemy.[40]

Bertrand de la Tour's models were intricately constructed. For the three subthemes which he derived from the interpretation of each initial Bible verse, Bertrand proposed further explanations in the form of distinctions. By doing so he wove a dense pattern of argument which filled the framework provided by the overall theme of 'divine guidance in war' from the particular angle chosen in each model. Although his texts are very short and, more often than not, his arguments are only indicated by a telegram-like listing of distinctions, Bertrand managed to offer a wealth of themes which a preacher could expand into a full-blown sermon. But since he connected his themes and arguments to a close, word-by-word interpretation of a single Bible verse, his models must have been difficult to adapt. Because of their dense structure they could really only be used with the one Bible verse proposed and according to the intricate pattern of argument suggested by Bertrand.

Lastly, Humbert of Romans's third model sermon for the preaching of the cross against heretics is constructed on the theme of 'heresy'. As was his manner of presenting his models, Humbert did not develop his theme with the help of an initial Bible verse. Instead, he chose four aspects of heresy which he treated in separate sections: the first section declares that the sin of heresy is the worst kind of sin, the second explains why heresy is such a noxious sin, the third describes how the Church deals with heresy, and the fourth justifies capital punishment for heretics with reference to Old Testament precepts.[41] This is followed by a *conclusio*, which is a suggestion for a formal invitation to take the cross against

---

[37] Bertrand II, 1.   [38] Bertrand II, 2, 3, 4.   [39] Bertrand III, 1.
[40] Bertrand III, 2, 3, 4.   [41] Humbert III, 1–3, 4–6, 7–10, 11–12.

heretics to be used at the end of a sermon.[42] It would have been up to the preacher using this model to choose an appropriate passage of the Bible and construct a sermon upon it which incorporated some or all of the aspects of heresy suggested by Humbert. As in all his models, Humbert proposed one possible biblical *thema* at the end.[43] But the fact that he structured his argument by developing a theme independent of a fixed biblical reading made this model potentially very flexible because it could easily be used with a variety of Bible verses.

STRUCTURING BY COMPARISONS

Four of the crusade model sermons presented here are constructed with the help of some type of comparison. The use of comparisons in the form of *exempla, narrationes, metaphorae* and *similitudines* was widely advocated by medieval sermon theorists.[44] The main use of these rhetorical devices generally was to make it easier for an audience to understand and remember a preacher's message. In these four model sermons they were also used as the main structuring elements for arranging a coherent overall argument. In one case, Eudes of Châteauroux's second model, the comparison was based on a parallel with an Old Testament episode. In the three other cases, the arguments of the models were developed with the help of metaphors or similitudes that were spun throughout the entire texts.

In his second model, Eudes of Châteauroux constructed the overall argument on the basis of a comparison between the crusade and the Israelites' war with Nicanor under Judas Maccabaeus as reported in 2 Maccabees. As the initial Bible verse and focus of the comparison, Eudes chose chapter 15, verse 16 ('Take the holy sword as a gift from God with which you will shatter the opponents of Israel my people'). At the beginning, he gave the context of the Old Testament passage, pointing out that it belonged to a dream that Judas Maccabaeus reported to his men in order to encourage them and raise their spirits. In the dream itself, the high priest Onias and the prophet Jeremiah appeared to Judas, offering him 'the holy sword'.[45] On the basis of this, Eudes explained that, just as Nicanor then wanted to destroy the Israelites, so today the enemies of the Lord wanted to destroy the Christians; because of this,

---

[42] Humbert III, 13–14.   [43] Humbert III, 15.

[44] L.-J. Bataillon, '*Similitudines* et *exempla* dans les sermons du XIIIe siècle', *The Bible in the Medieval World. Essays in Memory of Beryl Smalley*, ed. K. Walsh and D. Wood (Studies in Church History, Subsidia 4; Oxford, 1985), 191–205. Morenzoni, *Des écoles aux paroisses*, esp. pp. 120–1, 175–6. D'Avray, *The Preaching of the Friars*, 229–36.

[45] Eudes II, 1.

the Lord once again offered the 'holy' or 'golden sword' to the crusaders so that they might destroy 'the enemies of his people'.[46]

Eudes explored this comparison between the Old Testament wars and the crusade through two main parts of unequal length, in which he interpreted two sections of the initial Bible verse. In order to emphasise specific points, he drew on a number of additional biblical authorities. In the first part, in which he offered his reading of 'take the holy sword, a gift from God', Eudes explained that the Lord addressed the crusaders as his soldiers, and that he expected them to fight for him and his people.[47] In addition, Eudes offered an interpretation of the 'sword', comparing it to the crusader's 'cross' and explaining its significance.[48] In the much shorter second half, based on the second part of the initial Bible passage ('with which you will shatter the opponents of Israel, my people'), Eudes took up the theme of 'sinfulness', pointing out that the successful outcome predicted might be impeded by 'people's sins'.[49] The model ends with a suggestion for a formal invitation for the audience to take the cross.[50]

In his third model sermon, Eudes of Châteauroux chose as a comparison an allegorical image from the Bible. On the basis of Genesis 49: 21, Eudes compared the crusaders to 'Naphtali, the deer let loose who speaks beautifully'. Just as 'Jacob blessed his son Naphtali', Eudes explained, so 'the Lord today blesses [the crusaders]'.[51] He did not set out the comparison in terms of the biblical context or a theological exposition of this passage. Instead, he drew an allegorical comparison between deer and crusaders: just as deer leave their own habitat to find a mate during the mating season, so crusaders, 'burning with the love of God', leave their homes and cross the sea to go to foreign lands. The following exposition was again divided into two parts of unequal length. As in the second model, the interpretation of the first half of the initial Bible passage forms the first, much longer part. This is presented in two sections, one based on 'Naphtali' and the other on 'a deer let loose'.[52] In this first part, Eudes elaborated at great length on the theme of 'love' and the effects and implications of God's love on the crusaders. In the much shorter second part, Eudes suggested a prophetic reading of the remainder of Genesis 49: 12: 'who speaks beautifully'. This was to be understood as an indication that crusaders who trust in God will be saved after death.[53] The model concludes with an example of a prayer for those leaving on crusade and an invitation to those staying at home to join the crusade at a later stage or to support it in other ways.[54]

In his fourth model, Eudes of Châteauroux chose the metaphor of 'the

---

[46] Eudes II, 2.   [47] Eudes II, 2–8.   [48] Eudes II, 9–11.
[49] Eudes II, 12.   [50] Eudes II, 13.   [51] Eudes III, 1.
[52] Eudes III, 2–7, 8–10.   [53] Eudes III, 11.   [54] Eudes III, 12.

wood that sweetens' from Ecclesiasticus 38: 5, the initial Bible verse, as the structural leitmotiv. At the beginning, he applied this metaphor to the crusade, explaining that 'by taking the cross all bitterness of the heart is sweetened by the wood of the cross'.[55] The remainder of this relatively short model consists of a succession of points made as variations on this theme. By drawing on a number of additional biblical authorities, Eudes explored the metaphor of the 'wood that sweetens' throughout the entire sermon, showing how the cross generally sweetened the bitterness of life, and especially the crusader's life.[56] As in the other models, a formal invitation to take the cross follows at the end.[57]

These three models were probably derived from Eudes of Châteauroux's own crusade sermons preached during the 1240s.[58] This may explain why, compared to the other crusade model sermons, they present material for one clearly defined line of argument developed in direct relationship with the interpretation of one specific Bible passage. Preachers using these models were given a fairly complete structure for their sermons without much room for elaboration or adaptation to different biblical verses.

Finally, Gilbert of Tournai's second model was also constructed with the help of a comparison. He chose the metaphorical expression of 'the devil signing his followers with the sign of death' to describe those who are opposed to the crusade and thus 'follow the devil', in contrast to crusaders who 'follow Christ'.[59] Gilbert derived this metaphorical expresssion from what one might call an inverse interpretation of the initial Bible verse, Revelation 7: 2. At the beginning, he explained that the 'sign of the living God' was to be understood as 'the cross of Christ'.[60] By turning this round, Gilbert arrived at the metaphor of 'the devil signing his followers with the sign of death'. The remainder of the model consists of three parts in which Gilbert described various types of sinners who were signed by the devil: those given to bodily lust and pleasures, the envious, and the notorious sinners.[61] This model was clearly written to supply material for penitential sermons in which people were to be reminded of the consequences of their sins and offered a way of escaping these consequences by taking the cross.[62] Because of its loose three-partite structure and the fact that the overall theme and metaphor were only indirectly connected to the initial Bible verse, a preacher could have selected one or several sections of this model for composing a sermon based on Revelations 7: 2 or, indeed, some other Bible verse.

---

[55] Eudes IV, 1.   [56] Eudes IV, 2–14.   [57] Eudes IV, 15.
[58] See above pp. 9–10 and below p. 76.
[59] Gilbert II, 2.   [60] Gilbert II, 1.   [61] Gilbert II, 3, 4–6, 7–8.
[62] For a more detailed discussion of this point see below pp. 63–7.

Metaphors and similitudes were, of course, also used to illustrate individual points in sermons and to explain them in a more concrete, and often also more entertaining, manner.[63] At the same time, the visual quality of many similitudes and metaphors provided additional focal points for memorisation. There are numerous examples throughout most of the crusade model sermons of how a preacher could illustrate his argument by using visual language and mental pictures.

Similitudes involving animals appear particularly frequently: tigers, pelicans, eagles, dogs, birds, monkeys, donkeys, horses, wolves, dolphins, fish, bears, cattle, pigeons, snakes, deer, basilisks, lions and dragons.[64] James of Vitry, for example, used the image of a tiger throwing itself onto the hunter's spear to protect its cub as a comparison for Christ's dying on the cross for humankind.[65] He also compared Christ's act of redemption with the well-known picture of the pelican killing its young and reviving them with its own blood.[66] To explain the value of taking the cross, James suggested the image of an eagle fluttering above its nest in order to make its offspring fly up into the air to escape hunters coming to steal them; this was to be understood as a simile for Christ extending his arms over sinners, wanting them 'to climb the height of the cross' so as to escape the devil.[67] Elsewhere, Gilbert of Tournai compared crusaders, who were 'saved' from 'the storms of worldly things' by going to a 'foreign land', to 'little fish who hide under rocks to escape a storm and not be swept away by the current'.[68] In another section, describing the great value of joining the crusade despite its many hardships, Gilbert compared a person who considered a crusade too strenuous to undertake to a monkey that throws away a nut because it smells the bitterness of the shell and thus never gets to its sweet core. For the same purpose, Gilbert suggested a comparison with a donkey that does not even leave the mill when the mill has caught fire, or does not run away from the approaching wolf but instead hides its face in a bush even once the wolf starts eating at the donkey's flanks.[69] Like many other comparisons involving animals, these last three examples must have been meant as much for adding entertainment as for illustrating particular points.

Another popular domain for drawing images was daily life. The

---

[63] For a general discussion of images in sermons see N. Bériou, 'De la lecture aux épousailles. Le rôle des images dans la communication de la Parole de Dieu au XIIIe siècle', *Cristianesimo nella storia*, 14 (1993), 535–68.

[64] James II, 13, 14, 16, 25. Gilbert I, 13, 14, 22; II, 3; III, 9, 10. Eudes I, 20–1, 27; III, *passim*, 8; V, 9.

[65] James II, 13. Gilbert of Tournai took this passage over from James, see Gilbert III, 10.

[66] James II, 14.   [67] James II, 16.

[68] Gilbert II, 3.   [69] Gilbert I, 22.

domestic and personal sphere, in particular, provided numerous points of reference. Images of food, drink and cooking,[70] of clothing and jewellery,[71] of light and fire,[72] and of domestic handiwork[73] appear. Family life featured, as did relationships between people, such as marriage, friendship and sex.[74] Professional and public life provided stuff for comparisons, too. Once, for example, the task of the preacher is compared to that of a midwife,[75] another time the crusader's spiritual benefits are explained with reference to a poor artisan's wages.[76] Engraving featured, as did seafaring and the physician's craft.[77] Elsewhere, scenes from the marketplace and the tavern served as illustrations.[78] An important role was also played by scenes and symbols of feudal life, power and war. Images of feudal investiture,[79] court life,[80] fighting, weapons and war,[81] and symbols of power such as seals and coats of arms[82] appear in the texts. Last but not least, images from nature and the countryside were used, such as the sun, the sea, rivers, a rainbow, clouds, thunder, caves, trees or crossroads.[83]

Quite often, particularly in Eudes of Châteauroux's models, such visual language was derived from, or presented together with, a biblical passage in which they occurred. The choice of biblical images that could be translated, as it were, into the contemporary reality of the preacher's world added weight and authority to the preacher's message. It was particularly apt for the genre of sermon which, in essence, was an interpretation of the word of God in terms of the lives and aspirations of the audience. Thus, for example, Eudes derived his main image of the 'deer' in his third model from Genesis 49. Similarly, Gilbert of Tournai compared the effect of the 'divine radiance' on the hearts of the crusaders with a rainbow appearing through the clouds, which is an image taken from Genesis 9.[84] But authors also suggested images of altogether more mundane origin. Both James of Vitry and Gilbert of Tournai compared God offering 'his kingdom' to the crusaders 'for next to nothing' with a

[70] James I, 10, 11, 12; II, 25, 32. Gilbert I, 19; III, 9, 12. Eudes I, 12; IV, 2, 3.
[71] Gilbert I, 16; III, 7, 12.   [72] James I, 2–4. Gilbert II, 6.
[73] James, II, 5, 43.
[74] James I, 22; II, 37. Gilbert III, 8. Eudes I, 19; IV, 3, 7.
[75] James II, 2.   [76] James II, 23.
[77] Eudes II, 11; V, 10. Humbert III, 10.
[78] James II, 31, 37, 46. Gilbert II, 8; III, 22.
[79] James II, 46. Gilbert I, 21.
[80] James, II, 10. Gilbert I, 19; III, 8, 19.
[81] Gilbert I, 6, 10, 12, 13; III, 13, 14, 17. Eudes III, 4–11.
[82] James II, 3, 10, 44. Gilbert I, 13.
[83] James I, 4, 5, 10, 11; II, 5, 11. Gilbert I, 4, 8, 20; III, 7, 19. Eudes II, 11, IV, *passim*; V, 4. Humbert II, 8–9.
[84] Gilbert III, 19.

drunken trader on the market.[85] By the same token, most of the similitudes involving animals, like the ones of the monkey or the donkey mentioned above, were also not of biblical origin. Whatever their origin, such images and similitudes helped to make abstract meaning more concrete, they provided entertainment and they could easily be remembered for their visual vividness as well as, in some cases, their quirkiness.

STRUCTURING BY DISTINCTIONS

Scholastic distinctions were an important structuring element of medieval sermons generally and were often employed as devices for ordering thoughts and arguments in the model sermons presented here.[86] Bertrand de la Tour used them very systematically, but they appear more or less frequently in most other models. Five of the models in fact use a distinction for fashioning their overall argument, as the main structural backbone of the entire text: two each by Gilbert of Tournai and Humbert of Romans and one by Eudes of Châteauroux.

Gilbert of Tournai's first model sermon is divided into two main parts, both of which are structured by a different distinction. This bipartite structure can probably be explained by the fact that it is a multi-purpose model for the preaching on any saint's day as well as for the business of the cross.[87] The first part is fairly general in content, being suited for either purpose.[88] It is structured with the help of a distinction on 'saint' (*sanctus*), which is developed in three sections from a reading of the initial Bible verse, Revelation 7: 2: 'I saw a second angel rising where the sun rises, carrying the sign of the living God.' The distinction consists of three characteristic features of a saint's life: his 'office' (*officium*), the 'practice of virtues' (*virtutum exercitium*) and the 'sacred sign' (*signum deificum*) which he represents.[89] Gilbert ran through the three parts of the distinction one by one, showing how they linked up with the initial Bible verse and explaining their meaning with the help of other biblical authorities: the 'office' of the saint is that of an 'angel' or 'messenger'; his 'virtues' grow to perfection as '[the angel] rises from the sunrise'; he represents 'the sacred sign' because he carries the sign of the passion, 'the sign of the living God', in 'his own body'.[90]

---

[85] James II, 31. Gilbert III, 22.

[86] For the use of distinctions in sermons see L.-J. Bataillon, 'Intermédiaires entres les traités de morale pratique et les sermons: les *distinctiones* bibliques alphabétiques', *Les genres littéraires dans les sources théologiques et philosophiques médiévales. Actes du Colloque internationale de Louvain-la-Neuve, 25–27 mai 1981* (Louvain-la-Neuve, 1982), 213–26. D'Avray, *The Preaching of the Friars*, 172–9.

[87] Gilbert I, 1. See also above p. 30.

[88] Gilbert I, 2–5.   [89] Gilbert I, 2.   [90] Gilbert I, 3–5.

From the last element of the first distinction and the final section of
the initial Bible verse Gilbert launched into the second, much longer part
of the model which is clearly geared towards the preaching of the cross.[91]
He developed it with the help of a distinction on 'sign [of the cross]'
(*signum*), that is, a sign of 'direction' (*directivum*), 'distinction' (*discretivum*), 'recollection' (*rememorativum*) and 'reward' (*remunerativum*).[92]
Gilbert discussed these four parts of the distinction in turn, explaining
their meaning with regard to the crusade: the sign of the cross as a sign of
'direction' indicates 'the right way to salvation', as it makes 'devout
crusaders' who follow Christ;[93] the sign of the cross as a sign of
'distinction' marks the crusader as a soldier fighting for God;[94] the sign
of the cross was to be understood as a sign of 'recollection' because it
represents the friendship between the crusader and Christ;[95] and finally,
the sign of the cross was a sign of 'reward' because the crusaders obtained
a plenary indulgence.[96] The model ends with an *exemplum* taken from
James of Vitry and a short conclusion summarising the whole text.[97]

A preacher using this model for the preaching of the cross would
probably have had the choice between the material presented in the first
part and that of the second part. Even though the material in the first
part was primarily geared towards a saint's day sermon, it could
relatively easily be adapted for preaching the crusade. The second part,
however, contains much more material directly concerned with the
crusade; this would have been sufficient in itself as a basis for different
types of crusade sermons. Since the argument of the second part is
technically linked to the interpretation of the initial Bible verse, both
parts could, however, also have been used in combination.

Gilbert of Tournai's third model is also constructed with the help of a
distinction on the 'sign of the cross' (*signum crucis*). As in Gilbert's first
model, the key word is derived from an interpretation of Revelation 7: 2.
The four-part distinction divides the 'sign of the cross' into 'a sign of
clemency', 'victory', 'justice' and 'glory'.[98] Without further reference to
the interpretation of the initial Bible passage, these four themes are
discussed in the four main sections of the model.[99] By drawing on a
number of different biblical passages and patristic authorities, Gilbert
explained the significance of these themes for the crusader and the
crusade. Neither the single sections of the model nor the main parts of
the argument were closely interconnected. The entire model was kept
together only by the formal structure of the four-part distinction. A

---

[91] Gilbert I, 6–25.   [92] Gilbert I, 7.   [93] Gilbert I, 8–9.
[94] Gilbert I, 10–14.   [95] Gilbert I, 15–18.   [96] Gilbert I, 19–23.
[97] Gilbert I, 24, 25.   [98] Gilbert III, 2.
[99] Gilbert III, 3–6, 7–11, 12–16, 17–22.

preacher using this model could easily have constructed his sermon by taking over this four-partite structure. But because of the loose formal and argumentational cohesion between the single sections, he could also have chosen to select only one or two parts of the distinction for making up a sermon of his own. In addition, a preacher did not have to use the initial Bible verse suggested by Gilbert. Any Bible verse which could be associated with the theme of 'the cross' would have been suitable.

In this last respect, Eudes of Châteauroux's fifth model is different. Starting off from the same initial Bible verse, Revelation 7: 2–3, Eudes also came up with a four-part distinction on 'cross'. But this distinction is not presented in the usual neat scholastic form, rolling off the tongue through alliteration or rhyme. Instead, Eudes selected four aspects of the concept of 'cross' which he attached to an interpretation of four sections of the initial Bible passage: 'how much authority and virtue the cross has', 'who preached it openly for the first time', 'that through the virtue of the cross demons will be warded off' and 'that those signed with this sign are God's servants and will be saved'.[100] Before embarking on the development of the distinction, Eudes added a section in which he justified the interpretation of the 'second angel' from Revelation 7: 2 as Christ and, therefore, the 'sign' as the sign of the cross.[101]

In the four main sections that follow, Eudes discussed the four themes of the distinction in terms of an interpretation of four different parts of Revelation 7: 2–3.[102] As usual, the model ends with a suggestion for a formal invitation to take the cross.[103] In contrast to Gilbert's third model, the four parts of the distinction are much more closely connected to each other since they are part of a step-by-step interpretation of the initial Bible verse. Also judging by the length of the model, which is much shorter than Gilbert's, Eudes probably expected preachers to run through the entire sequence of the four-part distinction. In this sense, Eudes's model was less easily adaptable and less flexible than Gilbert's. It was more difficult to select any one part of the model because the line of argument ran through the whole text and was closely connected to a detailed interpretation of the initial Bible verse. It would, therefore, have been difficult to use this material in connection with a different passage of the Bible.

The first model by Humbert of Romans was designed as a three-part distinction on 'pilgrimage' (*peregrinatio*). In the first part he discussed the characteristics of a 'general pilgrimage' (*peregrinatio generalis*), meaning the ideal of a Christian life in general.[104] In the second part he commented on the 'special pilgrimage' (*peregrinatio specialis*), meaning

---

[100] Eudes V, 1.   [101] Eudes V, 2–3.
[102] Eudes V, 4–6, 7, 8–10, 11–13.   [103] Eudes V, 14.   [104] Humbert I, 1–2.

the visit to a saint's shrine for veneration.[105] In the third part Humbert explained why the crusade was a 'pilgrimage of outstanding excellence' (*peregrinatio prerogative excellentie*) and what that meant for the participants of a crusade.[106] Once again Humbert finished his model by suggesting one possible Bible verse which could be used to compose a sermon with the ingredients offered in his text.[107] As already mentioned in other contexts of this study, Humbert of Romans's models arguably were the most flexible because they were composed quite independently from a biblical authority.

Humbert of Romans's second model is also constructed with the help of a distinction. Humbert began by comparing God, who called the faithful to join the crusade, with a king gathering his people to fight a war.[108] Humbert then laid out a distinction on the 'sign of the cross' (*signum crucis*) by naming three aspects. He presented the sign of the cross as 'a sign that [people] take up this war for the faith of the Crucified', 'a sign that they are soldiers of the Crucified' and 'a sign that the large indulgences . . . are taken from the treasure of the passion of Christ'.[109] In the remainder of the model, Humbert discussed these three parts of the distinction in three separate sections.[110] At the end, he added a formal invitation to take the cross and, as usual, a suggestion for a biblical passage on which a sermon might be fashioned.[111]

In the texts collected here, distinctions were, of course, also used to structure individual sections. Bertrand de la Tour's models display the most systematic use of distinctions. Not only is the main theme structured by a distinction, but each section in itself contains between one and three distinctions which present individual points and subthemes.[112] At times, entire sections only consist of a string of distinctions with hardly any explanatory text in between.[113] The advantage of such a systematic use of distinctions is obvious: a large part of the argument of the sermon could be memorised via the key phrases of the distinctions, which together with the initial Bible verse and the final *exemplum* in each model gave a very comprehensive mnemonic framework for an entire sermon.

According to Richard of Thetford, a thirteenth-century sermon theorist, preachers were supposed to use distinctions sparingly when preaching to an unlearned audience, as the scholastic method of subdividing themes into individual aspects was in essence an academic exercise.[114] This

---

[105] Humbert I, 3.   [106] Humbert I, 4–6.   [107] Humbert I, 7.
[108] Humbert II, 1.   [109] Humbert II, 2.
[110] Humbert II, 3–5, 6–7, 8–9.   [111] Humbert II, 9, 10.
[112] Only the fourth section of the second model has no distinctions at all; see Bertrand II, 4.
[113] Bertrand II, 2, 3; III, 2.
[114] Cited in Morenzoni, *Des écoles aux paroisses*, 227–8.

probably explains why, with the exception of Bertrand de la Tour, the authors of crusade model sermons seldom suggested the use of distinctions given the fact that crusade sermons were in most cases preached to lay audiences.[115] At first sight, Bertrand de la Tour's models might, therefore, be considered to have been less suited for the preaching to unlearned lay audiences. Indeed, where the distinctions in his written texts depended on an exact Latin word or its spelling, it would have been impossible accurately to translate the distinction into the spoken vernacular.[116] A sermon preached on the basis of his models might, however, not have contained all or indeed any of the distinctions that appear in the texts. After all, the distinctions could have served primarily as mnemonic tools for the preacher to order and remember the structure of the argument. The material presented in the model could just as well have been turned into a straightforward prose narrative when actually delivered.

One way of rendering distinctions less abstract, and thus more acceptable for preaching to unlearned audiences, was to combine the individual divisions with a visual component and a concrete context. In his first model, Gilbert of Tournai explained the division of the 'sign of the cross' into 'a sign of direction, distinction, recollection and reward' by adding that these signs were used respectively 'in battles', 'at crossroads', 'for friendship' and 'as prizes'.[117] Similarly, in his third model, Gilbert attached concrete contexts to each of the divisions of another distinction on the 'sign of the cross': 'a sign of clemency for criminals, of victory for the doubtful and fearful, of righteousness for the holy and of glory for the perfect'.[118] It is probably no coincidence that the two distinctions on the 'sign of the cross' just mentioned both consist of four divisions. By imagining the sign of the cross, the theme of each division could, as it were, be attached to one of the branches of the cross. Thus the image of the sign of the cross not only served as a means of connecting the four abstracts to the key concept of the distinction but also as a mnemonic tool. In a similar case, Gilbert offered the biblical image of Jonathan's three arrows (1 Kings 20: 20) as a possible visual aid for remembering a tripartite distinction on the crusaders' 'righteousness', with each arrow standing for one of the three divisions.[119] By introducing such mental pictures a preacher could have made it easier for a lay audience to understand 'academic' divisions and helped them to memorise the themes represented in a distinction.

---

[115] There are distinctions in James II, 12. Gilbert I, 11; III, 14. Humbert III, 6, 7. Eudes V, 6, 12.

[116] See, for example, Bertrand I, 3 with a distinction on *eos* using the single letters of the word as divisions.

[117] Gilbert I, 7.   [118] Gilbert III, 2.   [119] Gilbert III, 14.

4

PORTRAYING THE CRUSADE

THE CONTRIBUTION of propaganda, and in particular sermons, to creating a public image of the crusade cannot be under-estimated. By the thirteenth century, crusade propaganda had come to play a considerable public role throughout most parts of Europe. As the century progressed, its volume and frequency continued to grow. The main factor in this growth was the ever more systematic organisation of crusade propaganda by the papacy. The involvement of the mendicant orders, in particular, meant that by the second half of the thirteenth century, there was a powerful machinery for crusade propaganda in place which could be put into action at relatively short notice and with a considerable degree of efficiency.[1] Even though we do not have any exact figures, it is probably no exaggeration to say that, theoretically, the great majority of inhabitants of Europe would have had the opportunity of listening to several crusade sermons during their lifetime. Even those who never actually made it to a crusade sermon would probably have heard reports from other people. This means that the impact of crusade sermons on the manner in which the public perceived of crusading and the crusade must have been considerable.

This chapter discusses how the model sermons presented here portray the crusade and the crusader. Even if crusade model sermons are no direct records of how crusade propaganda was actually delivered, these sermon texts are the next best sources for establishing the framework of ideas within which crusade propagandists worked. The discussion that follows is an attempt to describe some of the general ideas and common elements shared by all, or at least most, of the crusade model sermons. The emphasis is not so much on the exact presentation and development

[1] For this see Maier, *Preaching the Crusades*.

51

of these ideas in the individual models, but rather on exploring the scope
of these ideas and their variations across all the models.

TERMS FOR THE CRUSADE AND THE CRUSADER

Although by the end of the twelfth century a specific crusade terminology had emerged, there were still several different words used for
'crusade' and 'crusader' in the thirteenth century.[2] By the same token, the
authors of the crusade model sermons also used a variety of terms for
referring to the crusade and crusaders. Nevertheless, it is possible to
detect a tendency towards conceptual uniformity. Generally speaking,
the terms employed for 'crusader' and 'crusade' were based on one of
three concepts: 'pilgrimage', 'the sign of the cross', and 'being in the
service of Christ or God'. The expression 'business of the cross/faith'
(*negotium crucis/fidei*) hardly ever appears in these model sermons.[3]

Of these three concepts, 'pilgrimage' is the least frequently used.
Although in seven of the seventeen models the crusade is designated as a
'pilgrimage' (*peregrinatio*) at least once,[4] the only extensive use of the
concept of pilgrimage for describing the crusade occurs in Humbert of
Romans's first model sermon *Ad Peregrinos Crucesignatos*, where the
entire argument is based on the theme of 'pilgrimage'. Humbert called
life as such a 'general pilgrimage' (*peregrinatio generalis*), named the
journey to a saint's shrine for veneration a 'special pilgrimage' (*peregrinatio specialis*) and described the crusade as a 'pilgrimage of outstanding
excellence' (*peregrinatio prerogative excellentie*), because, as he pointed
out, it was a religious journey made 'for the sake . . . of Christ'.[5] The
concept of pilgrimage used by Humbert in this model is a fairly broad
one that was not uncommon at the time, describing any religious quest
or journey with a devout purpose.[6] This, of course, included the crusade.
By the same token, the term 'pilgrim' (*peregrinus*) also rarely crops up in
the model sermons studied here. Only Humbert, again in his first model
sermon, actually called crusaders 'pilgrims' (*peregrini*).[7] The only other
author to use pilgrim was Gilbert of Tournai, who once compared

---

[2] M. Markowski, '*Crucesignatus: Its Origins and Early Usage*', *Journal of Medieval
History*, 10 (1984), 157–65. C. Tyerman, *The Invention of the Crusades* (London,
1998), 49–55.

[3] Gilbert I, 1. Humbert II, 1.

[4] James II, 27, 33. Eudes I, 19; IV, 13. Gilbert I, 21; II, 5; III, 15, 22. Humbert I, 4–7.

[5] Humbert I, 1, 3, 4.

[6] J. A. Brundage, *Medieval Canon Law and the Crusader* (Madison, 1969), 3–18. See
also G. B. Ladner, '*Homo Viator*: Mediaeval Ideas on Alienation and Order',
Speculum, 42 (1967), 233–59.

[7] Humbert I, 4–7.

crusaders to 'good pilgrims' (*boni peregrini*) without, however, actually calling them pilgrims.[8]

If the authors of our model sermons only occasionally referred to the crusade as a pilgrimage, they much more commonly used the concepts of 'the sign of the cross' and being in the 'service of Christ or God' to describe the activity of crusading. By the thirteenth century, the standard Latin word for crusader was *crucesignatus* (or *crucesignata*).[9] The word described someone who had taken the crusading vow, which involved attaching a cross of cloth onto one's outer garments. Ideally, the cross was worn and publicly displayed from the moment of taking the vow until the end of the crusade. A crusader was, therefore, *crucesignatus*, that is, 'signed with the cross'. Wearing the cross not only visibly distinguished a crusader from the rest of society, it also marked the crusader's particular legal status, as guaranteed by the Church, and it was a reminder of the binding obligations which the crusading vow entailed.[10] Considering the symbolic content and legal importance of the crusader's cross, it comes as no surprise that *crucesignatus* became the most commonly used word for a crusader in the thirteenth century. This is also clearly reflected in the terminology of our crusade model sermons: they are directed *ad crucesignatos*,[11] designated for the preaching to *accipientibus crucem*,[12] called an *exhortatio ad assumendam crucem*[13] and an *invitatio ad crucem*,[14] or they are meant to be used for a *predicatio crucis*.[15]

In the texts themselves, *crucesignatus* and *accipiens crucem* are by far the most frequently terms for referring to a crusader.[16] By the same token, the act of becoming a crusader is usually described as *accipere crucem*, *suscipere crucem*, *recipere crucem* or *accedere ad crucem*.[17] The potent devotional symbolism of the cross was exploited by the authors of our crusade model sermons in two main ways. Firstly, the sign of the cross was said to symbolise the power and glory of God.[18] In particular, it stood for God's special protection in war which the crusaders were thought to enjoy.[19] Secondly, the sign of the cross was said to symbolise the power of redemption and salvation embodied in the penitential

---

[8] Gilbert II, 5.   [9] Markowski, '*Crucesignatus*', 160–4.

[10] Brundage, *Medieval Canon Law*, 115–90.

[11] James I, II. Gilbert I–III. Humbert I.   [12] Bertrand I–III.   [13] Eudes I.

[14] Eudes II–V.   [15] Humbert II–IV.

[16] See James I, 6, 21; II, 10, 18, 19, 21, 28, 40, 41. Eudes I, 24, 25, 26; II, 10, 12, 13; III, 5; V, 7, 9. Gilbert I, 6, 9, 11, 20, 21, 24; II, 3, 5; III, 5, 7, 14, 16, 18, 19, 20, 21, 22. Humbert I, 4, 7; II, 10; III, 14.

[17] James I, 7, 19, 21; II, 12, 36, 37, 38. Eudes I, 25; II, 11; IV, 1, 12, 14; V, 1, 11, 12, 13, 14. Gilbert I, 9, 14, 16, 18, 24; II, 7; III, 5, 11. Humbert II, 2, 10; III, 14; IV, 1.

[18] James I, 6; II, 12, 17. Eudes, V, 1, 12. Gilbert I, 6, 10, 13; III, 17, 19. Humbert II, 2.

[19] James I, 6; II, 12. Eudes V, 12. Gilbert I, 16. Bertrand III, 3.

aspect of the crusading and the crusader's indulgence.[20] Both these aspects will be discussed in greater detail below.

Since the crusader's cross represented the cross of Christ's passion, its symbolism and connotations were focused on the person of Christ or God. Crusaders were frequently referred to by the authors of the model sermons as 'soldiers' (*milites*), 'vassals' (*vassalli*), 'servants' (*servi*), 'friends' (*amici*) or 'associates' (*socii*) of Christ or God or the Crucified.[21] The majority of the expressions used for the crusade itself was based on the crusaders' association with Christ or God. When on crusade, crusaders were said to be in the 'service of Christ/God' (*servitium Christi/Dei*),[22] having joined the 'army or militia of Christ/God/the Lord/the Crucified' (*exercitus/militia Christi/Dei/Domini/Crucifixi*),[23] to fight 'God's war' (*pugna Dei*)[24] and 'for Christ' (*pro Christo pugnare*),[25] 'to hurry to the aid of the Lord' (*ad auxilium Domini properare*),[26] to defend 'Christ's cause' (*causa Christi*),[27] and to undertake 'the journey of the Lord' (*viae Domini*).[28] Referring to the crusade as an activity carried out with or for God or Christ was by far the most common way of describing what crusaders were doing.

THE CRUSADE AS WAR

When considering how the model sermons portray the crusade and the crusader, it is necessary to keep in mind that, by its very nature, preaching tends to focus on the devotional and moral aspects of life.[29] The characterisation of the crusade and the crusader in our model sermons, therefore, first and foremost tells us how their authors viewed crusading in terms of a devotional activity and with regard to its moral significance for the individual participant. In contrast, military, material or political aspects of crusading are less prominent features of these texts. The emphasis on the individual, moral and devotional can also in part be explained by the model character of these preaching aids: because they were written in order to supply materials for various types of sermons to be used in the context of any future crusade, the specific circumstances of a crusade could, of course, not be included. Generally speaking, it would have been the task of the preachers using these models to introduce into their sermons references to the political and military circumstances of the

---

[20] James I, 6; II, 9, 10, 11, 12. Eudes II, 11; IV, 1. Gilbert I, 5, 8, 9; II, 1, 2; III, 3, 20.
[21] James I, 7, 11, 13; II, 6, 26, 29, 46. Eudes II, 4; V, 1, 11, 12. Gilbert I, 6, 17, 18, 21. Humbert II, 2.
[22] James I, 13; II, 18, 19, 22, 23, 25. Eudes I, 7. Gilbert I, 20; III, 14.
[23] Eudes II, 4. Humbert III, 13, 14.   [24] Bertrand II, 1, 3.
[25] Gilbert III, 18.   [26] Eudes I, 26.   [27] Gilbert I, 9.   [28] Humbert I, 6.
[29] For a definition of preaching see Longère, *La prédication médiévale*, 12.

specific crusade they were promoting. Examples for how the context of a crusade could be included very effectively into a sermon can be seen in a number of sermons by Eudes of Châteauroux and Philip the Chancellor. The recorded versions of these still include clear references to the specific political and military contexts of the crusades they were concerned with.[30]

Even if the particular circumstances of a crusade could not be included in the models, the general aspects of the crusade as a war and of crusading as a military activity were not altogether absent. We have already seen that crusaders were portrayed as members of an army of the Lord and soldiers of Christ. Sermons also frequently employed biblical and historical figures and situations to serve as models and to illustrate how God influenced and interfered with human society in given situations. In the case of the crusade model sermons studied here, the examples range from Old Testament figures to near contemporaries such as the participants of the First Crusade. References to Old Testament figures were clearly in the majority, followed by those of the New Testament, post-biblical saints and other historical figures.[31]

Old Testament stories, in particular, were full of military heroes whose deeds could be held up as examples. Those who featured in the crusade model sermons were either fighters displaying extraordinary military prowess or war leaders who, trusting God's commands in war, successfully fought for the good of their people and religion. In one instance, James of Vitry gave a whole list of zealous fighters, namely Mattathias, the Maccabees, Phineas, Ehud, Shamgar and Samson, whose energy and dedication, he thought, might inspire the crusaders.[32] The two favourite Old Testament contexts serving as a foil for the crusades were the stories of the conquest of the Promised Land by the Israelites after the exodus from Egypt and the heroic fight of the Maccabbees against the enemies of Israel.[33] Both stories were perfect biblical examples of a war fought by God's people, led by the Lord against the enemies of his religion. They had been used widely in crusade propaganda since the First Crusade and

---

[30] See Cole, d'Avray and Riley-Smith, 'Application of Theology', 229–39. Cole, *The Preaching of the Crusades*, 235–43. Maier, 'Crusade and Rhetoric', 353–85. Maier, 'Crisis, Liturgy and the Crusade', 638–55.

[31] Old Testament: James I, 14, 17; II, 5, 24. Eudes I, 18, 19, 24, 25; II, *passim*; III, 1, 3, 6, 12; IV, 13; V, 11. Gilbert I, 12, 20; II, 3, 4; III, 10, 11. Humbert II, 4; III, 4, 15. Bertrand III, 1. New Testament (excluding references to Christ): Eudes I, *passim*; IV, 14. Gilbert II, 2; III, 20. Humbert II, 4. Post-biblical saints: Gilbert I, 13; III, 7. Humbert II, 4. Bertrand III, 5. Other historical figures: Eudes III, 3, 12; V, 12. Gilbert I, 24. Bertrand I, 5; II, 5; III, 5.

[32] James I, 17.

[33] Exodus–Promised Land: James I, 17. Eudes I, 18. Gilbert II, 3. Bertrand III, *passim*. Maccabbees: James I, 17. Eudes I, 25; II, *passim*. Gilbert I, 2. Humbert II, 4.

sometimes preachers managed to construct astonishing parallels between the crusades and parts of these biblical stories.[34] Comparing the crusades to the Israelites' wars in the Old Testament was an easy way of addressing the question of the justification of the crusade: if God directed and approved of the wars of his people in the Old Testament, there was prima facie no reason why he should not do so in the present time. Even though the logic of these comparisons might have seemed questionable, such arguments may well have worked as propaganda. In addition, if used in the preaching to crusaders in the field, Old Testament comparisons might also have given them courage and confirmed them in the belief that they were in fact guided by God and engaged upon a sacred enterprise.

THE CRUSADER AND GOD

An important image of the crusader put across in the model sermons is that of the follower of Christ or God. This concept offered a wide range of different aspects which made it possible to explore most of the ideological, devotional and penitential dimensions associated with crusading. The relationship between the crusader and Christ or God, as described by the authors of the crusade model sermons, was characterised by two main components: obligation and love.

In as much as crusaders were perceived as soldiers fighting a war in the service of God or Christ, they were considered to be bound to God by the terms of feudal obligation. The most elaborate expression of this was given by Humbert of Romans in his second model. Here, Humbert explicitly stated that the call for a crusade by the pope was to be understood as God calling on his 'faithful followers' (*fideles suos*) to join his army, just like a worldly king in times of war.[35] The comparison with contemporary feudal practice allowed Humbert to characterise the crusade further. Just as the grant of 'temporal things' from a 'worldly lord' carried with it an obligation between a man and his lord, so the fact that crusaders held their bodies and souls as a grant from God put them under an obligation to serve him in 'faithfulness' (*fidelitas*).[36] In return, again following the pattern of a feudal relationship, God was said to

---

[34] Cole, *The Preaching of the Crusades*, 21–30, 49, 69. J. Riley-Smith, *The First Crusade and the Idea of Crusading* (London, 1986), 91–2, 140–4, 147–8. Cole, d'Avray and Riley-Smith, 'Application of Theology', 233–9. See also the parallels between the conquest of Ai (Ios. viii) and the Albigensian Crusade of 1226 or the crusade against Lucera, Maier, 'Crisis, Liturgy and the Crusade', 646–8. Maier, 'Crusade and Rhetoric', 359–61.

[35] Humbert II, 1–2.   [36] Humbert II, 6–7.

reward crusaders for their service by granting them 'gifts' (*donaria, remunerationes*) in the form of the indulgence.[37]

The other authors did not use feudal terminology in quite the same systematic fashion, but they nevertheless advocated its usefulness. Thus, for example, a convenient way of presenting the crusade as a war with a religious character was to argue for the recovery of the Holy Land in terms of it being Christ's or God's 'patrimony' (*patria, patrimonium*) or '(hereditary) land's' (*hereditas, terra*).[38] There was also a range of expressions for describing the crusader's role in terms of feudal rank: Christ's or the Lord's 'vassal' (*vassalus*), 'liege-man' (*homo ligius*) 'arms-bearer' (*armiger*), 'standard-bearer' (*signifer*), 'key-bearer' (*claviger*), 'treasurer' (*thesaurarius*) or 'chancellor' (*cancellarius*).[39] By the same token, the spiritual rewards which the crusader was said to receive from God were described as God 'investing' the crusader 'with the heavenly kingdom',[40] or giving them 'benefices' (*beneficia*) or 'gifts' (*dona, donaria*).[41]

The use of feudal concepts for describing aspects of the crusade was, of course, not new in the thirteenth century. From the very beginning of the crusade movement, feudal terminology had an important place in crusade ideology and propaganda.[42] But the recurring use of feudal concepts in our crusade model sermons shows that, by the thirteenth century, the feudal model had become one of the established means of explaining what the crusade was all about: it could be used for justifying the crusade as God's war and explaining the nature of the crusader's relationship with God in terms of the duties and rewards which followed from service in the army of the Lord. All in all, there was an underlying consensus about the usefulness and appeal of portraying the crusader's relationship with God or Christ in terms of contemporary feudal practice.

Arguably even more important for characterising the relationship between the crusader and God was the second component, the model of love and friendship. James of Vitry, and Gilbert of Tournai following him, expressly stated that the crusader was to 'honour' (*honorare*) God by showing 'devotion' (*devotio*) and 'love' (*amor*) towards him.[43] In fact, the theme of the crusader's love of God, and of God's love for the

---

[37] Humbert II, 1, 6, 7, 9, 10.   [38] James I, 2, 8, 9, 20; II, 26. Gilbert I, 10, 12, 18.

[39] James II, 10, 46, 47. Eudes I, 24. Gilbert I, 18, 21.

[40] James II, 46. Gilbert I, 21.   [41] Eudes I, 9. Gilbert I, 18; III, 11. Humbert II, 1.

[42] See for example Cole, *The Preaching of the Crusades*. J. Riley-Smith, 'Crusading as an Act of Love', *History*, 65 (1980), 177–92. Riley-Smith, *The First Crusade*, 1–56. C. T. Maier, 'Kirche, Kreuz und Ritual: Eine Kreuzzugspredigt in Basel im Jahr 1200', *Deutsches Archiv für Erforschung des Mittelalters*, 55 (1999), 95–115.

[43] James I, 7.

crusader, is probably the single most consistent element used by the authors of our crusade model sermons for explaining the devotional dimension and penitential content of crusading.[44]

At times, the authors employed very striking imagery to explain the specific nature of the love between the crusader and God. We have already seen how Eudes of Châteauroux used the metaphorical expression of 'a deer during the mating season in search of new breeding grounds'.[45] In doing so, he compared the raw instinct of the animal's physical desire to the crusader's quest for the love of God. In the same context, Eudes also described the crusaders as 'burning with the love of God' and their hearts as 'enlarged' by God's love.[46] This was to be understood as follows: as the crusaders 'emptied their hearts through true penance and laid down the burden of their sins . . . the Lord enlarged their hearts through his love . . . so that they could contain the Lord'.[47] Elsewhere he described the crusaders' hearts as being set on fire by God's love.[48] Eudes obviously wanted to describe what he believed to be the spiritual side of crusading, namely the experience of God's love. The crusader's military expedition for the defence of religion was set against the devotional and penitential dimensions of a spiritual quest for God. Other authors used similarly expressive imagery to describe the love and friendship that they believed existed between God and the crusaders. James of Vitry, for example, suggested imagining that the crusader's cross was sewn onto their garments 'by the thread of God's love'.[49] By employing such visual and indeed sensuous images, the authors tried to explain the nature of the crusader's spiritual quest for the union with God through the bonds of mutual love that they believed went hand in hand with taking the cross.

One of the most powerful images of this kind appeared in Gilbert of Tournai's second model. There he described the effect of God's love on the crusader by painting the picture of Christ using 'a bellows [made] from his skin, the wood of the cross and the nails [of the cross]', with which 'the fire of his charity would be lighted in [the crusaders'] hearts'.[50] What is particularly interesting about this image is that it portrays Christ with the paraphernalia of the passion. Images of the passion and Christ's act of redemption on the cross were repeatedly used by the authors of our crusade model sermons when describing God's relationship with the crusaders.[51] In his first model in particular, Gilbert

---

[44] James I, 7, 8, 20, 23; II, 14, 19, 29, 43. Eudes I, 2–9; III, 1, 4, 5, 8, 9; IV, 10; V, 3. Gilbert I, 9, 15–17; II, 6; III, 9, 11.
[45] Eudes III. See above p. 42.   [46] Eudes III, 1, 4, 5.
[47] Eudes III, 3–7.   [48] Eudes I, 9.   [49] James II, 43.   [50] Gilbert II, 6.
[51] James, I, 7; II, 13–15, 26, 43. Eudes II, 7; IV, 10, 14–15. Gilbert I, 5, 12–13, 16; II, 6; III, 3–4, 6, 7, 10, 13.

clearly pointed out that the crusader's cross in fact represented the cross of the passion.[52] Both Eudes of Châteauroux and Gilbert of Tournai graphically explained the relationship between Christ's act of redemption and the effect of the indulgence by employing the image of the crusaders being washed in Christ's blood and thus cleansed of their sins.[53] By the same token, James of Vitry and Gilbert of Tournai, inspired by an Old Testament image, portrayed the crusaders as being signed with the redeeming blood of Christ.[54] The concept of the crusader experiencing the power of Christ's love at the moment of the passion was convenient for explaining the mechanism of the plenary indulgence promised to the crusader. In one of his models Humbert of Romans explicitly stated the connection between the passion and the indulgence by declaring that the 'indulgence which is granted [to the crusaders] is entirely taken from the treasure of Christ's passion which was filled up on the cross'.[55] At the time, people were well aware of the image of the passion and its redemptive significance through the regular celebration of the eucharist during mass.[56] Presenting crusaders as individuals who experienced God's love in the moment of the passion probably helped people to understand why crusaders, in particular, were said to be favoured recipients of God's grace who were to receive the fullest possible measure of the redemptive effect of Christ's death on the cross in the form of the plenary indulgence.

CRUSADERS FOLLOWING AND IMITATING CHRIST

One very useful and versatile concept which appears in our model sermons is that of the crusaders 'following' Christ. This was used by Eudes of Châteauroux, Humbert of Romans and Gilbert of Tournai, all of whom presented it in terms of the biblical precept in Luke: 'If anyone wants to come after me, let him renounce himself and take up his cross and follow me.'[57] The concept of following Christ carried with it a number of associations which could be exploited individually or merged for the sake of combining different aspects of crusading in one concept and image. Firstly, there was the aspect of following Christ into battle.

---

[52] Gilbert I, 5, 13, 16.   [53] Eudes II, 7. Gilbert III, 6, 7.
[54] James, II, 12. Gilbert III, 3–4.   [55] Humbert II, 2.
[56] M. Rubin, 'What did the Eucharist mean to Thirteenth-Century Villagers?', *Thirteenth Century England IV: Proceedings of the Newcastle Upon Tyne Conference. 1991*, ed. P. R. Coss and S. Lloyd (Woodbridge, 1992), 47–55. See also M. Rubin, *Corpus Christi. The Eucharist in Late Medieval Culture* (Cambridge, 1991), 83–163.
[57] Eudes I, 8, 20–4, 26, 28; IV, 12; V, 7, 13. Gilbert I, 9, 16; III, 12, 13, 15. Humbert I, 5, 7.

As we have seen, the prevailing tendency of the model sermons was to designate the crusaders as 'soldiers of Christ' and members of 'the army of the Lord'. On the basis of this understanding of the crusader's role, the biblical precept of taking up one's cross and following Christ could be interpreted as a direct incentive to join a crusade. Secondly, there was the devotional aspect of following Christ by going on crusade in the sense of seeking a spiritual union with Christ by experiencing his love. Eudes of Châteauroux presented someone going on crusade as striving to 'catch' (*comprehendere*) or 'hold' (*capere*) Christ in his heart.[58] Gilbert of Tournai even went one step further, describing the crusader's journey as an attempt to 'conform' (*conformari*) to Christ in the sense of a spiritual experience: when suffering hardship on their journey, crusaders could contemplate Christ's sufferings and tribulations. By doing so they spiritually 'conformed' to Christ.[59] In another context Gilbert suggested that the crusade to the Holy Land offered crusaders a particular benefit, because they could at the same time retrace the steps of the historical Christ.[60]

The concept of the crusader following Christ, however, also included a third aspect, namely that of following Christ into death. Gilbert of Tournai suggested that the crusaders were 'martyrs' who after death literally followed Christ into heaven.[61] When taking up his cross to follow Christ, the crusader could even be said to imitate Christ's passion, an idea which Gilbert of Tournai developed in some detail. At one point he explained that a crusader who truly loved Christ '[would] be ready to die for Christ', and added:

> May you have this cross of Christ in your heart and carry his stigmata on your body so that, offering the sacrifice of a burnt-offering inside, you have his skin on the outside. He who claims to remain in Christ through internal love must walk as he walked by the open imitation of his deeds and passion.[62]

This complex image of the crusader being consumed by the love of Christ and ready to die a sacrificial death on crusade in imitation of Christ's crucifixion combined the military, devotional and penitential aspects of crusading in an ideal way. Death on crusade was thus not only represented as martyrdom, but also as the ultimate proof of one's devotion to Christ by imitating his act of dying for the sake of others. Elsewhere, in another dramatic image, Gilbert managed to combine a similar mix of connotations. He suggested that crusaders going into battle might be encouraged to fight 'manfully' and 'to the blood' by conjuring up the vision of the wounded Christ on the cross actually

---

[58] Eudes I, 21.   [59] Gilbert III, 12, 15.   [60] Gilbert I, 9.
[61] Gilbert I, 8.   [62] Gilbert I, 15, 16.

present amongst them on the battlefield.[63] This again combines the ideas of the crusader following Christ into battle, sharing Christ's love in the moment of the passion, and possibly dying in imitation of Christ. Viewed in this way, crusading could be understood not only as one of the most extreme forms of devotion to Christ but also as one of the most complete acts of penance, because it consisted of surrendering one's earthly existence.

It may come as no surprise that the interpretation of crusading as conforming to the life of Christ and imitating his death was advanced by the Franciscan Gilbert of Tournai. The idea of life as a *devotio et imitatio Christi* was one of the most important principles on which the Franciscan order was founded.[64] To portray the crusader as imitating Christ might, therefore, have been particularly attractive to members of the Franciscan order who were generally keen on spreading their own ideas of a Christian life among the laity. But it would be wrong to describe the idea of crusading as an imitation of Christ's passion as exclusively Franciscan. The idea of the crusade as a ritual imitation of Christ's act of redemption was already advanced by Pope Innocent III at the beginning of the thirteenth century.[65] In general, the idea and practice of the imitation of Christ were popular at the time and even ritual imitations of the crucifixion were part of the religious experience outside the crusade movement and the Franciscan order.[66] The idea of the crusade as one form of ritual imitation of Christ's death on the cross may in fact have been much more widespread than our evidence suggests.

THE CRUSADER AND DEATH

Even if the idea of the crusader's sharing in Christ's passion was intriguing because of its intrinsic force and its different strands of meaning, its use in preaching and propaganda was probably not unproblematic, since it might be understood as necessarily involving the crusader's death. Unlike Gilbert of Tournai, the other authors made only occasional and indirect allusions to the crusader's possible death.[67] In one

---

[63] Gilbert I, 12.

[64] Moorman, *A History of the Franciscan Order*, 3–9, 256–72.

[65] For this see C. T. Maier, 'Mass, the Eucharist and the Cross: Innocent III and the Relocation of the Crusade', *Pope Innocent III and his World*, ed. J. C. Moore (Aldershot, 1999), 351–60.

[66] For the ideas and practice of *imitatio Christi* in the thirteenth century see G. Constable, *Three Studies in Medieval Religious and Social Thought. The Interpretation of Mary and Martha; The Ideal of the Imitation of Christ; The Orders of Society* (Cambridge, 1995), 190–217.

[67] E.g. James II, 18. Eudes I, 25; II, 7; V, 7. Humbert I, 5.

of his characteristically short statements, Humbert of Romans, for example, suggested that crusaders followed 'the example of Christ, who went to Calvary carrying his own cross', a metaphor which may or may not be understood as a hint at the crusader's possible death.[68] By the same token, Eudes said that crusaders ought to follow Christ after the example of St Paul; he added that the saint followed Christ to his own death, but did not elaborate that the same might happen to the crusaders.[69] Eudes elsewhere stated that crusaders 'exposed themselves to death' but again without actually talking about the crusader's death.[70] Although death on crusade did not infrequently occur, it is not surprising that model sermons did not, as a rule, suggest it as a theme for preaching the cross. Even where the crusade was concerned, too much talk of possible death would doubtless have had a negative effect on recruitment.

The authors of the crusade model sermons even avoided the theme of death when discussing the indulgence. They left little doubt that they believed the crusader's indulgence was a guarantee for salvation. Humbert of Romans stated that the indulgences granted to crusaders were 'large', 'very large' or 'plenary', without elaborating on the exact meaning of these terms.[71] James of Vitry, Eudes of Châteauroux and Gilbert of Tournai, on the other hand, clearly explained that they considered the indulgence to be a way of escaping the consequence of sin, to be as it were a passport to heaven.[72] Using an image which neatly fitted in with the idea of the crusader sharing Christ's love in the moment of the passion, both Eudes and Gilbert suggested that the crusaders were saved instantly by Christ and admitted into heaven like the good thief of the crucifixion.[73] The comparison of the crusader with the good thief, of course, carried with it the idea of the crusader dying. But here, as in the other passages concerning the indulgence, death was not mentioned openly, even though it played a decisive role. The crusader could only immediately follow the good thief thanks to the indulgence if he died on crusade; in the event of coming back he would start again to commit sins, for which new penance and works of satisfaction were required.

There was, however, one particular case where crusade propagandists may well have wanted openly to talk about death and the particular value of a crusade indulgence at death. As is well known, crusade recruitment

---

[68] Humbert I, 5.   [69] Eudes I, 21.   [70] Eudes V, 7.

[71] Humbert I, 5; II, 1, 2; III, 14. Bertrand de la Tour's models do not touch on the indulgence at all, probably because they were not exclusively written for crusade preaching.

[72] James I, 20, 23; II, 18–20, 27. Eudes II, 10; IV, 13–14; V, 1, 7. Gilbert I, 19–20; III, 20–2.

[73] Eudes IV, 13. Gilbert III, 20.

in the thirteenth century included *crucesignati* and *crucesignatae* who could not, or did not intend, to crusade in person either because of illness or old age, or because they were otherwise unfit to join an army.[74] Such people would have taken the crusade vow and subsequently redeemed it by paying a certain amount of money towards financing the crusade. Theoretically, the value of the indulgence received by a *crucesignatus* in such a deal was determined by the size of the subsidy he paid in aid of the business of the cross. If he paid enough money in relation to his wealth, he could gain a plenary indulgence, just as someone who actually joined a crusade.[75] Among the many crusaders who redeemed their vows, there was one group that was in a particularly favourable position, both with regard to having sufficient money to pay for a plenary indulgence and with regard to enjoying its full benefit. Those who took a crusade vow on their deathbed could, if they wished, invest their wealth, or part thereof, in a redemption payment likely to be high enough to gain a plenary indulgence. This was a particularly attractive proposition for the dying because it promised the full forgiveness of all their sins at a time when they were unlikely to commit many new ones. Being aware of the huge potential for recruitment among the mortally ill and dying, crusade propagandists particularly targeted this group of people.[76] It is in this context that crusade preachers might well have been more open about mentioning death in connection with taking the cross. The extent to which a preacher may have developed the theme of death tentatively suggested in a model sermon could well have depended on the particular occasion. Talking about death would have been comforting to the dying who took the cross, but might have been discouraging for all but the most fanatic of active crusaders.

FROM SINNER TO CRUSADER

As mentioned earlier, the model sermons tend to concentrate on the moral, devotional and penitential aspects of crusading. This was to some extent inescapable because a model could not supply information on the

---

[74] For this and the following see Maier, *Preaching the Crusades*, 135–60.

[75] This was laid down in the papal decree *Ad Liberandam* first issued at the Fourth Lateran Council, which was repeatedly re-issued and served as the main guideline throughout the thriteenth century. The only difference between an actual crusader and someone who redeemed a vow for sufficient money was that the former was promised 'a greater share of eternal salvation' in addition to the plenary indulgence. Exactly what this meant is a moot point. See *Conciliorum Oecumenicorum Decreta*, 243–7. For the re-issues see Maier, *Preaching the Crusades*, 80, 102–3, 158.

[76] Pope Innocent IV even encouraged crusade propagandists to concentrate special efforts on the dying. For this see Maier, *Preaching the Crusades*, 145–7.

political and military aspects of each individual crusade. But there were
other reasons. From the point of view of the psychology of recruitment,
the penitential and devotional aspects of the crusade were arguably the
most important. The notion of the crusade as penance rewarded by the
indulgence was probably the main incentive for the majority of people to
take the cross and, therefore, the main aspect preached by most propagandists. In the protheme of his second model James of Vitry clearly
stated that the first and foremost aim of preaching the cross was to lead
people away from their sins.[77] The model sermons generally address
potential crusaders as sinners while suggesting the taking of the crusade
vow as a way of turning away from a sinful life and dealing with the
consequences of sin. This is particularly evident in the models of James
of Vitry, Eudes of Châteauroux and Gilbert of Tournai. In his first model
sermon, for example, Eudes of Châteauroux suggested that taking the
cross amounted to a wholesale conversion to a truly Christian life. Using
the comparison of St Paul's conversion to God, he put this in very
general terms by saying that taking the cross liberated the crusader 'from
the fire of demons, desire, indulging and envy'.[78] In his third model,
Eudes suggested that only those people who emptied their hearts of all
sins could be true crusaders.[79] All three authors, in fact, built up an
image of crusaders as morally superior people: taking the cross not only
meant entering a life with exceptional devotional qualities because of the
crusader's special relationship with Christ, it also liberated the crusader
from all sins and thus distinguished him or her from the mass of ordinary
people.

While describing 'true' crusaders in ideal positive terms, the authors of
the model sermons painted a grim picture of 'anti'-crusaders, that is, all
those who refused to become crusaders or stood in the way of other
people taking the cross. The idea of dividing society into the virtuous
who supported the crusade and the non-virtuous who did not had its
origin in Pope Innocent III's grand design of the crusade, which was
adopted by popes and propagandists throughout the thirteenth century.
This was founded on the belief that there existed a duty for everybody to
contribute to the crusade effort, a belief which Innocent III so clearly
expressed in his influential bull *Quia Maior* and his seminal decree *Ad
Liberandam*.[80] With the establishment of various different ways of
joining in the crusade movement, from personal participation to paying
and praying for the crusade, it was indeed possible to expect everybody

---

[77] James II, 2–5.   [78] Eudes I, 18.   [79] Eudes III, 5–7.
[80] G. Tangl, *Studien zum Register Innocenz' III.* (Weimar, 1929), 88–97, and *PL*,
CCXVI, 817–22 (*Quia Maior*). *Conciliorum Oecumenicorum Decreta*, 243–7 (*Ad
Liberandam*).

to contribute to the crusade effort in one way or another.[81] In the radical thinking of crusade apologists, non-participation in the crusade was a sin because it constituted an act of disobedience towards God, whose war, they believed, the crusade was.

The authors of the crusade model sermons branded those who did not contribute to the crusade effort as morally destitute and evil, either because of a sinful disposition which prevented themselves from becoming crusaders or because they actively opposed the participation of others. The authors listed a number of common sins and specific moral shortcomings, explaining how these could be used to show up people who had no intention of supporting the crusade effort, and spur on those who, out of contrition and a desire to do penance, were prepared to take the cross. Generally speaking, there were three main types of people singled out for attack. The first group were lazy and sluggish people who could not gather the energy to get up and do something about the business of the cross; they kept postponing their decision to take the cross and in the end they were too late to help.[82] The second group were 'carnal' and 'worldly' people who were preoccupied with leading a life of pleasure; they had no time and interest for the crusade because their lives were ruled by the pursuit of carnal desires, wealth and worldly honour.[83] The third group of people were those who opposed participation in the crusade outright because they neither believed in the value nor the use of crusading.[84] This, incidentally, is the only context in which the role of women is explicitly mentioned. Referring to stock accusations used since the beginning of the crusade movement, the authors of the model sermons portrayed women as an impediment to crusading. They were accused of either actively trying to stop their husbands from taking the cross or being, together with their children, the reason why men did not want to go on crusade.[85]

In one of his models, Eudes of Châteauroux specifically attacked the educated, the rich and the powerful for attempting to prevent poor crusaders from taking the cross.[86] This seems to have been a recurrent problem which Eudes felt needed to be addressed separately. Since the introduction of widespread vow-redemptions at the beginning of the thirteenth century, crusade propaganda was directed not only at people

---

[81] For this see also Maier, 'Mass, the Eucharist and the Cross'.

[82] James I, 10, 19; II, 30, 38, 39. Gilbert I, 20, 22.

[83] James I, 9, 10, 14. Eudes I, 5, 18; IV, 3–7; V, 10. Gilbert II, 3; III, 13.

[84] James I, 13, 14; II, 38, 42–4. Gilbert I, 20; II, 7–8; III, 18.

[85] James II, 37, 38. Eudes I, 7; III, 9; IV, 3; V, 7. Gilbert II, 7; III, 8. For the role of women generally see E. Siberry, *Criticism of Crusading 1095–1274* (Oxford, 1985), 44–6, 90–1.

[86] Eudes I, 24, 25.

who would join a crusade army but also at those who were expected to take a crusade vow and redeem it for a money payment in support of the business of the cross. This led to situations where women, the poor, the elderly and ill, that is, people unfit for military service, either redeemed their vows for very little money, or in fact refused to redeem their vows and attempted to join the crusade armies. Both of these practices met with vehement criticism from those 'real' crusaders who were concerned about maintaining what they considered to be the dignity of the crusade vow and who had no interest in taking along on crusade people who could not effectively contribute to the military effort.[87]

During his close involvement in several crusade propaganda campaigns, Eudes of Châteauroux had probably witnessed many instances in which poor people were derided and discouraged from taking the cross by rich and powerful crusaders. Eudes attempted to counteract this problem for two reasons. Firstly, there was the danger that, even though the poor paid little money for a vow redemption, financial subsidies for the crusade might be curtailed as a result. In addition, such arrogant behaviour went against attempts by the Church to propagate the pastoral aspects of the crusade movement and make the devotional dimension and penitential benefits of the crusade vow available to everybody.[88] Eudes presumably wanted to make propagandists aware of such conflicts between powerful and poor crusaders and make sure that they were prepared to deal with them if and when they arose.

James of Vitry, Eudes of Châteauroux and Gilbert of Tournai all proposed the same dramatic picture from Ezekiel 9 as a warning for all those who were indifferent to the crusading effort: as God in the Old Testament purged the city of Jerusalem from all sinners and spared only those signed with the sign of thau, so only crusaders, that is, those signed with the cross, would be saved and all others would suffer God's wrath, either in this life or at the Last Judgement.[89] The most forceful expression of the difference between crusaders, who were said to free themselves from the burden of sins, and obstinate sinners, who refused to get involved in the business of the cross, can be found in Gilbert of Tournai's second model. Here, Gilbert set up a stark contrast between crusaders and 'anti'-crusaders by explaining that, as Christ signed crusaders with the cross, that is, the 'sign of life', so all sinners who disregarded Christ's call to the crusade were marked by the devil with the 'sign of death'.[90] At the same time, Gilbert contrasted to the portrayal of the crusader who imitated Christ that of the sinner who 'crucif[ied] Christ', a metaphor

---

[87] For this see Maier, *Preaching the Crusades*, 135–60.
[88] Maier, 'Mass, the Eucharist and the Cross'.
[89] James I, 13. Eudes V, 11. Gilbert I, 10.   [90] Gilbert II, 2. See also James I, 11.

which he also used in the same sense elsewhere.[91] Such dramatic and powerful metaphors and comparisons were obviously considered to make a strong impression on an audience's imagination. They were intended as a mirror in which members of the audience could see that their sinful lives prejudiced their own chances of salvation. Drawing on this kind of material, a preacher's task was to convince people that, in fact, they only had the choice between taking the cross, and thus dealing with the consequence of sins in a manner beneficial to themselves and the business of the cross, or persisting in their sinful lives and thus risking their own salvation, while damaging the business of the cross.

If this discussion has given the impression that all the *ad status* crusade model sermons project the same uniform picture of the activity of crusading, a note of caution must be issued because this is not so. Generally speaking, the authors worked within the same basic framework of ideas. In short, this consisted of the following elements: (i) the idea that the crusades were wars authorised and supported by God which could be understood as contemporary versions of Old Testament wars; (ii) the idea that participating in the crusade was a form of religious devotion which could be described in terms of a special relationship between the crusader and God or Christ; (iii) the idea that becoming a crusader was a form of conversion to a more thoroughly Christian life and one of the most efficient ways for the laity to deal with the consequence of sin. The authors thus couched the crusade in the great medieval narrative of redemption and salvation; indeed, by constructing a vital link between the individual crusader and Christ the Redeemer, they placed the business of the Cross at the very heart of this narrative. Within this basic framework of ideas the various models place different emphases. James of Vitry, Eudes of Châteauroux and Gilbert of Tournai primarily provided material that stressed the devotional and penitential aspects of crusading, whereas Humbert of Romans and Bertrand de la Tour were more concerned with the aspects of the crusade as war. One should, however, not attach any great meaning to the difference between the models of these two groups of authors. In principle, Humbert certainly had no tendency to play down the devotional and penitential aspects of crusading – quite the contrary. In his crusade preaching tract *De Predicatione S. Crucis*, he gave full treatment to all aspects of crusading, including the devotional and penitential. With Bertrand, the emphasis on the crusade as war can be explained by the fact that his models were written for the preaching to participants of any war: thus they were not exclusively directed towards crusaders. One should also

[91] Gilbert II, 2; III, 13, 18

bear in mind that these model sermons are no suitable guideline for what exactly crusade preachers said in their sermons. Thus, a sermon based on one of Bertrand de la Tour's models could very well be preached with a strong emphasis on penitence, for example, by developing certain aspects and adding other material. By the same token, Gilbert of Tournai's models, for example, could easily be used as a basis for a sermon expounding the military aspects of crusading.

Generally speaking, however, the hallmark of thirteenth and early fourteenth-century crusade preaching seems to have been a strong emphasis on the devotional and the penitential to judge by the model sermons studied here. This can, in part, be explained by the strong pastoral thrust of the crusade movement of the thirteenth century. For many, participation in the crusade consisted in supporting the crusade financially and by prayers rather than in actually joining a crusade army. This in turn meant that in propaganda the crusade had to be portrayed as profoundly relevant to people who might join for reasons that were not primarily connected to the military aspects of the crusade. Taking the cross was advertised above all as a way of showing one's devotion to Christ and of cleansing one's soul from sin, whether or not participation in the crusade meant fighting as a member of the army or supporting the business of the cross on the home front. This may, in part, explain why in the thirteenth century exponents of new forms of spirituality and pastoral reform, such as the two big mendicant orders of the Franciscans and the Dominicans, were often among the most fervent supporters of the crusade movement.

Part II

5

NOTES ON THE TRANSCRIPTION
AND TRANSLATION

WHEN EDITING a medieval document, the principles chosen for the transcription of the manuscript text must be determined in accordance with the purpose of the transcription. One of the principal interests of this study is the question of how crusade sermon models were used and turned into actual sermons by preachers of the cross. It is, therefore, more relevant to reproduce *a* version of each model as it appears in *a* manuscript than to assemble an 'authoritative' text based on an 'original' version or the 'best' readings of all the different variants and strands of textual transmission. The idea is to obtain a version of each model such as would have been used by a medieval preacher. For most of the crusade sermon models collected here, the different manuscript versions show very few significant differences that are not due to various types of scribal errors. Even where there exists a great number of manuscripts, which is the case for the models by James of Vitry, Gilbert of Tournai and Humbert of Romans, I have not been able to discern stemmatic traditions that, in terms of their content, yield significantly different versions of the models in question. The only exception concerns Bertrand de la Tour's models, which survived in three distinct versions of varying length.[1]

The texts reproduced here come close to what David d'Avray has called a 'critical transcription'.[2] For each sermon model one manuscript was chosen to supply the basic text. This was compared with all other known versions in the case of Eudes of Châteauroux's and Bertrand de la Tour's sermon models, for which only few manuscripts survive. For

---

[1] See below pp. 78–9.
[2] D. L. d'Avray, *Death and the Prince. Memorial Preaching before 1350* (Oxford, 1994), 8–10.

James of Vitry, Gilbert of Tournai and Humbert of Romans, whose sermon models have been transmitted in a great number of manuscripts, three additional manuscripts relating to different strands of textual transmission were chosen for comparison. Significant textual variants, that have a bearing on the meaning of the text, have been put in the footnotes in order to give an idea of the difference between different strands of textual transmissions and to indicate the place of the chosen text within the textual tradition. Minor differences, such as, for example, an *et* instead of an *atque*, *nota* instead of *notandum*, etc., and differences of spelling or scribal errors relating to one or two letters only have been ignored in order to keep the footnotes to a minimum. Textual variations in the additional manuscripts have only been included in the main text if the text of the basic manuscript was clearly faulty, that is, where the scribe missed out words or passages by mistake, obviously misread the text he was copying, or included grave grammatical errors that produce a misleading or garbled reading of the text. All in all, the text of the basic manuscript has normally been taken over without additions unless it makes no sense, whereas significant alternative readings from other manuscripts have been relegated to the footnotes.

Where inaccurate **grammar** or unusual or inconsistent **spelling** impinges on the modern reader's sensitivities, editorial alterations have been made. All these editorial corrections of grammar are indicated in the footnotes. If 'incorrect' grammar, however, simply reflects the uncertainty and idiosyncrasy of medieval usage but does not really make reading difficult, the original text has been recorded unaltered. This mainly concerns inconsistent use of the subjunctive and tenses, or different cases of nouns used with prepositions. As concerns spelling, a number of **normalisations** have been silently introduced. As a rule, *v* and *u* have been normalised to classical usage, as have *c* and *t*; *j* has been normalised to *i*. Unusual spellings have in most cases been taken over unless they are difficult to understand. In the latter case, the spelling of one of the alternative manuscripts has been adopted and the original spelling relegated to the footnotes.

Capitalisation is only used for proper names, titles of literary works and books of the Bible. As a rule, the **abbreviations** for the books of the Bible used by the scribe have been taken over; they have been extended only, for example, where the difference between Ecclesiastes and Ecclesiasticus is not made clear. Roman **numerals** have been adopted throughout, even where some manuscripts use Arabic numbers or a mixture of both. Numbers in the text that do not refer to a chapter or book of the Bible or another work are written out in words, such as *septem* for *vii*. **Quotations** from the Bible are marked by italics, quotations from other sources are written in single inverted commas.

The identification of unmarked biblical quotations and verse numbers are added in the text between square brackets. For this, the chapter and verse numberings and the abbreviations used in the Stuttgart edition of the Vulgate have been adopted,[3] except for Sm. i–ii and Sir., which have been replaced by Rg. i–ii and Ecclesiasticus in order to conform to the references used in the manuscripts. Bibliographical references to other quotations are footnoted in the text of the English translation. Modern **punctuation** has been adopted throughout to facilitate reading.

The texts have been divided into numbered **paragraphs** to make referencing easier. The paragraphs are, of course, not part of the original texts and the divisions chosen are to some extent arbitrary and only sometimes reflect divisions marked in the manuscripts. As a rule, I start a new paragraph where one train of thought ends unless the paragraphs determined in this way are too long and complicated, in which case I subdivide them again. One line inserted between paragraphs indicates the beginning of a new **section** or **subsection** within the texts as described above.[4] The **section titles** in James of Vitry's models, which are written in the margins of the manuscripts, are printed as section titles and are indicated by brackets (< >).

In translating the sermon texts edited here, I have tried to stay as close as possible to the Latin original in terms of word meaning, grammatical form and sentence structure. I have chosen to produce a word-by-word translation of the Latin text, which may sound a little artificial at times, in order to capture the exact meaning as well as the general flavour of the original. This procedure sometimes also produces renderings of the Latin Bible passages which sound unusual to those who are accustomed to modern standard translations. With regard to sentence structure, it has sometimes been necessary for the translation to break up overly long and intricately constructed Latin sentences; but here, too, an attempt has been made to reproduce the original flow of the text as best as possible.

One particular problem concerns the translation of the term *crucesignatus* or *cruce signatus*. Whether it is written in one or two words, the Latin term is based on the double meaning of 'crusader' and 'the one signed with the cross', and the authors often consciously play on this dual sense. There is, however, no equivalent term in English to convey this double meaning. One therefore always has to opt for one or the other translation, thus losing some of the connotations of the Latin expression.

[3] *Biblia Sacra Iuxta Vulgatam Versionem*, ed. R. Weber, 2 vols. (Stuttgart, 1969).
[4] See above pp. 32–50.

6

THE MANUSCRIPTS

Douai, Bibliothèque Municipale, 503 (= D), thirteenth century, containing James of Vitry's *Sermones de Sanctis*, his *Sermones Vulgares*, as well as one anonymous sermon.[1]

Paris, Bibliothèque Nationale de France, lat. 3284 (= P2), sixteenth century, containing James of Vitry's *Sermones Vulgares* as well as an incomplete text of his *Historia Transmarina*.[2]

Paris, Bibliothèque Nationale de France, lat. 17509 (= P6), thirteenth century, containing James of Vitry's *Sermones Vulgares*.[3]

Troyes, Bibliothèque Municipale, 228 (= T1), thirteenth century, consisting of three independent parts, of which one is an incomplete collection of James of Vitry's *Sermones Vulgares*.[4]

James of Vitry's *Sermones Vulgares* have survived in at least fourteen manuscripts.[5] T1 was chosen because it constitutes a good, carefully copied text of thirteenth-century date with a minimum of scribal errors. P2 is another very meticulously executed copy, which represents a

---

[1] Described in J. Longère, 'Un sermon inédit de Jacques de Vitry: *Si annis multis uixerit homo*', *L'Église et la mémoire des morts dans la France médiévale*, ed. J.-L. Lemaitre (Paris, 1986), 31–51, here pp. 34–5. See also *CGBP*, VI, 295–7 which, however, gives it a fourteenth-century date.

[2] *Catalogue général des manuscrits latins* [in progress] (Paris, 1939ff), V, 38–43. See also Longère, 'Quatre sermons', 218–19.

[3] L. Delisle, *Inventaire des manuscrits latin de N. Dame et d'autres fonds conservés à la Bibliothèque Nationale sous les no. 16719–18163* (Paris, 1871), 50. See also Longère, 'Quatre sermons', 220.

[4] *CGBP*, II, 118. See also Longère, 'Quatre sermons', 222.

[5] Schneyer, III, 220–1. Longère, 'Quatre sermons', 217–18.

manuscript tradition all of its own.[6] Because of this, it was selected as one of the additional manuscripts despite its late date. P6 and D were included because they are also of an early, that is, thirteenth-century date, but are not directly related to T1 in terms of manuscript traditions.[7]

EUDES OF CHÂTEAUROUX

Pisa, Biblioteca Cateriniana del Seminario, 21 (= Pa), third quarter of the thirteenth century, containing a selection of Eudes of Châteauroux's *Sermones de Tempore, de Sanctis, de Diversis Casibus* and *de Communi Sanctorum*.[8]

Paris, Bibliothèque Mazarine, 1010 (= P1), third quarter of the thirteenth century, containing a selection of Eudes of Châteauroux's *Sermones de Sanctis* and *de Communi Sanctorum* and produced by the cardinal's own scriptorium.[9]

Paris, Bibliothèque Nationale de France, lat. 15947 (= P4), mid-thirteenth century, containing Eudes of Châteauroux's *Sermones de Sanctis* and also produced by the cardinal's own scriptorium.[10]

Rome, Biblioteca Angelica, 157 (= R1), third quarter of the thirteenth century, containing Eudes of Châteauroux's *Sermones de Sanctis*, also produced by his own scriptorium.[11]

Rome, Archivio Generale dell'Ordine dei Predicatori, XIV.35 (= R2), third quarter of the thirteenth century, containing Eudes of Châteauroux's *Sermones de Sanctis*, also produced by his own scriptorium.[12]

Vatican, Biblioteca Apostolica, Pal. lat. 452 (= V1), beginning of the

---

[6] Longère, 'Quatre sermons', 219.   [7] Longère, 'Quatre sermons', 222.

[8] See the description in Iozzelli, *Odo da Châteauroux*, 51–66. Also Charansonnet, 'L'évolution', 114–15. Charansonnet, 'La tradition manuscrite'.

[9] A. Molinier, *Catalogue des manuscrits de la Bibliothèque Mazarine*, 4 vols. (Paris, 1885–92), I, 507–8. Also Charansonnet, 'L'évolution', 114–19. Charansonnet, 'La tradition manuscrite'.

[10] L. Delisle, *Le cabinet des manuscrits de la Bibliothèque Nationale*, vol. II (Paris, 1874), 165. For the date see Charansonnet, 'L'évolution', 114–19. Charansonnet, 'La tradition manuscrite'.

[11] Charansonnet, 'L'évolution', 114–19. Charansonnet, 'La tradition manuscrite'. H. Narducci, *Catalogus Codicum Manuscriptorum praeter Graecos et Orientales in Bibliotheca Angelica olim Coenobii Sancti Augustini de Urbe*, vol. I (Rome, 1893), 84; he gives it a fourteenth-century date.

[12] No description of this manuscript seems to exist. But see Charansonnet, 'L'évolution', 114–19. Charansonnet, 'La tradition manuscrite'.

fourteenth century, containing Eudes of Châteauroux's *Sermones de Sanctis*.[13]

Eudes of Châteauroux's sermons exist in two editions produced under his own guidance if not by himself.[14] Although for the crusade sermon texts the two editions hardly differ from each other, the second edition has been adopted as the basis of the edition. Four of the five sermon texts only exist in one manuscript of the second edition. R1 contains the second edition of Eudes's first model, R2 that of models two to four. The fifth model has survived in three copies of the second edition, Pa, P1 and R2. Pa was selected for the edition because it has the clearest text and is of virtually the same date as the other manuscripts. P4 and V1 were used as additional manuscripts and for the sake of comparison with the first edition.

Since Eudes's sermons were recorded so systematically, the manuscript tradition gives an indication as to when the models were written.[15] Since models one to four already appear in the first addition, they must have been composed before the late 1250s when the first edition was completed.[16] The fleeting reference to the Mongols in Eudes's second model suggests that he probably preached the cross against the Mongols around 1240 and that this experience contributed to his text.[17] The chronology of Eudes's collections also makes it likely that models one, three and four were linked to Eudes's activities as crusade propagandist during the preparations for Louis IX's first crusade in the late 1240s.[18] The fifth sermon model was probably written in the 1260s when the second edition of Eudes's sermons was under way.[19] This means that it could have been connected to Eudes's preaching in the context of one of the many crusade recruitment campaigns of the 1260s.[20]

GILBERT OF TOURNAI

Cambridge, University Library, Peterhouse 200 (= C), late thirteenth to early fourteenth century, containing in two independent parts John of

---

[13] No description of this manuscript seems to exist. But see Charansonnet, 'L'évolution', 114.

[14] Charansonnet, 'L'évolution', 114–15.

[15] Charansonnet, 'L'évolution', *passim*.

[16] Charansonnet, 'L'évolution', 117–19.

[17] For the crusade propaganda against the Mongols around 1240 see Maier, *Preaching the Crusades*, 59–60.

[18] See above pp. 9–10.   [19] Charansonnet, 'L'évolution', 120–1.

[20] Maier, *Preaching the Crusades*, 79–82.

Wales's *De IV Predicabilibus ad Omne Genus Hominum* and Gilbert of Tournai's *Sermones ad Status.*[21]

Marseille, Bibliothèque Municipale, 392 (= M), end of the thirteenth century, containing Gilbert of Tournai's *Sermones ad Status.*[22]

Paris, Bibliothèque Nationale de France, lat. 15943 (= P3), end of the thirteenth century, containing Gilbert of Tournai's *Sermones ad Status.*[23]

Paris, Bibliothèque Nationale de France, lat. 15953 (= P5), second half of the thirteenth century, containing a selection of sermons by individual preachers (Guillaume of Mailly, Nicolas of Le Mans, Walter of Château-Thierry, Eudes of Châteauroux, Guiard of Laon, William of Auvergne, Nicolas of Biard, Nicholas of Gorran), Stephen Bourbon's *De Septem Bonis* and Gilbert of Tournai's *Sermones ad Status.* It was owned by Peter of Limoges, who donated it to the Sorbonne at his death in 1306.[24]

So far, between sixty and seventy manuscripts containing some or all of Gilbert of Tournai's *Sermones ad Status* have been discovered.[25] P5 was selected because it seemed the clearest and least faulty of the ones consulted, probably owing to the careful editing by its thirteenth-century owner, Peter of Limoges. The three additional manuscripts were chosen because they are carefully copied thirteenth-century manuscripts that seem to belong to different strands of textual transmission.[26]

HUMBERT OF ROMANS

Avignon, Bibliothèque Municipale, Musée Calvet 327 (= A), fifteenth century, containing a selection of Humbert of Romans's *Sermones ad Omnes Status.*[27]

---

[21] M. R. James, *A Descriptive Catalogue of the Manuscripts of the Library of Peterhouse* (Cambridge, 1899), 235–6.

[22] J. Longère, 'Guibert de Tournai (d. 1284). Sermon aux chanoines réguliers: *Considerate lilia agri quomodo crescunt (Mat. VI, 28)*', *Revue Mabillon*, n. s. 3 (1992), 103–15, here p. 106. N. Bériou and F.-O. Touati, *Voluntate Dei Leprosus. Les lépreux entre conversion et exclusion aux XIIème et XIIIème siècles* (Testi, Studi, Strumenti 4; Spoleto, 1991), 86. See also *CGBP*, XV, 135.

[23] L. Delisle, *Inventaire des manuscrits de la Sorbonne* (Paris, 1870), 29. For a recent description see Bériou and Touati, *Voluntate Dei Leprosus*, 87. Also Longère, 'Guibert de Tournai', 105.

[24] Delisle, *Inventaire des manuscrits de la Sorbonne*, 30. For a recent description see Bériou and Touati, *Voluntate Dei Leprosus*, 87–8. Also Longère, 'Guibert de Tournai', 105.

[25] Schneyer, II, 306–7. See also Bériou and Touati, *Voluntate Dei Leprosus*, 84.

[26] For the various 'families' of manuscripts see Bériou and Touati, *Voluntate Dei Leprosus*, 89–91.

[27] *CGBP*, XXVII, 237–8.

Frankfurt a. M., Stadt- und Universitätsbibliothek, Praed. 29 (= F), mid-fifteenth century, containing Humbert of Romans's *De Praedicatione S. Crucis*, the part of his *De Eruditione Praedicatorum* which contains the *Sermones ad Omnes Status*, and his *Expositio Regulae Beati Augustini*.[28]

Reims, Bibliothèque Municipale, 612, (= Re), early fourteenth century, containing Humbert of Romans's *Sermones ad Omnes Status*.[29]

Segovia, Catedral Estanceria B 331 (= S), dated 1477 in the manuscript itself, containing Humbert of Romans's *Sermones ad Omnes Status*.[30]

The majority of Humbert of Romans's *Sermones ad Omnes Status* have survived in at least nineteen manuscripts, most of which date from the fifteenth century.[31] The text does not vary greatly between the many different manuscripts and 'families' of manuscripts. The difference rather lies in the care with which the manuscripts were executed. Simon Tugwell's analysis of the manuscript tradition has established that, generally speaking, A is a very carefully produced manuscript.[32] It was therefore chosen as the basis for the edition. S was selected as an additional manuscript because it seems to belong to the same strand of transmission as A, while F represents a different 'family' of manuscripts.[33] Re was included because it is one of the few earlier manuscripts which contains all four models, even though it has a fair number of scribal errors.

BERTRAND DE LA TOUR

Barcelona, Archivo de la Corona de Aragon, Ripoll 187 (= B), early fourteenth century, containing Bertrand de la Tour's *Collationes Abbreviate*, which feature his *ad status* model sermons.[34]

Naples, Biblioteca Nazionale, VIII.A.36 (= N), composite manuscript with a fourteenth-century part and a part of the late fourteenth to early

---

[28] G. Powitz, *Die Handschriften des Dominikanerklosters und des Leonhardsstifts in Frankfurt a. M.* (Die Kataloge der Stadt- und Universitätsbibliothek Frankfurt a. M. 2; Frankfurt a. M., 1968), 68–9.

[29] *CGBP*, XXXVIII, 803–4.

[30] No description of this manuscript seems to exist.

[31] Kaeppeli, *Scriptores Ordinis Praedicatorum*, II, 287–8. Bériou and Touati, *Voluntate Dei Leprosus*, 92–3.

[32] Simon Tugwell very kindly allowed me to work with his collation of nineteen manuscripts of the *Liber de Eruditione Predicatorum* which contains the *sermones ad status*. See also Bériou and Touati, *Voluntate Dei Leprosus*, 92.

[33] Bériou and Touati, *Voluntate Dei Leprosus*, 92.

[34] No description of this manuscript seems to exist.

fifteenth century; the earlier part contains a selection of Bertrand de la Tour's *Collationes Abbreviate* including his *ad status* models.[35]

Troyes, Bibliothèque Municipale, 2001 (= T2), fourteenth century, containing three independent collections of model sermons, of which one consists of Bertrand de la Tour's *Collationes Abbreviate* including his *ad status* models.[36]

Vatican, Biblioteca Apostolica, Archivio Capitolare di S. Pietro, G. 48 (= V2), containing a selection of Bertrand de la Tour's *Collationes Abbreviate* including his *ad status* models.[37]

The four manuscripts containing Bertrand de la Tour's crusade model sermons represent three different text versions. Compared to the sermon texts by the other four authors, Bertrand's texts underwent a much greater degree of change during the process of transmission. It seems that the scribes sometimes wanted to improve the text that they copied by changing individual words or adding short phrases and sometimes replacing obviously incorrect readings. But the main difference between the three versions is the number of *exempla* added at the end of the models. B seems to represent the standard version with one *exemplum* at the end of each model. Because of this it was selected as the basis of the edition. N and V2 also have the *exemplum* at the end of the first model, but omit it at the end of the second and the third. T2 has the same *exempla* as B, but has an additional one at the end of the first and the second models.

[35] C. Cenci, *Manoscritti Francescani della Biblioteca Nazionale di Napoli*, 2 vols. (Spicilegium Bonaventurianum 7, 8; Grottaferrata, 1971), II, 726–9.
[36] *CGBP,* II, 820.   [37] No description of this manuscript seems to exist.

7

THE SERMONS

James of Vitry

SERMO I

T1 = Troyes, Bibliothèque Municipale, 228, ff. 148rb–149rb

Additional manuscripts
D = Douai, Bibliothèque Municipale, 503, ff. 363v-365r
P2 = Paris, Bibothèque Nationale de France, lat. 3284, ff. 123rb-125rb
P6 = Paris, Bibliothèque Nationale de France, lat. 17509, ff. 92^4-94^2

Reference
Schneyer, III, 216, no. 413

Sermo ad crucesignatos vel -signandos

1 Thema sumptum ex Apoc. [vii, 2–3]:[1] *Vidi angelum ascendentem ab ortu solis habentem signum Dei vivi, et clamavit voce magna quatuor angelis quibus datum est nocere terre et mari dicens: Nolite nocere terre et mari neque arboribus, quousque signemus servos Dei nostri in frontibus eorum.*

< De instantia predicationis et de lampade[2] >
2 *Propter Syon non tacebo et propter Ierusalem non quiescam, donec egrediatur ut splendor iustus eius et salvator eius ut lampas accendatur.* Hiis verbis ostendit Ysa. [lxii, 1] quam instanter et diligenter verbum Dei vobis debeamus[3] predicare et maxime quando predicamus *propter Syon*

---

[1] The chapters of the books of the Bible are sometimes noted in the margin.
[2] Throughout the sermon the manuscript supplies the section titles in the margin.
[3] debeamus T1, D] debemus P2, debeatis *post corr.* P6

James of Vitry

SERMON I

Sermon to those who are or will become crusaders

1 Theme taken from Apocalypse: *I saw an angel rising from the sunrise carrying the sign of the living God, and he called in a powerful voice to the four angels whose duty was to devastate land and sea: Do not devastate land and sea nor the trees, until we have signed the servants of our God on their foreheads.*

< About the force of preaching and about the lamp >
2 *For Zion's sake I will not be silent, for Jerusalem's sake I shall not rest, until her right shines forth like a bright light and her salvation is lit like a lamp.* With these words Isaiah shows how much more forcefully and diligently we must preach the word of God to you and in particular

et *Ierusalem*, ut scilicet Terra Sancta de manibus inimicorum liberetur. Non enim dare debemus *sompnum oculis nostris aut palpebris vestris dormitationem* [Ps. cxxxi, 4–5], *sompnum* scilicet negligentie vel *dormitationem* torporis et ignavie, *aut requiem temporibus nostris, donec inveniamus* et recuperemus *locum Domino*, in quo scilicet loco Dominus tamquam in patria sua corporaliter habitavit, *et tabernaculum Deo Iacob*, in quo scilicet Dominus contra diabolum militavit et ipsum expugnavit [cf. Mt. iv].

3 Vel *propter Syon non tacebo*, sed loquar id est propter ecclesiam, et *propter Ierusalem non quiescam*, laborando scilicet et predicando propter animas convertendas et multiplicandam ecclesiam,[4] *donec egrediatur ut splendor iustus eius*, id est cognoscatur per predicationem meam, et *salvator eius ut lampas accendatur* in cordibus auditorum. Per lampadem Christus designatur, unde in Zach. [iv, 2] dicitur quod lampas super candelabrum erat, id est Christus super ecclesiam, cuius caro vitro assimilatur, quia pura fuit et fragilis sicut vitrum. Et sicut vitrum ligno[5] adaptatur, ut melius ymago inspicientis resultet, ita in crucis speculo adaptata Christi carne quilibet imaginem suam potest cognoscere, ut ex medicine qualitate infirmitatem suam agnoscat.

4 Lampadibus autem divites non utuntur sed contempnunt, et Christus a divitibus et secularibus hominibus contempnitur, unde Iob [xii, 5]: *Lampas contempta apud cogitationem divitum*, et Ysa. [xlix, 7] de Christo ait: *Hec dicit Dominus ad animam contemptibilem*. Predicta tamen verba possunt intelligi contra contemptores verbi Dei, ut per *Syon* principes et per *Ierusalem* sacerdotes intelligantur, qui ora prophetarum obstruere nitebantur, unde Ysa. [xlv, 10]: *Ve qui dicit patri: Quid generas*, patri scilicet spirituali, *et mulieri: Quid parturis*, id est ecclesie? Et Bernardus ait: 'Irascitur homo medicanti et applaudit sagittanti', id est adulatori. Qui autem noluerunt audire levem sibilum predicationis saltem audiant magnum clamorem Crucifixi, alioquin audituri sunt tonitruum terribilis vocis: *Ite, maledicti* [Mt. xxv, 41]! Orate igitur Dominum, ut ex[6] lampade, que est Christus, hodie nobis infundat oleum pietatis et splendorem cognitionis.

---

[4] ecclesiam] Dei *praem.* D, P2, P6
[5] vitrum ligno D, P2, P6] lignum vitro T1
[6] ex D, P2, P6] *om.* T1

when we preach *about Zion* and *Jerusalem*, so that the Holy Land may be freed from the hands of the enemies. We must not give *sleep to our eyes or drowsiness to your lids*, the *sleep* of negligence or the *drowsiness* of sluggishness and idleness, *or rest in our life-times, until we find* and recover *for the Lord the place,* where the Lord lived bodily as in his fatherland, *and a dwelling place of the God of Jacob,* where the Lord fought against the devil and defeated him.

3 Or, *for Zion's sake I will not be silent*, but speak for the church, and *for Jerusalem's sake I shall not rest*, but labour and preach to convert souls and enlarge the church, *until her right shines forth like a bright light*, that is [until] it is made known through my preaching, and *her salvation is lit like a lamp* in the hearts of the listeners. The lamp means Christ, whence in Zechariah it says that there was a lamp above the candle-holder, that is Christ above the church, whose flesh is likened to glass, because it was as pure and fragile as glass. And as glass is fitted to wood, so that a better likeness of the onlooker results, so, with Christ's flesh fitted to it, anyone can recognise his own likeness in the mirror of the cross, so that he may behold his weakness in medical terms.

4 The rich do not use lamps but despise them, and Christ is despised by rich and worldly people, whence Job: *The lamp is despised in the thoughts of the rich*, and Isaiah says of Christ: *The Lord said this to the despisable soul*. The above words can be understood [as being directed] against those who despise the word of God, just as by *Zion* the princes are understood and by *Jerusalem* the priests who strive to muzzle the mouths of the prophets, whence Isaiah: *Woe to anyone who asks his father*, that is the spiritual father: *What do you beget, and his mother*, that is the church: *What do you give birth to?* And Bernard says: 'People get angry with him who heals and applaud him who shoots arrows',[1] that is a flatterer. Those who do not want to listen to the soft murmur of the sermon, should at least listen to the loud call of the Crucified, else they will hear the thunder of a dreadful voice: Go, *you who are cursed*! Therefore, pray to the Lord, that today he may pour for us from the lamp, that is Christ, the oil of piety and the bright light of understanding.

---

[1] Bernardus, 'Super Cantica', *S. Bernardi Opera*, ed. J. Leclerq, C. H. Talbot and H. M. Rochais, 9 vols. (Rome, 1957–77), II, 34.

< Expositio thematis et de angelo ascendente >

5 *Vidi angelum ascendentem ab ortu solis* etc. Angelus iste est Christus, paterne voluntatis nuntius, qui ascendere dicitur, dum suos ascendere facit de virtute in virtutem de bono in melius perficiendo. *Ab ortu solis* ascendit, dum paulatim per predicatores mundum illuminavit, sicut sol paulatim crescit usque ad perfectum diem; *ab ortu* etiam *solis* ascendit, id est a Patre, de diabolo triumphans.

< De signo crucis et signatis >

6 Habet hic angelus *signum Dei vivi,* id est signum crucis, quo suos signat ad distinctionem, ut discernantur ab infide- [f. 148va] libus et reprobis, et munit ad deffensionem, ne ledantur ab inimicis, unde in Ezech. [ix, 3] dicitur: *Vocavit virum qui indutus erat lineis,* id est Deus Pater Christum veste candida indutum, qui sacerdos in eternum est, *et attramentarium scriptoris habebat in lumbis suis,* ut scilicet omnium peccata scriberet et sanctorum numerum a peccatoribus segregaret. *Et dixit Dominus ad eum: Transi per mediam civitatem in medio Ierusalem et signa thau super frontes virorum gementium et dolentium super cunctis abhominationibus, que fiunt in medio eius* [Ez. ix, 4], et paulo post: *Omnem super quem videritis thau ne occidatis et a sanctuario meo incipite* [Ez. ix, 6]. 'Thau littera crucis habet similitudinem', qua solebant olim uti Hebrei, 'Samaritani usque hodie', teste Ieronimo, hac littera 'utuntur'. Aliis autem occisis liberati sunt cruce signati. *A sanctuario* autem, id est a sacerdotibus, incipere precipiuntur quia, sicut in libro Sapie. [vi, 6] dicitur, maioribus maior instat cruciatus et *iudicium durissimum hiis qui presunt fiet.*[7]

< Quod Christus cruce signatus fuit et de sepulcro Domini >

7 Patet igitur quod *signum Dei vivi* habet Christus, ut signet milites suos; qui etiam prior cruce signari voluit, ut alios precederet cum vexillo crucis. *Hunc enim Deus Pater signavit* [Io. vi, 27], cuius carni crux clavis ferreis affixa est, que molli filo affigitur palliis vestris. Unde Ysa. [xi, 10]: *Radix Iesse, qui stat in signum populorum; ipsum gentes deprecabuntur et erit sepulcrum eius gloriosum. Radix* enim *Iesse,* id est Christus, stetit *in signum populorum,* id est in cruce, qua signatur Dei populus; *ipsum*

---

[7] fiet D, P6] *om.* T1, P2

< Exposition of the theme and about the rising angel >

5 *I saw an angel rising from the sunrise* etc. This angel is Christ, the messenger of his Father's will, who is said to rise as he makes his people rise from virtue to virtue by making them better and better. He rises *from the sunrise* as he slowly enlightens the world through his preachers, just as the sun slowly rises until the height of the day; he also rises *from the sunrise*, that is from the Father, triumphing over the devil.

< About the sign of the cross and those who are signed >

6 This angel has *the sign of the living God*, that is the sign of the cross, with which he signs his people to distinguish them, so that they can be told apart from the unfaithful and reprobate, and he arms them for defence, so that they may not be hurt by the enemies, whence it says in Ezekiel: *He called the man dressed in linen*, that is God the Father [called] Christ dressed in a white garment, who is a priest in eternity, *and has the scribe's ink-horn round his loins*, so that he may write down everybody's sins and separate the number of the saints from the sinners. *And the Lord said to him: Go all through the city, all through Jerusalem and mark a thau on the foreheads of the men who grieve and lament over all the abominations which happen inside it*, and a little later: *Do not kill anyone on whom you see the thau and begin at my sanctuary.* 'The letter *thau*', which the Hebrews once used, 'resembles the cross', and according to Jerome,[2] the Samaritans still 'use' this letter today. While the others were killed, those signed with the cross were freed. They were told to begin *at the sanctuary*, which means with the priests, because, as it says in the book of Wisdom, the mighty are mightily tormented and *on the highly placed a most harsh judgement falls.*

< That Christ was signed with the cross and about the Lord's sepulchre >

7 It is clear that Christ has *the sign of the living God*, so that he may sign his soldiers; he also wanted to be signed with the cross first, so that he could precede all others with the banner of the cross. *God Father signed him*, to whose flesh the cross, that is fixed with a soft thread to your coats, was fixed with iron nails. Whence Isaiah: *The root of Jesse, standing as a sign for the people; the nations will beseech him and his sepulchre will be glorious. The root of Jesse*, that is Christ, stood *as a sign for the people*, namely on the cross, with which God's people are signed;

---

[2] Hieronymus, 'Commentariorum in Hiezechielem Libri xiv', *CCSL*, LXXV, 3–743, here p. 106.

gentes deprecabuntur, maxime post resurrectionem et ascensionem, et *sepulcrum,* in quo iacuit, *gloriosum* est quia ab omnibus Christi fidelibus habetur in honore in tantum quod multi pre amore Christi et devotione asumpto salutifere crucis signaculo per terram et mare laborant, ut ipsum corporaliter videre valeant et honorare.

<De armis Christi et militum eius et contra illos qui de Terra Sancta non curant>
8 Magnum honorem reputantes, si eisdem vestibus induantur, quibus rex eorum est indutus, et si eodem caractere insignantur. Non reputantes vere Christi milites qui aliquid[8] panicellum, quod vulgari Gallico 'pannuncel' appellatur; de armis eius[9] non habent. Et quoniam scriptum est: *Si oblitus fuero tui Ierusalem, oblivioni detur dextera mea* [Ps. cxxxvi, 5], qui veri filii sunt patriam patris sui suam reputant patriam et amore trahuntur ad videndam civitatem illam, in qua Dominus *operatus est salutem* nostram [Ps. lxxiii, 12]. De qua Ysa. [lx, 12] ait: *Gens et regnum, quod non servierit tibi, peribit et gentes solitudine vastabuntur,* id est a Deo delinquntur qui nolunt servire Ierusalem et succurere ei ac deffendere ab inimicis. Unde et Ysa. [lxiiii, 10–1] eius desolationem in spiritu previdens, dolens et merens ait: *Civitas sancti tui facta est deserta, deserta Syon, deserta facta est Ierusalem, desolata est domus sacrificationis nostre et glorie nostre ubi laudaverunt te patres nostri, facta est in exustionem ignis et omnia desiderabilia nostra versa sunt in ruinas.*

<De refrenatione[10] quatuor angelorum et quod nocent terre et mari et arboribus>
9 *Vidi angelum ascendentem ab ortu solis habentem signum Dei vivi, et clamavit voce magna quatuor angelis, quibus datum est nocere terre et mari.* Clamare Dei est malitiam demonum refrenare. *Datum est* autem *quatuor angelis,* id est demonibus habitantibus in quatuor mundi climatibus; permissum est *nocere terre,* id est amantibus terrena, quos amor terrenus retinet, ut de cruce [f. 148vb] accipienda non curent vel de hereditate Domini ab hostibus liberanda. *Datum est* insuper *nocere mari,* id est amaris et fetidis peccatoribus, qui variis fluctibus curarum et

---

8 aliquid T1, P2] aliud signum vel D, P6
9 eius D, P2, P6] *om.* T1
10 refrenatione T1, D, P2] reformatione P6

the nations will beseech him, in particular after the resurrection and ascension, and *the sepulchre*, in which he lay, is *glorious* because it is held in honour by all faithful Christians in as much as many, after they have taken the sign of the salutary cross out of the love of Christ and out of devotion, exert themselves on land and at sea, so that they may see and honour [the sepulchre] in person.

< About the arms of Christ and his soldiers and against those who do not care about the Holy Land >
8 They are greatly honoured [who] wear the same garments that their king wore and [who] are signed with the same mark. Those who [wear] just any coat, which is called 'pannuncel' in the French vernacular, are not really known as soldiers of Christ; they do not carry his arms. And since it is written: *If I forget you, Jerusalem, may my right hand wither*, those who are true sons consider their father's fatherland their own fatherland and are drawn by love to see the city where the Lord *has worked* our *salvation*. Isaiah says about this: *For the nation and kingdom that will not serve you will perish and the nations will be destroyed by depravation*; this means that those will be abandoned by God who do not want to serve Jerusalem and come to its aid and defend it against the enemies. Whence, foreseeing its desolation in his mind, again Isaiah rightly said with pain: *Your holy city has been made a desert, Zion has been made a desert, Jerusalem has been made a desert, the house of our sacrifice and our glory, where our fathers praised you, has been abandoned, it has been burned down and all our delight lies in ruins.*

< About restraining the four angels and that they devastate the land and the sea and the trees >
9 *I saw an angel rising from the sunrise carrying the sign of the living God, and he called in a powerful voice to the four angels whose duty was to devastate land and sea.* To call to God means to restrain the wickedness of the demons. *It is the duty of the four angels*, that is the demons living in the four regions of the world; they are allowed *to devastate the earth*, this means the lovers of worldly things who are held back by worldly love, so that they do not care about taking the cross or about liberating the inheritance of the Lord from the enemies. *It is* also *their duty to devastate the sea*, that is the bitter and fetid sinners who are frightened by the changing currents of sorrows and anxieties and so feel

sollicitudinum anxiantur, itaque desolationi Terre Sancte non compatiantur. Unde vera Christi membra dici nequeunt qui capitis lesionem non sentiunt.

< Contra pigros et accidiosos >

10 Permissum est insuper angelis Sathane *nocere arboribus* infructuosis, pigris scilicet et accidiosis et otiosis. Si quidem otia corpus alunt, sed animam destruunt, e contra teste Philosopho: 'Generosos animos labor nutrit', teste autem Gregorio: 'Ut caro mollibus, sic spiritus duris nutritur.' Illa delectationibus pascitur, hic amaritudine vegetatur, et inde in perpetuum spiritus interit, unde ad horam caro suaviter vivit. Dicunt autem physici quod partes animalis que magis sunt in motu saniores sunt ad comedendum; 'et vitium capiunt, ni moveantur, aque'. Sicut autem navis sine aliquo pondere non potest mare transire, sed[11] fluctibus iactatur et levitate sua evagando periclitatur, ita sine pondere et labore non valet homo ad portum quietis pervenire.

11 Arbores igitur infructuose diabolo exponuntur, que sicce sunt sine humore gratie, non habentes 'fructum bonorum operum' vel folia bonorum verborum. Nam teste Iohanne in Apoc. [xii, 4]: *Draco traxit tertiam partem stellarum,* una pars que fidem deffendit verbo sicut doctores contra hereticos, alia que fidem deffendit gladio sicut Christi milites, tertia que nec verbo nec gladio, et isti sunt pars diaboli. Nam sicut in Parab. [xx, 17] dicitur: *Suavis est homini panis mendacii, sed os eius implebitur calculo. Panis mendacii* voluptas carnalis, que mentitur se esse panem. *Panis* quidem natura est satiare et confortare, quod non facit mendax voluptas; *calculus* autem dicitur pena eterna, que masticari non potest pre nimia duritia, quia intollerabilis et inconsumabilis pena gehenne, nec glutiri potest, quia est magnus et ignitus.

12 Teste autem Ecclesiastico [xxiii, 22]: *Anima calida velut ignis; donec aliquid glutierit, non extinguetur.* Ergo numquam ille ignis *extinguetur,* quia nunquam poterit calculus ille glutiri. Et quoniam diabolus tibi cyphum porrexit et tu spumam voluptatis bibisti in hoc seculo, feces inexhaustibiles pene eterne bibes in alio, cuius *fex non est exinanita* [Ps. lxxiv, 9].

---

[11] sed D, P2, P6] nec T1

no pity for the desolation of the Holy Land. Whence those who do not feel the wound of the head cannot be called true limbs of Christ.

< Against the lazy and slack >

10 The angels of Satan are also allowed *to devastate the trees* that do not carry fruit, that is the lazy, slack and idle. Even though idleness strengthens the body, it destroys the soul, as against the Philosopher's testimony: 'Work nourishes the noble souls;'[3] [see] moreover Gregory's testimony: 'As the flesh is nourished by softness, so is the soul by harshness.'[4] [The flesh] is fed on pleasures, [the soul] thrives on bitterness; thence the soul will exist in eternity, whereas the flesh sweetly lives only once. Physicians say that those parts of an animal that are most frequently in motion are healthier to eat; 'and water acquires a taint unless it is in motion'.[5] As a ship cannot sail across the sea without any weight but is thrown about by currents and in danger of lingering because of its lightness, thus people cannot reach the haven of calm without heavy and harsh work.

11 The trees that carry no fruit are exposed to the devil; they are dry without the humidity of grace, they do not carry 'the fruits of good works'[6] or the leaves of good words. According to John's testimony in Apocalypse: *The dragon swept the third part of the stars*; the first part defends the faith with the word like the doctors against the heretics, the second part defends the faith with the sword like the soldiers of Christ, the third part defends neither with the word nor with the sword and they are the devil's part. As it says in Proverbs: *The bread of deceit is sweet to man, but his mouth will be filled with grit. The bread of deceit* [means] carnal pleasure, which pretends to be bread. The nature of *bread* is to stop hunger and to strengthen, which deceitful pleasure does not do; *grit*, which cannot be digested because it is too hard, means eternal punishment, because the punishment of hell is unbearable and cannot be consumed, and it cannot be swallowed since it is big and fiery.

12 According to the testimony of Ecclesiasticus: *The hot soul is like fire; it will not be extinquished until it has swallowed something*. This *fire will* never *be extinguished* because this grit can never be swallowed. And since the devil offered you a cup and you drank the froth of pleasure in this world, you will drink the inexhaustible lye of eternal punishment in the next, whose *lye has not been emptied*.

---

[3] Walther, II/1, 872, no. 6968.
[4] Gregorius Magnus, 'Moralia in Iob libri i-x', *CCSL*, CXLIII, 567.
[5] Ovidus, 'Ex Ponto', *P. Ovidi Nasonis Tristium Libri Quinque, Ibis, Ex Ponto Libri Quattuor, Halieutica, Fragmenta*, ed. S. G. Owen (Oxford, 1915), I, v, 6.
[6] Ambrosius Mediolanensis, 'De Ioseph', *CSEL*, XXXII/2, 75.

< Qui signati non sunt diabolo exponuntur et contra illos qui dedecus Domini sui nolunt vindicare >

13 Cum igitur dicatur predictis angelis malis: *Nolite nocere terre et mari neque arboribus, quousque signemus servos Dei nostri*, valde timendum est hiis qui signari nolunt sed in fecibus consuetis malunt manere quam in servitio Dei laborare ne, postquam signati fuerint servi Dei, ipsi malignis spiritibus *quibus datum est nocere terre et mari* exponantur, dicente Domino per Ezech. [ix, 4–6]: *Transite per mediam civitatem et percutite et non parcat oculus vester neque misereatur; omnem autem super quem videritis thau ne occidatis!* Soli autem gementes et dolentes super abhominationibus, que fiunt in Ierusalem, a percussoribus signo thau deffenduntur.

14 Non enim dignus est misericordia qui pectus ferreum habet et de vituperio patris sui non dolet, cum etiam de Hely sacerdote licet alias malus esset legamus [cf. i Rg. iiii, 11–22] quod, statim cum audivit archam Domini captam esse, pre nimio dolore corruit de sella et expiravit. Quid igitur de illis qui audiunt Terram [f. 149ra] Sanctam ab inimicis Christi conculcari et nec dolore moventur nec curare videntur, contra quos Dominus per Aggeum [i, 9] ait: *Domus mea deserta est et vos festinatis unusquisque in domum suam?* De Uria etiam legimus [ii Rg. xi, 11] quod in domum suam intrare noluit nec vacare deliciis, quamdiu fratres sui in exercitu suo laborabant et *archa* Dei Israel esset *in papilionibus.*

< De destructione et desolatione Terre Sancte, de multiplici eius commendatione et lamentatione eius >

15 Hodie autem *domina gentium, princeps provinciarum facta est sub tributo* [Lam. i, 1], et usque ad nobilius membrum, ad interiora viscerum, ad pupillam oculi extenderunt manus sacrilegas inimici crucis Christi inpugnantes et expugnantes civitatem redemptionis nostre, que mater est fidei: *Quia de Syon exivit lex et verbum Domini de Ierusalem* [Is. ii, 3], in qua *est operatus* Dominus *salutem in medio terre* [Ps. lxxiii, 12], in qua *corpus suum dedit percutientibus et genas suas vellentibus, ubi faciem suam non avertit ab increpantibus et conspuentibus*[12] *in ipsum* [Is. l, 6], ubi *peccata nostra portavit in corpore suo super lignum* [i Pe. ii, 24]. Nunc

---

[12] et conspuentibus D, P2, P6] *om.* T1

< [That] those who are not signed are exposed to the devil and against those who do not want to avenge their Lord's dishonour >

13 As it says about the above-mentioned bad angels: *Do not devastate land and sea nor trees, until we have signed the servants of our God*, those who do not want to be signed but would rather remain in the lye that they are used to than labour in the service of God must fear that, after the servants of God are signed, they will be exposed to those evil spirits *whose duty is to devastate land and sea*, as the Lord says through Ezekiel: *Go all through the city and kill and your eye shall spare and pity [no one]; but do not kill anyone on whom you see the thau!* Only those who lament and pine over the abominations which happen in Jerusalem are defended against the killers by the sign of the thau.

14 He who has a breast of iron and does not pine over the blame of his father is not worthy of pity, as we read about Eli the priest that, even though he was once bad, he fell from his seat and died from too much pain as soon as he heard that the ark of the Lord was captured. So what about those who hear that the Holy Land is overthrown by the enemies of Christ and are not moved by pain and do not appear to care, against whom the Lord says through Haggai: *My house lies in ruin and each of you is busy with his own house?* About Uriah we read that he did not want to enter his house and enjoy any pleasures while his brothers laboured in his army and *the ark* of the Lord was *in tents*.

< About the destruction and desolation of the Holy Land, about its multiform recommendation and its lamentation >

15 Today too, *the mistress of the nations, the princess of the provinces has been made a tributary,* and the enemies of the cross of Christ reached out their sacrilegious hands as far as the most noble limb, the inner organs and the pupil of the eye, attacking and conquering the city of our redemption, that is the mother of faith: *For the law went forth from Zion and the word of the Lord from Jerusalem,* where the Lord *has worked our salvation in the midst of the earth,* where *he gave his body to those who struck [him] and his cheeks to those who plucked out [his beard],* where *he did not turn his face away from those who insulted him and spat on him,* where *he bore our sins in his body on the wood.* Now she has been made *the nest of*

autem facta est *cubile draconum et pascua structionum* [Is. xxxiv, 13], et quotquot Christiani in ea habitant in servitute sunt Sarracenorum et in periculo personarum.

16 *Periit sacrificium et libatio de templo Domini* [Ioel i, 9] et in eo nomen Machometi iugiter invocatur. Et secundum Dan. [ix, 27] vaticinium, *defecit ibi hostia et sacrificium et in templo abhominatio desolationis*; *tulerunt enim iuge sacrificium et deiecerunt locum sacrificationis* [Dn. viii, 11]; *incenderunt igni sanctuarium Domini, in terra polluerunt tabernaculum nominis eius* [Ps. lxxiii, 7], sicut scriptum est in Daniele [viii, 12]: *Prosternetur veritas in terra et faciet et prosperabitur*, et ut verbis Ysa. [i, 21] loquitur: *Facta est meretrix civitas fidelis*; *urbs quondam perfecti decoris, gaudium universe terre* [Lam. ii, 15]; *iustitia habitavit in ea nunc autem homicide* [Is. i, 21]; *dominator enim exercituum et Dominus abstulit ab ea validum et fortem, omne robur panis et omne robur aque* [Is. iii, 1], et sicut ait Iere. [vii, 34]: *Quiescere fecit de urbibus Iuda et de plateis Ierusalem vocem gaudii et vocem letitie, vocem sponsi et vocem sponse. Facti sunt hostes eius in capite* [Lam. i, 5], id est superiores. Et sicut in libro [i] Machab. [i, 41–2] dicitur: *Sanctificatio desolata est sicut solitudo, dies festi conversi sunt in luctum, sabbata eius in obprobrium, honor eius in nichilum, secundum gloriam eius multiplicata est ignomina eius*, nam teste Ioel [i, 9, 11]: *Periit sacrificium et libatio de domo Domini; confusi sunt agricole, ululaverunt vinitores.*

17 Et cum scriptum sit in Apoc. [xi, 2]: *Civitatem sanctam conculcaverunt mensibus quadraginta duobus*; peccatis exigentibus annus pro mense[13] datus nobis. Ubi igitur est quem *comedit zelus domus* Domini [Ps. lxviii, 10], ubi gemitus et anxietates Mathatie [cf. i Mcc. ii], ubi Machabeorum fortitudo [cf. i Mcc. iii], ubi zelus et pugio Phinees [cf. Nm. xxv], ubi gladius Aioth elimatus [cf. Idc. iii, 15–16], ubi vomer Sangar [cf. Idc. iii, 31], et *maxilla asini* in manu Samsonis [Idc. xv, 15], ubi est qui *ascendat ex adverso* [Ez. xiii, 5] et capiat vulpeculas demolientes vineas Domini [cf. Ct. ii, 15]? *Vix est qui consoletur eam ex omnibus caris suis* [Lam. i, 2], que tamen continue clamare non cessat: *Miseremini mei, miseremini mei saltem vos amici mei* [Iob xix, 21]! *Filios enutrivi et exaltavi, ipsi autem spreverunt me* [Is. i, 2]. Et Isa. [li, 18] ait:

---

[13] pro mense D, P2, P6] per mensem T1

dragons and the pasture of ostriches, and all the Christians who live there are enslaved by the Saracens and in fear of their lives.

16 *The offering and libation are cut off from the temple of the Lord* and in it the name of Mohammed is invoked continuously. And in accordance with Daniel's prophecy, *oblations and offering no longer take place there and in the temple [there is] the abomination of desolation; they abolished perpetual offering and ruined the place of worship; they set fire to the sanctuary of the Lord and they dragged the dwelling-place of his name in the mud*, as it is written in Daniel: *Truth is flung to the ground and it will practice and prosper*, and in the words of Isaiah it says: *The faithful city has been made a whore; once the city of perfect beauty, the joy of the whole world; justice used to dwell in her, but now murderers; the ruler of the armies and Lord deprived her of [all that is] mighty and strong, all resources of bread and all resources of water*; and as Jeremiah says, *he silenced the voice of rejoicing and the voice of mirth, the voice of the bridegroom and the voice of the bride in the towns of Judah and the streets of Jerusalem. Her enemies have been put at the head*, that is [they are made] superior. And as it says in the book of Maccabees: *Her sanctuary is as forsaken as a desert, her feastdays have been turned into mourning, her Sabbaths into disgrace, her honour into nothing, her shame has been multiplied to match her glory*, because according to Joel's testimony: *The offering and libation are cut off from the house of the Lord; the farmers were dismayed, the workers of the vineyards lamented.*

17 And as it is written in Apocalypse: *They have trampled the holy city for forty-two months*; because of our sins a year has been handed to us for each month. Where is he who is *eaten up with zeal for the house* of the Lord, where are the sighs and anxieties of Mattathias, where the courage of the Maccabees, where the zeal and the dagger of Phineas, where is Ehud's sharpened sword, where Shamgar's ploughshare and *the jawbone of a donkey* in Samson's hand, where is he *who rises out of misfortune* and catches the little foxes who demolish the Lord's vines? *There is hardly anyone of all her loved ones to comfort her* who still does not cease to call incessantly: *Pity me, pity me, at least you my friends! I have reared and brought up children, but they spurned me.* And Isaiah

Non est qui sustentet[14] *eam ex omnibus filiis, quos genuit; non est qui apprehendat manum eius ex omnibus filiis quos enutrivit.*

18 Igitur secundum Iere. [li, 50] consilium: *Nolite stare, recordamini procul Domini, et Ierusalem ascendat super cor vestrum.* Et ut verbis Baruch [iv, 9–13] loquitur in persona Ierusalem: *Audite, civitates Syon, adduxit michi Deus luctum magnum, vidi enim captivitatem populi mei, filiorum meorum et filiarum mearum; nurtrivi illos cum iocunditate, dimisi autem illos cum fletu et luctu. Nemo gaudeat super me viduam et desolatam a multis;* [f. 149rb] *derelicta sum propter peccata filiorum meorum, quia declinaverunt a lege Dei; iustitias autem ipsius nescierunt nec ambulaverunt per vias mandatorum Dei*; et paulo post [19–23]: *Ambulate filii, ambulate, ego enim derelicta sum sola, exui me stola pacis, indui autem me sacco obsecrationis et clamabo ad Altissimum in diebus meis! Animequiores estote, filii, et clamate ad Deum altissimum, et erripiet vos de via principum iniquorum. Emisi vos cum luctu et ploratu, reducet autem vos michi Deus cum gaudio et iocunditate in eternum.*

< Contra illos qui differunt signari et tardant succurere Terre Sancte >
19 Nolite igitur, fratres, dicere sicut reprobi Iudei, de quibus Aggeus [i, 2, 6, 9] ait: *Populus iste ait: Nondum venit tempus domus Domini edifficare,* et subiungit: *Numquid tempus*[15] *est vobis ut habitetis in domibus laqueatis, et domus ista sit deserta? Domus mea deserta est et vos festinatis unusquisque in domum suam.*

< Quod Dominus occasione Terre Sancte vult probare suos et de indulgentia et merito signatorum >
20 Posuit autem Dominus, sicut Zach. [xii, 3] ait, *Ierusalem lapidem oneris cunctis gentibus,* ut scilicet probet qui sint amici eius et qui doleant vices ipsius; teste enim Ecc[us]. [xii, 8]: *Non agnoscitur in bonis amicus,* id est in prosperis non facile cognoscitur, *et non abscondetur in malis inimicus.* Sicut autem lapidem ponderosum solent proicere ad probandas vires, ita Dominus per civitatem illam probat qui fortes sint animo et qui pusillanimes et qui sint amici eius, nam sicut in Parab. Salo. [xvii, 17] ait: *Omni tempore diligit qui amicus est,* verus scilicet amicus, *et frater in*

---

[14]   sustentet D, P2] susteniet T1, sustet P6
[15]   tempus D, P2, P6] templum T1

says: *There is no one to support her of all the children she has borne, and no one to take her hand of all the children she has reared.*

18 Thus the advice according to Jeremiah: *Do not wait, remember the Lord from afar, and may Jerusalem come into your heart.* And as in the words of Baruch Jerusalem as a person says: *Listen, burghers of Zion, God has sent me great sorrow, I have seen the captivity of my people, my sons and my daughters; I reared them joyfully, in tears and sorrow I let them go. Do not, any of you, exult over me, a widow, deserted by so many; I am bereaved because of the sins of my sons, because they turned away from the law of God, they did not know his precepts and did not follow the ways of God's commandments*; and a little later: *Go sons, go away, because I am bereft and lonely, I have taken off the clothes of peace and put on the sackcloth of entreaty and I will cry to the Almighty all my life! Take courage, sons, and call to almighty God, and he will deliver you from the way of the unjust princes! In tears and sorrow I let you go, but God will lead you back to me in joy and gladness in eternity.*

< Against those who put off being signed and are slow in coming to the aid of the Holy Land >

19 You must not, brothers, speak like the reprobate Jews, about whom Haggai says: *This people says: The time has not yet come to build the house of the Lord*, and adds: *Is this a time for you to live in your panelled houses, when this house lies in ruins? My house lies in ruins and each of you is busy with his own house.*

< That the Lord wants to test his followers by way of the Holy Land and about the indulgence and the merit of those who are signed >

20 As Zechariah says, the Lord placed *Jerusalem as a stone of weight for all people*, so that he could test who are his friends and suffer on his behalf, because according to the testimony of Ecclesiasticus: *You cannot tell a friend in good times*, that is he cannot be recognised easily in times of prosperity, *but in adversity you cannot lose sight of an enemy.* Just as [people] often throw a heavy stone to prove their strength, thus the Lord through this city wants to find out who are the strong in spirit and who are faltering and who are his friends, because as it says in the Proverbs of Solomon: *A friend*, that is a true friend, *loves all the time, and a brother*

angustiis probatur. Dominus quidem affligitur in patrimonii sui amissione et vult amicos probare et experiri si fideles eius vasalli estis. Qui enim a domino ligio tenent feodum, si desit illi dum inpugnatur et hereditas sua illi aufertur, merito feodo privatur. Vos autem corpus et animam et quicquid habetis a summo imperatore tenetis, qui vos hodie citari facit, ut ei in prelio succuratis, et licet iure feodi non teneremini. Tanta et talia stipendia offert vobis quod sponte currere deberetis, remissionem cunctorum scilicet peccatorum quantum ad penam et culpam et insuper vitam eternam.

< Exemplum de beata Maria que filium suum dabat accipientibus crucis signum >
21 Memini cum aliquando in quadam ecclesia de cruce suscipienda[16] predicarem, aderat ibi quidam sanctus homo Cysterciensis ordinis conversus, qui frater Symon vocabatur, qui frequenter divinas revelationes et secreta Dei consilia videbat. Cumque cum lacrimis videret[17] multos relictis uxoribus et filiis et patria atque possessionibus ad crucem accedere, supplicavit Domino ut ei ostenderet, quale premium crucesignatis collaturus esset. Qui statim in spiritu vidit Beatam Virginem filium suum tenentem et secundum quod unusquisque signum crucis corde contrito recipiebat filium suum illi dabat. Non igitur deesse debetis vero amico, qui vobis non defuit, sed se ipsum pro vobis morti tradidit, qui vobis in necessitate succurreret quando alii amici vestri succurrere non valebant.

< Exemplum de tribus amicis >
22 Tres quidem amici vestri in hoc seculo sunt: carnis suavitas, rerum habundantia, consanguineorum societas. Primus relinquit in infirmitate, secundus in morte, tertius in sepultura.

23 Verus autem et fidelis amicus vester, si nunc ei in hac necessitate succurratis, in omnibus necessitatibus vestris succurreret vobis, conferendo vobis in presenti gratiam suam, omnium peccatorum integram remissionem, in futuro vero vitam eternam: Dominus Noster Ihesus Christus, cui est honor et gloria in secula seculorum. Amen.

[16] suscipienda D, P2, P6] suspendenda T1
[17] videret D, P2, P6] audiret T1

proves himself in hard times. The Lord has indeed suffered the loss of his patrimony and wants to test [his] friends and find out if you are his faithful vassals. He who holds a fief from a liege lord is rightfully deprived of his fief if he abandons him, when he is involved in a war and his inheritance is taken away from him. You hold your body and soul and all that you have from the highest emperor, who has you summoned today to come to his aid in battle, even if you are not bound by feudal law. He offers you such great payment that you ought to rush willingly, namely the remission of all sins with regard to punishment and guilt, and in addition eternal life.

< Exemplum about Saint Mary who gave her son to those who took the cross[7] >
21 I remember when I once preached about taking of the cross in some church, there was a certain saintly man, a lay brother of the Cistercian order called Brother Symon, who often had divine revelations and visions of God's secret plans. When he saw with tears that many people took the cross while leaving their spouses, children, fatherland and possessions behind, he asked the Lord to show him what kind of a reward the crusaders were given. At once he saw in his mind the Holy Virgin holding her son and that she gave her son to everyone who received the cross with a contrite heart. Therefore, you must not abandon a true friend, who did not abandon you, but turned himself over to death for you, who would come to your aid in need when all your other friends cannot help you.

< Exemplum about the three friends >
22 We have three friends in this world: the sweetness of the flesh, the abundance of things [and] the company of relatives. The first stays behind in illness, the second in death and the third in burial.

23 If you now come to his aid in this time of need, your true and faithful friend will come to your aid in all your needs, granting you his grace in the present time, the full remission of all sins, and in the future eternal life: Our Lord Jesus Christ, whose is the honour and the glory for ever and ever. Amen.

[7] Crane, no. cxxi, 55; Tubach, no. 5128.

James of Vitry

SERMO II

T1 = Troyes, Bibliothèque Municipale, 228, ff. 149rb-151va

Additional manuscripts
D = Douai, Bibliothèque Municipale, 503, ff. 365r-368v
P2 = Paris, Bibliothèque Nationale de France, lat. 3284, ff. 125rb-128va
P6 = Paris, Bibliothèque Nationale de France, lat. 17509, ff. 94²-96⁴

Reference
Schneyer, III, 216, no. 414

Item sermo ad crucesignatos vel -signandos

1 Thema sumptum ex Iere. [iv, 6]:[1] *Levate signum in Syon, confortamini et nolite* [f. 149va] *stare!*

< De officio predicatoris et virtute predicationis[2] >
2 *Educ foras populum cecum et oculos habentem, surdum et aures ei sunt.*
Hiis verbis ostendit Ysa. [xliii, 8] officium predicatoris et virtutem predicationis. Predicator quidem verbo et exemplo debet educere peccatores de conversatione mala velut aspidem de caverna, ut sicut dicitur in Iob [xxvi, 13]: *Obstetricante manu sapientie educatur coluber tortuosus.* Caute enim et suaviter debet tractare infirmos peccatores sicut obstetrices mulieres, et hoc per manum bene operationis et sapientiam predicationis. Illi quidem nuntio creditur qui litteras habet, idest scientiam scriptur-

---

[1] The chapters of the books of the Bible are sometimes noted in the margin.
[2] Throughout the sermon the manuscript supplies the section titles in the margin.

James of Vitry

SERMON II

Another sermon to those who are or will become crusaders

1 Theme taken from Jeremiah: *Raise a sign in Zion, be strong and do not delay!*

< About the preacher's task and the virtue of preaching >
2 *Lead out the people that are blind yet have eyes, that are deaf yet have ears.* With these words Isaiah explains the preacher's task and the virtue of preaching. By his word and example a preacher must lead sinners away from a bad way of life as the adder [is led] from its cave, as it says in Job: *The crooked snake is led out by the midwife's hand of wisdom.* He must treat weak sinners carefully and gently as midwives [treat] women, and this with the hand of good works and the wisdom of preaching. People believe a messenger who is educated, that is who has knowledge

arum, et sigillum, id est impressionem conversationis sancte, per quam valeat alios informare.

3 In quibusdam vero sigillis littere transverse sunt, sicut fieri solet in sigillo materiali: dum bona predicant et contrarium faciunt, hii non bene *populum cecum* a tenebris *foras* educunt, quia doctrinam suam malis operibus destruunt. Bonus vero predicator verbo et exemplo *populum cecum foras* educit clamando Christi exemplo: *Lazare, veni foras* [Io. xi, 43]! Cecus autem dicitur predicator quamdiu in tenebris peccatorum commoratur licet *oculos* habeat, idest rationem et intellectum; sed quia *maculam habet* [Lv. xxi, 23] in oculo, dum luto carnalis voluptatis vel fumo secularis vanitatis vel terra mundane cupiditatis oculus mentis involvitur, cecus reputatur.

4 Sed et surdus dicitur, licet *aures* habeat corporis, dum diabolus ita obturat aures cordis quod nec audit tonitrua comminationum nec attendit voces blandas promissionum nec audire curat clamorem illum de quo dicitur quod Christus *voce magna clamans* [Lc. xxiii, 46] emisit spiritum. Cum tamen per Iob [xvi, 19] Dominus dicat: *Terra, ne operias sanguinem meum nec inveniat in te locum latendi clamor meus*; sanguis Christi *terra* operitur, dum per terrena desideria de memoria hominis deletur; *clamor* autem in illo absorbetur et latet qui Christo clamanti non respondet.

< De fune[3] coccineo et funiculo distributionis[4] >

5 Orate igitur Dominum, ut hodie crucis Christi funiculo de cavernis suis peccatores foras educantur. Hic est enim funis coccineus per quem Raab[5] liberata est aliis pereuntibus [cf. Ios. ii, 6]; sicut hiis diebus pereuntibus duris et obstinatis alii[6] funiculo crucis ad Christum trahuntur, quibus *dividit Dominus terram* promissionis *in funiculo distributionis* [Ps. lxxvii, 54].

< De signo crucis exaltando et quod ad[7] vexillum crucis congregari debent Christi[8] milites >

6 *Levate signum in Syon* etc. Precipit nobis Dominus ut *signum* crucis tamquam vexillum summi regis levemus *in Syon*, id est in ecclesia Dei,

---

[3] fune T1] funiculo P2, *om.* D, P6
[4] de . . . distributionis T1, P2] *om.* D, P6
[5] Raab T1, D, P2] Moab P6   [6] alii D, P2, P6] aliis T1
[7] ad D, P2, P6] *om.* T1   [8] Christi D, P2, P6] *om.* T1

of the scriptures, and has a seal, that is the impression of a saintly way of life, with which he can instruct others.

3 On some seals the letters are intertwined, as is normally the case on a real seal: those who preach good things but do the contrary do not lead well *the people that is blind out* of darkness, because they destroy their teaching by bad works. But a good preacher leads *the people that is blind out* by word and example, calling after the example of Christ: *Lazarus, come out!* A preacher is called blind if he stays in the darkness of sins even though he has *eyes*, that is reason and intellect; he is considered to be blind as *he has a blemish* in the eye, when his mind's eye is drawn towards the filth of carnal pleasure, the smoke of worldly vanity or the world of earthly desire.

4 But he is also called deaf, even though he has bodily *ears*, when the devil stops up the ears of the heart so that he does not hear the noise of threats, pays no attention to the flattering voices of promises nor cares to hear the call with which it says that Christ let his spirit go out *calling in a loud voice*. As the Lord said through Job: *O earth, do not cover my blood and let my cry find no place to hide;* the blood of Christ is *covered* by earth since it is effaced from the memory of man by earthly desires; *the call* is swallowed up by it and he who does not respond to the call of Christ conceals himself.

< About the scarlet string and the line of distribution >

5 Therefore, pray to the Lord that today the sinners may be led out of their caves by the string of the cross of Christ. This is the scarlet string by which Rahab was freed while the others perished; thus today, while the hardened and obstinate perish, the others, amongst whom *the Lord divided the* promised *land by the line of distribution*, are drawn to Christ by the string of the cross.

< About exalting the sign of the cross and that the soldiers of Christ must gather at the banner of the cross >

6 *Raise a sign in Zion* etc. The Lord orders us to raise the *sign* of the cross as the banner of the highest king *in Zion*, that is in the church of

crucis virtutem predicando et voce preconia laudes crucis attollendo et populum ad crucem invitando. Unde Dominus per Ysa. [xlix, 22]: *Ecce levabo ad gentes manum meam et exaltabo ad populos signum meum.* Manus suas *ad gentes* levavit dum eas in cruce extendit, sicut scriptum est [Ps. cxl, 2]: *Elevatio manuum mearum sacrificium vespertinum.* Hodie enim manum suam elevat et erigit, dum per predicatores suos crucem vobis porrigit, unde per Ysa. [lxvi, 18–9]: *Videbunt gloriam meam et ponam in eis signum. Ad populos* vero signum exaltatur quando virtus crucis declaratur et eius misterium populis predicatur.

7 Et iterum Ysa. ait [xi, 12]: *Levabit Dominus signum in nationes et congregabit profugos Israel et dispersos Iuda*[9] *colliget a quatuor plagis terre. Levabit signum* crucis ut profugi a Deo et per diversa vitia dispersi ad hoc signum revertantur et *a quatuor plagis terre*, id est ab universo mundo, ad crucis vexillum populi congregentur. Unde et destructores Babilonis alloquens Ysa. [xiii, 2] ait: *Super montem calliginosum levate signum, exaltate vocem, levate manum, ingrediantur portas duces. Super montem caliginosum signum* levamus, cum potentibus huius seculi tenebris peccatorum involutis crucem Domini baiulandam predicamus.

8 Non solum autem *vocem* sed et *manum* debent levare qui crucis gloriam aliis volunt predicare, [f. 149vb] ut *portas* aurium et cordium exhortationis sermo valeat penetrare. Quid enim prodest si vox fuerit exaltata et manus depressa? Cum dicat Ecc[us]. [iv, 34]: *Noli esse citatus in lingua tua et inutilis et remissus in operibus tuis!* Qui igitur summi imperatoris signiferi esse debent, si signum quod exaltandum susceperunt male vivendo deprimunt, merito proditionis argui possunt sicut terreni regis signifer, si in conflictu vexillum negligentia[10] vel timore depresserit, proditionis reatum incurrit.

9 Signum igitur levamus dum crucis gloriam predicamus, unde **Iere.** [li, 27]: *Levate signum in terra, clangite buccina* in montibus; et Ysa. [xviii, 3] ait: *Omnes habitatores orbis, qui moramini in terra, cum elevatum*[11] *fuerit signum in montibus, videbitis et clangorem tube audietis.* Hanc prophetiam hodie impletam videtis: *in montibus* enim, id est aperte et cunctis cernentibus, *signum* crucis elevamus, dum eius virtutem commendamus et clangendo tuba predicationis declaramus. Tandem autem in

[9] Iuda D, P2, P6] Iude T1
[10] negligentia D, P2, P6] *om.* T1
[11] elevatum D, P2, P6] elevatus T1

God, by preaching the virtue of the cross, singing the praises of the cross with the voice of the herald and inviting the people to [take] the cross. Whence the Lord [says] through Isaiah: *Look, I shall raise up my hand to the nations and hoist my sign to the peoples.* He raised up his hands *to the nations* when he stretched them out on the cross, as it is written: *The lifting up of my hands [is like] an evening sacrifice.* So today he lifts up his hand and holds it up, while offering you the cross through his preachers, whence in Isaiah: *They will witness my glory and I shall give them a sign.* The sign is hoisted *to the peoples* when the virtue of the cross is proclaimed and its mystery is preached to the peoples.

7 And again Isaiah says: *The Lord will raise a sign for the nations, assemble the outcasts of Israel and gather the scattered people of Judah from the four corners of the earth.* He will raise the sign of the cross so that those outcast from God and scattered by various vices may return to this sign, and that the peoples may come together *from the four corners of the earth*, that is from all over the world, to the banner of the cross. Whence Isaiah says, speaking to those who destroyed Babylon: *Hoist a sign on the cloudy mountain, raise your voice, lift up your hand so that the nobles may go through the gates.* We hoist *the sign on the cloudy mountain* when we preach to the powerful of this world, who are wrapped in the darkness of sins, to carry the cross of the Lord.

8 Those who want to preach the glory of the cross to others must not only raise their *voice* but also their *hand*, so that the exhortatory sermon may enter the *gates* of [people's] ears and hearts. What good is it if the voice is raised and the hand stays down? As Ecclesiasticus says: *Do not be bold of tongue and idle and slack in your deeds!* Those who must be the standard-bearers of the highest emperor can rightly be accused of treason if, by living badly, they keep down the sign which they were given to exalt, just as the standard-bearer of an earthly king is charged with treason if he holds down the banner in battle out of negligence or fear.

9 Thus we set up the sign when we preach the glory of the cross, whence Jeremiah: *Raise a sign throughout the world, sound the trumpet* on the mountains; and Isaiah says: *All inhabitants of the world, you who people the earth, when the sign is raised on the mountains, you will see and you will hear the sound of the trumpet.* You see this prophecy fulfilled today: we raise the *sign* of the cross *on the mountains*, that is openly and for everybody to see, when we commend its virtue and reveal it by sounding the trumpet of preaching. At the last, the sign of the cross

iudicio signum crucis in supernis apparebit: hoc enim signum crucis erit in celo cum *Dominus ad iudicandum* [Is. iii, 13] venerit et tunc omnes audient novissime *tube clangorem.*

< De signiferis et clavigeris, thesaurariis et cancellariis summi regis >
10 Qui igitur accipiunt signum crucis signiferi sunt summi regis et clavigeri domus eius. Crux enim clavis est reserans portas paradisi, unde Ysa. [xxii, 22]: *Ponam clavem domus David super humerum eius,* quod adimpletum est quando Christus in humeris suis crucem baiulavit [cf. Io. xix, 17]. Crux quidem aliis est clavis, aliis est clava: *Posita enim est in ruinam et in resurrectionem multorum* [Lc. ii, 34]. Non solum autem clavigeri sed thesaurarii Christi et cancellarii sunt crucesignati, habentes clavem celestis thesauri et sigillum cui impressa fuit caro Christi. Sicut autem domus Dei cognoscitur per crucem superpositam, sic homo dignoscitur domus Dei per crucem humeris suis affixam.

< Quod sine cruce ad patriam celestem non possumus pervenire et de multiplici virtute crucis et ipsius commendatione >
11 Et quoniam ab ipso baptismo cruce signati sumus, crucis signum abnegare non debemus. Nam sicut homo in modum[12] crucis natat, navis in modum crucis currit et avis in modum crucis volat, ita et vos sine cruce mare huius seculi non potestis transire nec ad supernam Ierusalem pervenire. Unde Iacob in Gen. [xxxii, 10] ait: *In baculo meo transivi Iordanem istum,* id est cum baculo crucis hius mortalis vite fluxum. Nam sicut archa Domini vectibus ligneis portata est trans Iordanem et in terra promissionis inducta [cf. Ios. iii], sic ecclesia in ligno crucis torrentem hius mundi pertransiens transfertur in regnum celorum.
12 Hec est potentia quam dedit Dominus mundo in senectute sua, qua sustentaretur ne caderet. Hec est columpna, seu 'estache',[13] in qua affixi sunt clavi, ut suspendamus pondera nostra in ligno crucis, unde Ysa. [xxii, 23–4]: *Ponam illum paxillum in loco fideli et suspendam in eo gloriam patris eius.* Hec est *quasi therebinthus expandens ramos suos* [Ecc(us). xxiv, 22], ut sit nobis obumbratio seu 'escramal' contra[14] ignem vitiorum. Hec est virga illa de qua in Levit. [xxvii, 32] dicitur quod

---

[12] modum D, P2, P6] signum T1
[13] estache T1] enstache D, P2, astache P6, Gallice *add. in marg.* P2
[14] escramal contra T1] escramail contra D, estivale circa P2, escrail contra P6

will also appear on high at the time of judgement: this sign of the cross will be in the heavens when *the Lord* comes *to judge* and then everybody will hear anew *the sound of the trumpet.*

< About the standard-bearers and the key-bearers, the treasurers and the chancellors of the highest king >
10 Those who take the sign of the cross are the standard-bearers of the highest king and the key-bearers of his house. The cross is the key that opens the gates of paradise, whence Isaiah: *I shall place the key of David's house on his shoulder,* which was fulfilled when Christ carried the cross on his shoulders. For some the cross is a key, for others a mace: *It is placed for the fall and the resurrection of many.* Crusaders are not only key-bearers but treasurers and chancellors of Christ, holding the key to the heavenly treasure and the seal with which the flesh of Christ was stamped. As the house of God is recognised by the cross on top of it, so a man of the house of God is recognised by the cross put on his shoulders.

< That we cannot reach the heavenly fatherland without the cross and about the multiform virtue of the cross and its recommendation >
11 Since we were signed with the cross from baptism alone, we cannot forgo the sign of the cross. As a man swims in the manner of the cross and a ship sails in the manner of the cross and a bird flies in the manner of the cross, so you, too, cannot cross the sea of this world and reach the heavenly Jerusalem without the cross. Whence Jacob says in Genesis: *With my staff I crossed the Jordan,* that is with the staff of the cross the stream of this mortal life. As the ark of the Lord was carried across the Jordan on wooden poles and taken to the promised land, so the church, travelling on the wood of the cross through the torrent of this world, is carried to the heavenly kingdom.
12 It is the power which the Lord gave to the world in its old age, by which it could be supported so it would not fall. It is the pillar, or 'estache', on which the keys are hung so that we may hang our burdens on the wood of the cross, whence Isaiah: *I shall put this post in a trusted place and I shall hang upon it the glory of his father.* It is *like a terebinth spreading its branches,* so that it may give us shade or a screen against the fire of vices. It is the staff about which it is said in Leviticus that *all that*

quicquid sub virga pastoris transierit sanctificatum erit Domino. Ad litteram pastor habebat virgam sanguine tinctam et *quicquid decimum* de grege transibat tangebat et sanguine signans Domino sanctificabat. Virga enim crucis et sanguine Christi Domino sanctificamur et ab aliis non signatis discernimur. Sicut autem *ferrum securis in aquis* [iv Rg. vi, 5] submersum ad manubrium supernatavit, ita ad crucis lignum supernatant et ab aquis vitiorum sublevantur qui corde contrito crucis caractere signantur. Hec est *paxillus in loco fideli*, id est in ecclesia, fixus ut ipsum apprehendant qui in aquis huius maris periculose laborant. Hec est scala Iacob [cf. Gn. xxviii, 12], cui innixus est Dominus, ut ascendentes sursum trahat et adiuvet et descendentes precipitet. Hec singulare presidium, ultimum remedium, portus naufragis, salus in periculis. Defficiente enim [f. 150ra] iustitia et succumbentibus meritis illa succurrit in qua est salus, vita et resurrectio nostra: salus quantum ad redemptionem, vita quantum ad gratiam, resurrectio quantum ad gloriam. Unde Iere. [viii, 22]: *Numquid resina non est in Galaat? Quare non est abducta cicatrix populi mei?* Quasi diceret Dominus: per me non stat, parata est medicina. Hec est medicina contra omnes infirmitates, dulcedo contra omnes amaritudines, unde Ecc[us]. [xxxviii, 4–5]: *Altissimus de terra creavit medicinam, et vir prudens non abhorrebit eam. Nonne a ligno dulcorata est aqua amara?* Pone igitur te crucem assumendo in statera crucis, et Dominus preponderans sublevabit te ad gloriam resurrectionis. Hec est suprema tabula mundo naufraganti, vite lignum, iustitie libra, sceptrum regni, regum diadema, thronus imperialis, arbor obumbrationis, virga correctionis, baculus sustentationis, vexillum Christi sanguine rubricatum, quo viso ad prelium incitamur. Misso autem Iona [i, 15] in mari *stat mare a fervore suo*, quia quod prius videbatur importabile exemplo Crucifixi fit leve, qui se *exinanivit* usque ad carnem, usque ad crucem, *usque ad mortem* [Phil. ii, 7–8].

< Exemplum de tigride et venatoribus et quanta Christus pro nobis fecit>

13 Sicut enim tigris rabido cursu insequitur venatorem et tanto affectu prosequitur fetum ut se mittat in venatoris spiculum, ita Christus ut nos eriperet de manu venatoris, id est diaboli, in spiculum mortis se misit.

14 Et ideo, teste Augustino, cum Christus per alia beneficia ad amorem

passes under the shepherd's staff will be consecrated to the Lord. Literally, the shepherd had a staff daubed in blood and touched *every tenth* animal that went by and signed it for the Lord with blood. We now are consecrated to the Lord by the staff of the cross and the blood of Christ and are so distinguished from the others who have not been signed. As *the iron axehead* thrown *in the water* floated by the haft, so those who are signed by the symbol of the cross with a contrite heart float by the wood of the cross and are raised from the waters of vices. It is the *post in a trusted place*, that is in the church, put up so that those who labour in the waters of this dangerous sea may behold it. It is Jacob's ladder, at the top of which stands the Lord, so that he may pull up those who go up and help them and throw down those who descend. It [is] a unique aid, the ultimate remedy, the port for the shipwrecked, salvation when in danger. When there is no justice and righteousness succumbs, it, in which our salvation and resurrection lies, comes to [our] aid: salvation in terms of redemption, life in terms of grace, resurrection in terms of glory. Whence Jeremiah: *Is there no more resin in Gilead? Why has the scar on my people not been removed?* As if the Lord were saying: It does not depend on me; the medicine is ready. It is the medicine against all illnesses, a sweetener for all bitterness, whence Ecclesiasticus: *The Almighty has brought forth medicine from the ground, and no sensible man will despise it. Is not bitter water sweetened by a piece of wood?* So put yourself into the balance of the cross by taking the cross, and the Lord, who is weighing, will raise you up to the glory of the resurrection. It is the last plank for a shipwrecked world, the wood of life, the scales of justice, the king's sceptre, the diadem of kings, the imperial throne, the shading tree, the staff of punishment, the supporting stick, the banner made red by the blood of Christ, by the sight of which we are encouraged to fight. When Jonah was thrown into the sea, *the sea stopped raging,* because what earlier seemed unbearable is made easy by the example of the Crucified, who *emptied himself* unto the flesh, unto the cross, *unto death.*

< Exemplum about the tiger and the hunters and how many things Christ has done for us >
13 Just as the tiger runs after the hunter in a wild chase and follows his cub with such affection that it throws itself onto the hunter's spear, so Christ threw himself onto the spear of death to snatch us from the hunter's, that is the devil's, hand.

14 And likewise, according to Augustine's testimony,[1] while Christ

---

[1] I have not been able to identify this reference.

suum nos incitaverit, per mortis beneficium nos coegit. Hic est vere ille de quo in Ezech. [x, 2] dicitur quod manus suas igne implevit et super civitatem proiecit; omnia enim opera eius plena sunt caritatis igne, et maxime quando manus suas in cruce extendit, proiecit ignem super civitatem ecclesie et eam caritate inflammavit. Ipse quidem similis factus est pellicano solitudinis qui proprios pullos occidit, quia contra ipsum erigunt rostra sua, sed postmodum sanguinem proprium super pullos mortuos stillat et sic illos vivificat.

15 Ita primi parentes, quia contra Deum rostra sua per inobedientiam erexerunt, ab ipso occisi sunt [cf. Gn. ii, iii], sed postea sanguine in cruce effuso vivificati. Qui enim per lignum vetitum cecidimus per lignum crucis surreximus. *Sub arbore quidem malo suscitavit* [Ct. viii, 5] genus humanum, id est Adam et filios eius, quos *redemit de manu inimici, de regionibus congregavit eos a solis ortu et occasu, ab aquilone et mari* [Ps. cvi, 2–3], quod significatum est in quatuor partibus crucis que terrarum comprehendit quatuor confinia. Unde Origenes: 'Tanta est virtus crucis Christi ut, si in mente fideliter habeatur, nulla libido dominatur, nulla peccati[15] prevalere poterit malitia, sed continuo ad memoriam eius totus peccati et mortis fugit exercitus.'

16 Sicut autem aquila provocans ad volandum pullos suos volitat ipse super illos dum homines rapere volunt illos, sic Dominus super peccatores brachia sua extendit provocans eos, ut nidum peccatorum relinquant et altitudinem crucis, ad quam diabolus non potest attingere, ascendant. Per hanc Christus humiliavit calumpniatorem. Dicebat enim diabolus: Meum est genus humanum, cartam habeo in qua scriptum est: *Quacumque die comederis ex eo morte morieris* [Gn. ii, 17]. Respondit Dominus: Falsarius es, addisti de tuo: *Nequaquam moriemini* [Gn. iii, 4], unde privilegium amittere meruisti. Dicebat calumpniator: Tutus sum prescriptione. Cui Dominus: Multotiens interrupta est dum predicatores misi qui dicerent: *Dimitte populum meum, ut sacrificet michi in deserto* [Ex. v, 1]; et maxime interrupta fuit in diluvio [cf. Gn. vi–viii]. Dixit calumpniator: Ponderentur bona et mala, veniamus ad stateram. Videns

---

[15] peccati D, P2, P6] *om.* T1

encourages us to love him by other favours, he forced us to it by the favour of his death. It is he about whom it is said in Ezekiel that he took a handful of burning coals and threw them over the city; all his works are full of the fire of charity, and in particular when he stretched out his hands on the cross, he threw fire over the city of the church and enflamed it with charity. He is like the pelican of the desert that kills its own offspring because they raise their beaks at it, but afterwards spills its own blood over its dead offspring and thus revives them.[2]

15 In the same way, the first parents, who raised their beaks against God in their disobedience, were killed by him, but were afterwards revived by the blood that was spilled on the cross. We who fell through the forbidden wood stood up again through the wood of the cross. *Under the apple tree he awakened* humankind, that is Adam and his sons, *whom he redeemed from the hand of the enemy, he brought them back from foreign lands, from the east and west, north and south*, which is signified by the four parts of the cross, which embraces the four regions of the world. Whence Origen: 'The virtue of the cross of Christ is so great that, if it was held faithfully in the mind, no passion would rule, no cunning of sin could prevail, but the whole army of sin and death would flee at once at the memory [of the cross].'[3]

16 As the eagle flutters above its offspring in order to make them fly when people want to steal them, so the Lord extends his arms over the sinners so that they leave their nest of sins and climb the height of the cross where the devil cannot reach. Thus Christ humiliated the challenger. The devil said: Humankind belongs to me, I have a charter in which is written: *The day you eat of that you will die your death*. The Lord replied: You are a forger, you have added your own bit: *You will certainly not die*, wherefore you deserve to lose your privilege. The challenger said: I am safe because of [the right of] prescription. The Lord [replied] to him: It lapsed many times when I sent preachers who said: *Let my people go, so that they may make sacrifices to me in the desert*; and it above all lapsed during the flood. Then the challenger said: Let good and evil be weighed, let us go to the balance. When God saw that

---

[2] The description of the pelican goes back to Isidore of Seville, see Isidorus Hispalensis, *Etymologiae Liber xii*, ed. J. André (Paris, 1986), VII, 26, p. 245.
[3] I have not been able to identify this quotation.

Deus quod mala in infinitum preponderarent, misit se ipsum in alia parte statere crucis; que statera facta est corporis predamque tulit tartaris.

< De gloria crucis et quod in illa debemus gloriari et de magnitudine indulgentie et quod prodest uxoribus, filiis et parentibus signatorum tam vivis quam mortuis >

17 Merito igitur Apostolus [Gal. vi, 14] ait: *Michi absit gloriari nisi in cruce Domini Nostri Ihesu Christi,* ac si diceret: Quidam gloriantur [f. 150rb] in potentia honoris, alii in nobilitate generis, alii in pulcritudine carnis, alii in viribus corporis, alii in velocitate currendi, alii in peritia loquendi. Nos autem *gloriari* oportet *in cruce Domini Nostri Ihesu Christi;* qui enim crucis virtutem intrinsecus intuetur, merito in ipsa gloriatur.

18 Unde et crucesignati qui vere contriti et confessi ad Dei servitium accinguntur, dum in Christi servitio moriuntur, vere martires reputantur, liberati a peccatis venialibus simul et mortalibus, ab omni penitentia sibi iniuncta, absoluti a pena peccatorum in hoc seculo, a pena purgatorii in alio, securi a tormentis gehenne, gloria et honore coronandi in eterna beatitudine.

19 Uxores autem et filii sicut participes sunt expensarum ita particeps sunt meritorum. Sed et parentibus defunctis qui bona sua[16] illis reli-querunt, si hac intentione ut eis subveniant crucem accipiunt, multum eis succurrere possunt. Si enim elemosinis et aliis bonis operibus potest mortuis subveniri, que maior elemosina quam se et sua Deo offere et animam pro Christo ponere, uxorem, filios, consanguineos et natale solum pro Christi servitio relinquere, periculis in terra, periculis in mare, periculis latronum, periculis predonum, periculis preliorum pro amore Crucifixi se exponere? Unde nullo modo dubitetis quod non solum vobis ad remissionem peccatorum et eterne vite premium valet hec peregrinatio sed etiam uxoribus, filiis, parentibus, tam vivis quam defunctis, multum proderit quidquid boni feceritis in hac via pro ipsis.

20 Hec enim plena et integra indulgentia quam vobis summus pontifex secundum claves a Deo sibi commissas concedit. Est quasi *fons patens domui David in ablutionem* [Za. xiii, 1] omnium peccatorum et in acquisitione celestium premiorum.

---

[16] sua D, P2, P6] *om.* T1

evil would be infinitely heavier, he put himself in the other part of the balance of the cross; this balance was made of the body and he carried his booty away from hell.

< About the glory of the cross and that we must be glorified in it and about the magnitude of the indulgence and that it is of benefit to the spouses, children and parents of those signed, those alive and those dead >

17 The Apostle says rightly: *Far be it from me that I should boast except of the cross of our Lord Jesus Christ*, as if he were saying: Some boast of the power of their honour, others of the nobility of their descent, others of the beauty of their flesh, others of the strength of their body, others of how fast they can run, others of their skill of speech. But we ought *to boast of the cross of our Lord Jesus Christ*; he who beholds the virtue of the cross inwardly, boasts of it by right.

18 Because of this, those crusaders who prepare themselves for the service of God, truly confessed and contrite, are considered true martyrs while they are in the service of Christ, freed from venial and also mortal sins, from all the penitence enjoined upon them, absolved from the punishment for their sins in this world and the punishment of purgatory in the next, safe from the tortures of hell, in the glory and honour of being crowned in eternal beatitude.

19 The spouses and children are included in these benefits in as much as they contribute to expenses. But [crusaders] can also greatly help their deceased parents who have left their goods to them, if [the crusaders] take the cross with the intention of helping [their parents]. If it is possible to come to the aid of the dead by giving alms and doing other good works, what greater alms are there but to offer oneself and one's belongings to God and pledge one's soul to Christ, to leave behind one's spouse, children, relatives and birthplace for the service of Christ alone, to expose oneself to dangers on land, dangers on sea, the dangers of thieves, the dangers of predators, the dangers of battles for the love of the Crucified? Therefore, have no doubt at all that this pilgrimage affords not only you the remission of sins and the reward of eternal life, but that whatever good you do on this journey on behalf of your spouses, children and parents, whether living or dead, will profit them greatly.

20 This is the full and plenary indulgence that the pope concedes to you according to the keys that were given to him by God. This is like *the fountain open to the house of David for washing away* all sins and acquiring heavenly rewards.

<De altari crucis et titulo>

21 Quemadmodum Ysa. [xix, 19] ait: *In die illa erit altare Domini in medio Egipti et titulus iuxta terminum eius.* Altare in quo oblatus est Christus dicitur crux ipsius, que *in medio* terre *Egypti*, id est huius mundi tenebrosi, esse dicitur, quia communiter crucis beneficium cunctis offertur. *Et titulus iuxta terminum eius*, quia statim et quasi inmediate veri crucesignati obtenta indulgentia et servata post *terminum* vite presentis eterne beatitudinis titulum consequuntur.

<De labore modico et premio immenso>

22 Nec enim de misericordia et largitate illius diffidimus, de quo scriptum est: *Pro nichilo salvos faciet illos* [Ps. lv, 8]. Nam quicquid pro ipso sustinebits modicum est et quasi nichilum respectu premii interminabilis neque, enim si mille annis homo serviret Deo, posset mereri ex condigno, ut una modica hora videret illum *in quem desiderant angeli conspicere* [i Pt. i, 12], 'cuius pulcritudinem sol et luna mirantur'.

23 Et hoc vos valde debet ad Dei servitium et ad labores pro Christo sustinendos animare, sicut pauper homo qui manibus operando non nisi sex denarios pro labore meretur, si ei centum marce[17] pro dieta sua promitterentur, letus et cum gaudio portaret *pondus diei et estus* [Mt. xx, 12], nec pro labore murmuraret, licet frigus aut calorem maximum sustineret dum quantitatem premii attenderet, ut pro modico labore qui semper in paupertate et miseria fuit ultra modum dives fieret et de cetero in deliciis quiescere posset.

24 Unde de Iacob legimus, quod *septem annis servivit pro Rahel et pre magnitudine amoris videbantur ei pauci dies* [Gn. xxix, 20]. Ita dies presentis tribulationis breves et leves reputantur respectu interminabilis et inestimabilis premii: *Non enim sunt condigne passiones huius temporis ad futuram gloriam que revelabitur in nobis* [Rm. viii, 18]. Si Noe centum annis laboravit fabricando archam [cf. Gn. vi-viii], ut [f. 150va] evaderet mortem temporalem, quanto magis vos paucis annis laborare debetis, ut evadatis eternam mortem et acquiratis vitam sempiternam.

25 Unde Ecc[us]. [vi, 20] ait: *In opere Domini modicum laborabis et cito edes de generatione illius*; quasi dicat: labor brevis et merces immanis,[18]

---

[17] marce T1] marce auri D, P2, P6
[18] immanis P2] manis T1, ianuis D, etiam P6

< About the altar of the cross and the sign-post >

21 As Isaiah says: *That day there will be an altar to the Lord in the centre of Egypt and a sign-post at the frontier.* The *altar* on which Christ was sacrificed is called his cross, that is said to be *in the centre of Egypt*, meaning of this gloomy world, because the benefice of the cross is offered to all communally. *And [there will be] a sign-post at the frontier,* because true crusaders follow the sign-post of eternal beatitude at once and immediately after the end of their present life, having obtained the indulgence and having served [their term].

< About the modest labour and the immense reward >

22 We have no doubt about his mercy and generosity, of whom it is written: *He shall save them for nothing in return.* Whatever you sustain for him is little, practically nothing with regard to the infinite reward, and, even if man served God for a thousand years, he could not in return earn [the right] to see for one short hour him *whom the angels long to catch a glimpse of,* 'whose handsomeness the sun and the moon admire'.[4]

23 This really ought to motivate you to take upon yourselves the service of God and the labours for Christ, just as a poor man who, doing manual work, earns only six pennies for his labour would, if he was promised one hundred marks for his day's work, gladly and joyfully carry *the weight and heat of the day*, and he would not complain about the labour, even if he suffered cold or extreme heat while waiting for the great reward, so that, for the little bit of work, he who had always been in poverty and misery would become rich beyond measure and from then onwards be at rest with his pleasures.

24 Whence we read about Jacob that *he worked for seven years for Rachel and they seemed to him like a few days because of the greatness of his love.* In the same way the days of present tribulation are considered short and light compared to the infinite and unimaginable reward: *All that we suffer in the present time is nothing in comparison with the future glory which will be disclosed to us.* If Noah worked one hundred years to build the ark in order to escape death in this life, how much more ought you to work a few years in order to escape eternal death and to acquire everlasting life!

25 Whence Ecclesiasticus says: *In the work of the Lord you will labour little and you will quickly overcome his creation*, as if he were saying: the

---

[4] Hesbert, III, 117, no. 1968.

quia *cum dederit dilectis suis sompnum,*[19] *ecce hereditas Domini* [Ps. cxxvi, 2–3]. Unde cum gaudio magno laborare debent qui post laborem requiem sine fine expectant, sicut vulgariter dici solet: 'Secure potat qui lectum paratum spectat'; 'potat ad affectum qui presto videt sibi lectum'. Pedes ire non metuit qui iuxta se palefridum suum ducit et quando fatigatus est ascendit. Paratus est lectus vester in paradiso. Si moriamini in Dei servitio, parati sunt angeli sancti ut animas vestras ferant et presentent Deo. Et tunc coram ipso cantare poteritis *canticum novum* [Ps. xcvii, 1]: *Sicut audivimus sic vidimus in civitate Domini virtutum* [Ps. xlvii, 9].

< Quare Deus terram suam[20] ab inimicis occupari sustinuit nec statim eam liberare voluit et quantus fructus ex hoc pervenit >

26 Hoc autem diligenter debetis attendere quod, cum Deus terram suam uno verbo per se posset liberare, ipse tamen servos suos honorare vult et socios habere in eius liberatione, dans vobis occasionem salvandi animas vestras, quas redemit et pro quibus sanguinem suum fudit [cf. Lc. xxii, 20], unde non eas libenter perdit.

27 Multi quidem per hanc sanctam peregrinationem salvati sunt qui in peccatis suis remansissent, si a principio Dominus per se terram illam liberasset. Propterea in libro Sapie. [x, 17] dicitur: *Reddet* Deus *mercedem laborum* sanctorum *suorum*; non dicit fructum: ipse enim non remunerat secundum rei eventum. Unde quamvis Terram Sanctam non recuperaverunt Christiani, nichilominus eternum premium reportaverunt qui pro ipsa recuperanda laboraverunt.

28 Multos insuper lucratus est Dominus qui signum crucis accipientes ex cordis contriti devotione se ipsos voto solempni Domino obligaverunt, unde licet preventi sint morte, quia per eos non stetit. Confidimus in Domino quod tam sancte voluntatis non privabuntur premio: talis enim voluntas pro facto reputatur in ipsis, ut impleatur in eis quod scriptum est in Ecc[co]. [xx, 12]: *Est qui multa redimat modico tempore.* Et in libro Sapie. [iv, 7, 13] dicitur: *Iustus si morte preocupatus fuerit in refrigerio, erit consummatus in brevi, explevit tempora multa.*

[19] sompnum D, P2, P6] sopnum T1
[20] suam P2] *om.* T1, D, P6

work is short and the wages immense, because *when he gave his dear ones sleep, it was the inheritance of the Lord*. Because of this, they must labour with great joy who hope for rest without end after the work [is done], as one usually says in the vernacular: 'He who has a ready bed drinks safely';[5] 'he who has a bed for himself before his eyes drinks merrily'.[6] He who leads a palfrey with him is not afraid to walk and when he is tired he gets on the horse. Your bed is ready in paradise. If you stay in the service of God, the holy angels are ready to carry your souls and present them to God. And then you can *sing a new song* before him: *What we heard we saw for ourselves in the city of the Lord of virtues.*

< Why God let his land be occupied by the enemies and did not want to liberate it immediately and how much good comes from this >

26 You must note carefully that, although God could liberate his land by himself with one word, he wants to honour his servants and wants to have companions in its liberation, giving you the chance to save your souls, which he redeemed and for which he spilled his blood and therefore does not like to lose them.

27 Many have been saved by this holy pilgrimage who would have remained in their sins if the Lord had liberated this land by himself in the first place. This is why it says in the book of Wisdom: God *pays back the wages for their* holy *labours*; it does not say fruit since he does not remunerate according to the result of the matter. Which is why, although the Christians have not recovered the Holy Land, those who laboured for its recovery nevertheless received the eternal reward.

28 In addition, the Lord rewarded many who took the sign of the cross out of devotion with a contrite heart and pledged themselves to the Lord by a solemn vow, even though they were prevented by death [from fulfilling their vow], since it was not through any fault of their own. We trust in the Lord that they are not deprived of the reward for such a holy resolve: for them such a resolve counts as the deed, so that it is fulfilled in them what is written in Ecclesiasticus: *There is a person who buys much for little time.* And in the book of Wisdom it says: *The just person will be refreshed even if he dies before his time, having come to perfection so soon, he has lived a long time.*

---

[5] Walther, II/4, 760, no. 27794.   [6] Walther, II/3, 907, no. 22092.

29 Unde in eodem libro Sapie. [i, 1] dicitur: *Sentite de Domino in bonitate*. Ipse quidem bonus est et largus in miserationibus, indulgentiis et remunerationibus et tribuit servis suis et amicis dona secundum magnificentiam regiam. Unde non est petendus ab illo obulus temporalium, quia paratus est dare eterni premii thesaurum.

< Contra illos qui magis diligunt paleam quam granum et vile quam pretiosum et de bono foro quod facit Dominus >

30 Multi tamen hodie currunt et properant dum pecunia modica illis offertur, quos tamen pigros videmus dum regnum celorum cum cruce illis offerimus. Et ut iuxta vulgare Gallicum loquimur: si clamaretur: 'Gueagne maalle!', accurrerent multi, dum clamatur: 'Gueagne paradis!' vel: 'Avuot, avuot ad paradis!', accurrunt pauci.

31 *Querite igitur Dominum dum inveniri potest, invocate eum dum prope est* [Is. lv, 6]. Dici enim solet quod bonum forum trahit de bursa denarium. Non igitur in bursa diaboli remaneatis, nec Domino clamanti et offerenti vobis paradisum surdam aurem faciatis! 'Qui non dat, quod amat, non accipit ille, quod optat.' Dominus velut ebrius modo facit bonum forum et quasi pro nichilo dat regnum suum. Regno quidem Dei nichil vilius cum emitur, nichil carius cum possidetur.

32 Ipse vero, tanquam crapulatus potens a vino, cito excitabitur [f. 150vb] et manum suam retrahens percutiet inimicos suos in posteriora post hanc vitam et opprobrium sempiternum dabit illis post mortem. Ut sicut Dominus per precones suos modo clamat et non exaudiunt, ita ipsi clamabunt et non exaudientur [cf. Prv. xxi, 13]. Sicut scriptum est in Parab. [i, 24–26]: *Vocavi et renuistis, extendi manum meam,* offerendo scilicet vobis crucem et indulgentiam, *et non fuit qui aspiceret; despexistis omne consilium meum; ego quoquoe in interitu vestro ridebo et subsannabo, cum vobis quod timebatis advenerit.* Et per Iob [xix, 16] Dominus ait: *Vocavi servum meum et non respondit michi, ore proprio deprecabar illum.*

< De bonis que proveniunt ex predicatione crucis et ex hac peregrinatione >

33 Valde quidem negligentes sunt vel potius concutientes qui non aspiciunt nec attendunt quot bona ex hac predicatione et tam sancta peregrinatione proveniunt.

29 Whence it says in the same book of Wisdom: *Be properly disposed towards the Lord*. He is good and generous with mercy, indulgences and rewards and he gives presents to his servants and friends in accordance with [his] royal magnificence. Hence he should not be asked for a halfpenny's worth of worldly goods, since he is prepared to give a treasure of eternal reward.

< Against those who prefer the chaff to the grain and the base to the precious and about the good bargain that the Lord makes >
30 Many today make haste and run when they are offered a little money, but we see them lazy when we offer them the kingdom of heaven with the cross. In vernacular French we say: if someone shouts: Gueagne maalle! [i.e. Have a halfpenny!], many come running; when someone shouts: Gueagne paradis! [i.e. Have paradise!] or : Avuot, avuot ad paradis! [i.e. Hurry up to paradise!], few come.
31 *Seek out the Lord while he can still be found, call to him while he is still near*. One usually says that a good bargain draws the penny from the purse. Therefore, do not stay in the purse of the devil and do not close your ears to the Lord, who calls you and offers you paradise. 'He who does not give what he loves does not receive what he wishes.'[7] As if drunk, the Lord now makes a good bargain and gives his kingdom for just about nothing. There is nothing cheaper to buy than the kingdom of God and nothing dearer to possess.

32 Like a powerful man drunk with wine, he will soon be aroused and, pulling back his hand, he will strike down his enemies from behind at the end of this life and will give them eternal shame after death. As the Lord now calls through his preachers and people do not hear, so [these people] will call and will not be heard. As it is written in Proverbs: *I called and you refused me, I held out my hand*, offering you the cross and the indulgence, *and there was no one who looked; you disregarded all my advice; I shall laugh at your distress and jeer when what you fear befalls you*. And the Lord says through Job: *I called my servant and he did not answer me, I shall ask him with my own mouth*.

< About the good things that derive from the preaching of the cross and this pilgrimage >
33 Those who do not notice and are not aware of how much good derives from this preaching and from so holy a pilgrimage are very disregarding, [sometimes] even alarmed.

---

[7] Petrus Abaelardus, *Carmen ad Astralabium*, ed. J. M. A. Rubingh-Bosscher (Groningen, 1987), 139, verse 579 (= Walther, II/4, 222, no. 24391).

34 Primum quidem bonum quod multi hac occasione ad verbum Dei convenientes multa peccata et lascivias dimittunt, quas diebus festivis facere consueverunt et, ad predicationem compuncti dum peccata sua cognoscunt, ad confessionem currunt.

35 Secundum bonum quod venientibus ad sermonem viginti vel quadraginta dies aliquando de penitentia relaxantur, quod multum proderit eis maxime post mortem in purgatorio, quando pro unius hore relaxatione, si possibile esset, magnum thesaurum dedisse voluissent.

36 Tertium bonum quod multi incitantur ad idem faciendum dum alios currere vident ad bonum forum; multos enim vidimus qui in corde suo proposuerant non signari, venientes tamen ut viderent qui crucem acciperent, ipsi primi ad crucem currebant.

< Exemplum de illo qui abscondit se in solario ut non signarebitur et de bono exemplo aliis ostendendo >

37 Nam et ego cum aliquando in quadam villa predicarem, quidam uxore sua dissuadente ad sermonem cum aliis noluit venire. Cepit tamen quasi ex curiositate de solario per fenestram inspicere et quid ego dicerem latenter auscultare. Cumque audisset quod per crucis compendium absque alia penitentia tantam indulgentiam obtinerent quantam plerumque non obtinent qui per annos sexaginta ieiunant et portant cilicium et nichil enim amplius potest remitti quam totum – dominus enim papa nichil excipit sed universaliter omnia dimittit tanquam Dei minister qui non vult esse avarus ubi Dominus est largus –, audiens insuper quod pro labore modici temporis penitentia huius seculi et pena purgatorii remittitur et pena gehenne evitatur regnumque celorum acquiritur, ipse valde compunctus et a Deo inspiratus, timens uxorem, que ostium clauserat et ne exgrederetur, observabat per fenestram, in turbam exilivit et ipse primus ad crucem venit. Et quia bonum aliis prebuit exemplum et multi secuti sunt eum, ipse particeps extitit meriti universorum. Qui enim malo exemplo multos corrumpit bono exemplo debet restituere Deo quod illi abstulit; iustum quidem est ut qui cum multorum destructione se prodidit cum multorum edificatione se redimat.

34 The first good [is] that many who come together on this occasion to [hear] the word of God leave aside many of the sins and lascivious acts that they usually commit on feastdays and, made remorseful by the sermon when they realise their sins, they go to confession.

35 The second good [is] that those who come to the sermon are granted a remission of their penance of twenty or forty days, which does them much good especially in purgatory after death, when they would have wished to have given a great treasure for just one single hour of remission, if it were possible.

36 The third good [is] that many are encouraged to do the same when they see others rushing to the good bargain; in fact, we have seen many, who having decided in their heart not to be signed but coming to see who would take the cross, were the first to hurry to the cross.

< Exemplum about the man who hid in a loft so that he would not be signed and about the good example to show others[8] >

37 Once when I preached in some town, one man did not want to come to the sermon with the others since his wife objected. But he began to watch through a window in the loft out of curiosity and listen secretly to what I would say. When he heard that through the properties of the cross and without any other penitence people received such a great indulgence as people mostly do not obtain who fast and wear a hairshirt for sixty years and that nothing less than the whole may be remitted – the lord pope left nothing out but remitted everything altogether like a minister of God who does not want to be greedy where the Lord is generous –, when he also heard that for the labour of a short time the penance in this world and the punishment of purgatory were remitted, the punishment of hell avoided and the kingdom of heaven gained, he was full of remorse and inspired by God; afraid of his spouse, who had locked the door so that he would not leave, he was watching from the window and jumped out into the crowd and was the first to come to the cross. And since he showed a good example to others and many followed him, he is now enjoying all universal benefits. He who corrupts many by bad example must give back to God by good example what he took away from him; it is just that he who took advantage by pulling down many should redeem himself by edifying many.

---

8 Crane, no. cxxii, 56; Tubach, no. 1062.

< Contra illos qui differunt signari et contra illos qui impediunt alios ne signentur >

38 Unde valde bonum est coram cunctis crucem accipere et alios bono exemplo invitare, maxime quia bona voluntas cito refrigescit et diabolus per uxorem vel per seculares amicos bonum propositum frequenter extinguit. Quando peccata facere solebatis, de malo faciendo non accipiebatis consilium nec erubescebatis. Quare ergo verecundamini accipere crucem in aperto, ut bonum exemplum aliis detis et confundatis diabolum coram omnibus, sicut confunditur latro quando deprehenditur in furto et in pilori ponitur in medio foro? Non accipiebatis consilium ab uxoribus eundi ad diabolum; quare expectatis consilium eundi ad Deum?

39 In Deut. [xxv, 17–8] quidem legitur quod Amalech *ex-* [f. 151ra] *tremos agminis qui* pigri erant *et lassi* interfecit. Hic est diabolus: caveatis ne sitis de extremis, ne sitis tardi ad bonum faciendum. Illi autem qui bonum impediunt, damnationem reportabunt, unde in Parab. [iii, 27]: *Noli prohibere bene facere eum qui potest; si vales et ipse benefac*; et iterum in Parab. [iii, 28]: *Noli dicere amico tuo: Vade et revertere et cras dabo tibi, cum statim possis dare.* 'Qui non est hodie, cras minus aptus erit.' Hii vero qui prohibent dissuadendo, detrahendo et malum exemplum dando, similes sunt cani nequam, qui iacet super fenum et manducare nequit nec cetera animalia, que comedere possent, maducare sinit.

40 Quartum bonum ex hoc sancto negotio provenit: Nam multi qui ire non possunt pro se mittunt et euntibus tanta de bonis suis largiuntur quod indulgentiam consequntur. Sed illi qui cruce signati sunt dum morte preveniuntur, ad subsidium Terre Sancte mittunt ea que ferre debuerunt.

41 Quintum autem et precipuum bonum est quod, postquam cruce signati sunt, ne tantum premium laboris sui ammitant, ad confessionem currunt et de cetero a peccatis abstinere student ne tantum bonum perdant.

< Against those who put off being signed and against those who prevent others from being signed >

38 Because of this it is a very good thing to take the cross in front of everybody and invite others by good example, especially since good intention cools down quickly and the devil often extinguishes a good proposal through the spouse or worldly friends. When you used to commit sins, you did not take any advice about doing evil and you did not blush. Why then are you ashamed to take the cross openly, so that you might give a good example to others and embarrass the devil in front of everybody, just as a thief is embarrassed when he is caught in a robbery and is put in pillory in the middle of the market place? You did not take the advice to go to the devil from your wives; why do you wait for advice to go to God?

39 One reads in Deuteronomy that Amalek killed *the last in the row who were* lazy and *weary*. He is the devil: watch out that you are not among the last, that you are not late for doing good. Those who prevent good bring about damnation, whence in Proverbs: *Do not prevent from doing good someone who can do it; if it is in your power, do good yourself;* and again in Proverbs: *Do not say to your friend: Go away and come back another time and I shall give it to you tomorrow, when you can give it immediately.* 'He who cannot do it today will be even less able tomorrow.'[9] Those who hinder [others] by dissuading, distracting and giving a bad example are like a useless dog who lies in the hay and cannot eat [it] and does not let other animals eat that could eat [it].

40 The fourth good that derives from this holy business: Many who cannot go send [others] for themselves and grant those who go so much of their goods that they [themselves] obtain the indulgence. But if those who are signed with the cross are prevented by death, they send that which they would have had to take with them as a subsidy to the Holy Land.

41 The fifth and most important good is that, after having been signed with the cross, people go to confession so as not to lose so great a reward of their labour, and to strive to abstain from sins so as not to lose so great a benefit.

---

[9] Ovidus, 'Remedia Amoris', *P. Ovidi Nasonis Amores, Medicamina Facei Feminae, Ars Amatoria, Remedia Amoris*, ed. E. J. Kenney (Oxford, 1961), verse 94 (= Walther, IV/4, 223, no. 24398).

< Contra pusillanimes et meticulosos et contra duros et obstinatos >

42 Multaque alia bona inde proveniunt, que miseri non advertant, qui ita pusillanimes sunt et putridi quod crux illis non potest assui, qui tamquam panni[21] vetustate consumpti et nulli usui apti suturam retinere non valent. Hii sunt formidolosi qui ad bellum non sunt ydonei, sed a Domino reprobentur [cf. Dt. xx, 8].

43 Alii sunt ita duri et obstinati quod de indulgentia non curant nec acu timoris Dei penetrari possunt, ut humeris eorum crux assuatur vel filo amoris Dei illis astringatur. Cum igitur Dominus radios gratie sue per universum mundum diffundat, quidam pussilanimes velud cera ad hunc solem ita liquescunt quod sigillum crucis non recipiunt, in quo sigillata fuit caro Christi.

44 Alii vero velut lutum ad hunc solem indurantur ut sigilli impressionem non recipiant, et ideo caractere bestie sigillantur [cf. Apc. xiii, 16], dum diabolum imitantur. Quia noluerunt benedicitonem, elongabitur ab eis, et quoniam quando possunt nolunt, quando vellent non poterunt.

< Exemplum de Carolo et filiis eius >

45 Exemplo cuiusdam filii imperatoris Caroli qui vocabatur Gobaut, volens etiam Carolus, ut dicunt, probare filiorum obedientiam. Accepta parte pomi quam in manibus tenebat dixit: Gobaude, aperi os tuum et accipe! Respondit quod non aperiret nec tantum vituperium pro patre sustineret. Tunc pater vocato alio filio nomine Ludovico dixit: Aperi os et accipe quod tibi porrigo! Cui ille: Sicut placet vobis; de me tamquam de servo vestro facite. Et aperto ore pomum de manu patris accepit. Cui pater statim subjunxit: Et ego do tibi regnum Francie. Et cum tertio filio, qui Loerins vocabatur, preciperet ut coram cunctis os aperiret, pater aperienti dixit: Per partem pomi quam recepisti in ore investio te de ducatu Lothorengie. Tunc Gobaudus sero penitens ait patri: Pater, ecce aperio os meum; da michi partem pomi! Cui pater: Tarde aperuisti, nec pomum nec terram dabo tibi. Et ceperunt omnes deridere eum dicentes: 'A tart bea Gobard', id est tarde hyavit Gobardus.

---

[21] panni D, P2, P6] *om.* T1

< Against the fearful and timid and against the stubborn and obstinate >

42 Many other good things derive from this that the wretched people are not aware of, they who are so weak and rotten that the cross cannot be sewn onto them; like old pieces of cloth that are worn out by age and are no longer useful for anything, they cannot hold a seam. They are fearful people who are not suitable for war and they will be condemned by the Lord.

43 Others are so stubborn and obstinate that they do not care about the indulgence, nor can they be reached by the needle of the fear of God so that the cross might be sewn onto their shoulders or tied onto them with the thread of God's love. As the Lord pours out the rays of his grace over the whole world, some fearful people melt like wax in this sun, so that they do not obtain the seal of the cross, into which the flesh of Christ was stamped.

44 Other people become hard as clay in this sun, so that they do not take the impression of the seal, and because of this they are stamped with the symbol of the beast, as they imitate the devil. Because they do not want the blessing, it will be taken away from them, and because when they could they did not want, they will not be able to when they want.

< Exemplum about Charles and his sons[10] >

45 According to an exemplum about a son of the Emperor Charles who was called Gobaud[us], Charles wanted, as they say, to test his sons' obedience. Taking part of an apple that he held in his hand he said: Gobaud, open your mouth and take this! He replied that he would not open it and would not suffer so much shame for his father. After calling his second son, named Ludovicus, the father said: Open your mouth and take what I give you! He [replied] to him: As you please; treat me as you would treat your servant. And having opened his mouth he accepted the apple from his father's hand. The father added, [saying] to him at once: I shall give you the kingdom of Francia. When he ordered his third son, who was called Loerins, to open his mouth in front of everybody, the father said to him who had opened [his mouth]: By the part of the apple that you received with your mouth I invest you with the duchy of Lotharingia. Then Gobaudus, regretting too late, said to his father: Father, see I open my mouth, give me a part of the apple! The father [replied] to him: You have opened it [too] late, I shall give you no apple and no land. And everybody began making fun of him saying: 'A tard bea Gobard', meaning Gobardus gaped too late.

---

[10] Crane, no. cxxiii (false cxxx); Tubach, no. 947.

< Quod per rem modicam investitur homo, de magna possessione et de fardello quid facit Dominus >

46 Consuetudo quidem est nobilium et potentium quod per cirothecam vel aliam rem vilis pretii vasallos suos investiunt de feodis pretiosis, sicut Dominus per crucem ex modico filo vel panno vasallos suos investit de[22] celesti regno. Et more ludentium ad aleas vel decios ingenti exposito fardello vos invitat. In hoc tam sancto ludo aut tenes aut dimittis: si tenes lucraris, si dimittis amittis. Vide quid facias! Optio tibi datur! Non remanebit in Deo nisi in te remaneat.

47 Obsecro igitur vos, [f. 151rb] fratres, per misericordiam Ihesu Christi et per aspersionem sanguinis Crucifixi quatenus non solum Domino, qui privatus est hereditate sua, tanquam fideles vasalli et homines ligii succurratis, sed vobismetipsis subveniatis nec tantam gratiam in vacuum recipiatis. *Ecce nunc tempus acceptabile, ecce nunc dies salutis* [ii Cor. vi, 2]. *Levate signum* crucis salutifere, *confortamini et nolite stare*, sed currite *ad bravium vocationis superne* [Phil. iii, 14]! Et vocanti vos per predicationem respondeatis per obedientiam Domino Nostro Ihesu Christo, cui est honor et gloria in secula seculorum. Amen.

---

[22] feodis . . . de D, P2, P6] *om.* T1

< That man is invested by modest things, about the large possession and the prize that the Lord makes >

46 It is a custom among noble and powerful men to invest their vassals with precious fiefs by a glove or some other object of little worth, just as the Lord invests his vassals with the heavenly kingdom by the cross [made] of ordinary thread or cloth. He invites you in the manner of those who play at hazard or dice, having shown you the enormous prize. In this holy game you either hold or throw away: if you hold you win, if you throw away you lose. Watch out what you do! You are given the choice! It will not hold with God unless it holds with you.

47 I beseech you, brothers, by the mercy of Jesus Christ and by the shedding of the blood of the Crucified that you come not only to the aid of the Lord, who has been deprived of his inheritance, like faithful vassals and liege men, but also to your own aid, and that you may not receive such great grace in vain. *See, now is the right time, now is the day of salvation. Raise the sign* of the salutary cross, *be strong and do not delay*, but run *towards the prize of the heavenly call!* May you respond by obedience to Our Lord Jesus Christ, who calls you through the sermon and whose is the honour and the glory for ever and ever. Amen.

Eudes of Châteauroux

SERMO I

R1 = Rome, Biblioteca Angelica, 157, ff. 137vb-140ra

Additional manuscripts
P4 = Paris, Bibliothèque Nationale de France, lat. 15947, ff. 90ra-92va
V1 = Vatican, Biblioteca Apostolica, Pal. lat. 452, ff. 69rb-71rb

Reference
Schneyer IV, 439, no. 562

Sermo in conversione sancti Pauli et exhortatio ad assumendam crucem

1 Matheo xix [28]: *Amen dico vobis, quod vos qui reliquistis omnia et secuti estis me in regeneratione, cum sederit Filius Hominis in sede magestatis sue, sedebitis et vos super sedes duodecim, iudicantes duodecim tribus Israel.* In his verbis nobis ostendit Spiritus Sanctus tria. Conversionem peccatoris ad Deum, et precipue beati Pauli, cuius conversionem hodie celebramus, cum dicit: *Vos qui relequistis.* Secundo, vitam ipsius post conversionem, ibi: *Et secuti estis me.* Tertio, premium pro utroque, cum dicit: *Sedebitis* etc.

2 Dicit itaque: *Amen dico vobis, quod vos qui reliquistis omnia* etc. Beatus Paulus, quando conversus fuit ad Dominum, propter ipsum omnia dereliquit. Immo ipsa eius conversio nichil aliud fuit quam omnium derelictio, neque converti ad Dominum aliud[1] quam relinquere omnia uno modo, sicut convertere se ad mundum nichil aliud est quam

---

[1] aliud P4, V1] nichil aliud est R1

128

Eudes of Châteauroux

SERMON I

Sermon for the Conversion of St Paul and exhortation to take the cross

1 Matthew 19: *In truth I tell you who have left everything and followed me: When everything is made new again and the Son of Man is seated on the throne of his glory, you yourselves will be seated on twelve thrones to judge the twelve tribes of Israel.* In these words the Holy Spirit shows us three things: The sinner's conversion to God, and especially that of Saint Paul, whose conversion we celebrate today, when it says: *You who have left.* Secondly, his life after conversion, here: *And you followed me.* Thirdly, the reward for both of these, when it says: *You will be seated* etc.

2 Thus it says: *In truth I tell you who have left everything* etc. When Saint Paul was converted to the Lord, he renounced everything for him. As his conversion was nothing short of renouncing everything, and as to convert to the Lord means to leave behind everything in the same way, so to convert to the world is nothing short of renouncing the Lord.

Dominum derelinquere. Sicut quando aliqui convertunt se ad aliquem regem, eo ipso regem alium inimicantem illi[2] derelinquunt, unde Matheo vi [24]: *Nemo potest duobus dominis ser-* [f. 138ra] *vire: Aut enim unum odio habebit et alterum diliget aut unum sustinebit et alterum contempnet.*

3 Conversio ista fit per amorem eo ipso enim quo quis ponit amorem in creatura; nisi propter Deum hoc faciat, eo ipso cor suum avertit a Deo. Sicut enim corpus tuum non potest esse in duobus locis simul, sic nec cor. Et dicit Dominus, Matheo vi [21]: *Ubi est thesaurus tuus, ibi est cor tuum.* Unde si *thesaurus tuus* est in Deo, *ibi est et cor tuum*, ergo non alibi. Unde Iacobus iiii [4]: *Adulteri, nescitis quia amicitia huius mundi inimica est Deo? Quicumque ergo voluerit amicus esse huius seculi inimicus Dei constituitur.*

4 Sed dicetis: Ergo non contingit nisi amare unum, quia, ut dicetis, cor non potest esse nisi in uno loco? Quod concedo, sicut secundum beatum Augustinum in dilligendo proximum ex caritate non diligimus nisi Deum, sic et in omnibus aliis que diligimus propter Deum. Quid est enim diligere Deum nisi velle honorem eius et gloriam?

5 Quicquid vero diligimus non propter Deum diligimus aut propter utilitatem nostram aut propter delicias nostras aut propter nostrum honorem. Unde in his que diligimus propter Deum non diligimus nisi propter unum. Similiter in hiis que diligimus propter nos non diligimus nisi unum, nos ipsos scilicet. Et loquimur de amore libidinoso qui illicitus est, non de amore naturali qui licitus est. Qui quomodo licitus sit, magna questio est eo quod videtur esse quedam fruitio nature.[3]

6 Sic ergo hec conversio fit per amorem. Et ex quo convertit se quis ad Dominum per amorem, mundum et ea que in mundo sunt derelinquit, ut non amet ea. Et quando crescit amor Dei, ut zelus fiat, vel quando convertitur amor in zelum, tunc derelictio in tedium, ut etiam ipsum mundum sustinere non possit, [f. 138rb] immo eum a se omnino abicit. Sic in beato Paulo factum est, qui conversus est ad Deum per amorem. Sed amor iste conversus in ardorem et zelum mutavit dilectionem in odium, ut omnia que sunt mundi a se abiceret.

7 Non diligere enim mundum incipientium est, abicere vero perfectorum est. Et signum est quod homo Deum diligat, qui mundum abicit.

---

[2] illi] alii R1, P4, V1   [3] Et loquimur . . . nature R1] *om.* P4, V1

When people convert to some king, they of course renounce another king who is hostile, whence Matthew 6: *No one can serve two masters: He will either hate the one and love the other or he will support the one and despise the other.*

3 This conversion happens through love, through which, of course, someone puts his love in the creation; he turns his heart from God unless, of course, he does it for the sake of God. Just as your body cannot be in two places at the same time, neither can your heart. The Lord says, Matthew 6: *Where your treasure is, there is your heart.* Thus, if your treasure is in God, *your heart is also there*, and therefore not elsewhere. Whence James 4: *Adulterers! Do you not know that love for this world is hatred of God? Anyone who chooses to be a friend of this world is constituted an enemy of God.*

4 But you say: Can you therefore only love the one, since, as you say, the heart can only be in one place? I grant you this; as according to Saint Augustine[1] we in fact love but God when we love our neighbour out of charity, this also goes for all other things that we love for the sake of God. What does it mean to love God if not to wish for his honour and glory?

5 Whatever we do not love for the sake of God we love either for our convenience or for our pleasure or for our own honour. This is why we love those things which we love for the sake of God for one reason only. In the same way we love those things which we love for our own sake for only one reason, namely ourselves. And here we are talking about lustful love which is illicit, not about natural love which is licit. In what way it is licit is a big question, since it seems to be an enjoyment of nature.

6 This conversion thus happens through love. And when someone converts to the Lord through love, he renounces the world and everything that is of the world, so that he may not love them. And when his love of God grows, so that it becomes zeal, or when his love is turned into zeal, then his renouncement [is turned into] tedium, so that he cannot stand this world any more and he casts it off altogether. This happened to Saint Paul who was converted to God through love. This love was converted into ardour and zeal and turned his fondness into hatred, so that he cast off everything that was of the world.

7 Not to love the world is what beginners do, to cast it off is what the perfect do. And it is a sign that man loves God, when he casts off the

---

[1] Cf. Augustinus, 'In Iohannis Evangelium Tractatus cxxiv', *PL*, XXXV, 1809.

Sic signum manifestum est quod homo dilectione Dei ardeat et zelo, qui propter Deum patriam, possessiones, domos, filios, uxores derelinquit vadens ultra mare in servitio Ihesu Christi, ut possit dicere cum Psalmista [xxi, 15]: *Factum est cor meum tanquam cera liquescens in medio ventris mei.*

8 Ad hoc enim venit Filius Dei in mundum, ut homines non tantummodo eum diligerent, quia hoc ante incarnationem faciebant, immo potius ut amore eius arderent et ut iste ignis vehementius inflammaretur. Se ipsum misit in hunc ignem quasi adipem, sicut legimus ministros Nabugodonosor fecisse in fornace ignis, Daniel iii [46–7]: *Non cessebant qui miserant eos ministri regis succendere fornacem napta et stupa et pice maleolis, et effundebatur flamma iginis super fornacem cubitis quadraginta novem.*

9 Sic ipse Dominus, etsi multa beneficia et etiam omnes creaturas posuisset in hunc ignem, donaria enim fomes sunt amoris, ad ultimum se posuit in hunc ignem et se ipsum hoc igne concremavit, ut nos ardere faceret amore suo. Se ipsum enim dedit. Hec enim recogitatio debet totum cor hominis inflammare, sicut dicit Ps. [xxxviii, 4]: *In meditatione mea exardescet ignis.* Et ut dictum est certissimum indicium est quod illi amore eius ardeant qui assumpta cruce eum secuntur.

10 Sed potest conqueri Dominus de quibusdam, sicut legimus in Ier. vi [29]: *Defecit sufflatorium in igne,* [f. 138va] *consumptum est plumbum,* quasi dicat: Nichil valet sufflare. Sicut enim diabolus sufflatores suos habet, scilicet[4] eos quorum verbis vel suggestione amor malus succendetur – secundum illud Ysaye liiii [16]: *Creavit fabrum sufflantem prunas in igne*; Iob xli[5] [12]: *Alitus eius prunas ardere facit* – , sic et Deus habet folles suos, id est predicatores, sed deficiunt quantum ad quosdam.

11 *Plumbum* etiam *consumptum est,* id est Christus, et pro nichilo tanto amore se concremavit, unde ipse dicit per Ysayam xlix [4]: *Ego dixi: In vacuum laboravi sine causa et vane fortitudinem meam consumpsi, ergo iudicium meum cum Domino.* Sed quod erit hoc *iudicium*? Ut qui noluerint ardere hoc igne in futuro ardeant igne gehenne. Sed michi timendum est ne forte ex parte follis sit quod iste ignis minus ardeat, quia qui non ardet non incendit; legitur Ecc[co]. xlviii[6] [1]: *Surrexit Helias quasi ignis et sermo eius quasi facula ardebat.*

---

⁴ scilicet V1] *om.* R1, P4   ⁵ xli] xl R1, P4, V1   ⁶ xlviii] l R1, P4, V1

world. Thus it is a sure sign that a man burns with the love of God and with zeal if he leaves his fatherland, possessions, houses, sons [and] spouses for the sake of God to go across the sea in the service of Jesus Christ, so that he may say with the Psalmist: *My heart is made like wax melting in the midst of my bowels.*

8 The Son of God came into the world not just so that people would love him, because they did this before the incarnation, but rather that they burn with his love and that this fire be ignited more fervently. He put himself into this fire as if he were oil, as the servants of Nabuchadnezzar did in the fiery furnace, as we read in Daniel 3: *The king's servants, who had thrown them in, did not stop stoking the furnace with oil, tow and pitch of brushwood, and the flame of the fire rose forty-nine cubits above the furnace.*

9 Thus the Lord himself, although he might have put many a favour and also all creatures into this fire, since offerings are the tinder of love, finally put himself into this fire and burned himself in this fire, so that he could make us burn with his love. He in fact gave himself. This thought ought to set on fire the whole human heart, as the Psalmist says: *While I was musing, the fire burned.* And as has been said, the clearest indication is that they who have taken the cross and follow him burn with this love.

10 But the Lord can complain loudly about some people, as we read in Jeremiah 6: *The bellows are burned by the fire, the lead is consumed*, as if to say: it is not worth blowing. As the devil has his own blowers, namely they by whose words and instigation bad love is fired up – according to Isaiah 54: *He has made a smith who blows the coals in the fire*; Job 41: *His breath makes coals burn* –, so God has his own bellows, meaning his preachers, but these are fewer than they.

11 Also *the lead is consumed*, meaning Christ, since he burned himself out of such great love for nothing in return, as he himself said through Isaiah 49: *I said: I laboured in vain without reason and I spent my strength for nothing, yet my judgement is with the Lord.* But what will this *judgement* be? Those who do not want to burn in this fire will burn in the fire of hell in the future. But I fear that this fire may burn less well unless perhaps for the bellows, because he who does not burn cannot light a fire; one reads in Ecclesiasticus 48: *Elija rose like a fire and his words burned like a torch.*

12 Tamen video quod de calculo ignis egreditur et materia preparata incenditur. Quamvis calculus non ardeat, sic licet ego non ardeam, tamen si preparati essetis, nichilominus arderetis; legitur Iudic. vi [21]: *Extendit angelus Domini summitatem virge, quam tenebat in manu, et tetigit carnes et azimos panes, ascenditque ignis de petra.* Per *carnes* verba moralia que dulcia sunt et nutriunt hominem interiorem, per *panem* verba que fidem astruunt et interiorem hominem fortem faciunt in fide. Quando quis proposse suo hec verba sincere aliis preponit, licet *petra* sit et durus ac expers ignis, tamen per tactum *virge*, id est per auxilium Domnini, ignis erumpit et alios inflammat.

13 Sed dicitur in Ps. [ciii, 4]: *Qui facit angelos suos spiritus et ministros suos* [f. 138vb] *ignem urentem.* Qui sunt isti ministri nisi clerici, qui pre aliis ardere deberent? Angeli enim qui vicinius Deum contemplantur ab ardore seraphin nuncupantur, id est ardentes. Quare ergo theologi minus ardent?

14 Legitur Apo. xxi [16]: *Civitas in quadrum posita, longitudo eius tanta quanta est latitudo.* Et sancti dicunt quod quatuor latera sunt: fides, spes, caritas et operatio. Quantum enim quis credit tantum sperat, tantum diligit, tantum operatur. Per fidem autem cognoscitur Deus, sed videtur quod cognitioni non equatur amor, quia qui magis cognoscunt minus diligunt. Sed hoc est quia vere non cognoscunt aut quia spem non habent, que debet intervenire media.

15 Sic ergo, ut dictum est, debemus non tantummodo diligere Deum, immo amore eius ardere et inflammari. Si enim eum diligeremus, tunc omnia delinqueremus corde nichil diligendo nisi propter ipsum vel in ipso, et si arderemus eius amore, tunc etiam omnino omnia abdicaremus sicut Paulus de quo loquimur, quia arsit ideo omnia dereliquit, unde fuit de numero eorum de quibus dicit Dominus: *Amen dico vobis, vos qui reliquistis omnia.*

16 Sed quid dereliquit? Ipse dixit Ad Phil. iii [4–8]: *Si quis alius videtur confidere in carne, ego magis: Circumcisus octava die ex genere Israel de tribu Beniamin, Hebreus ex Hebreis, secundum legem Phariseus; sed que michi fuerunt lucra, hoc arbitratus sum propter Christum detrimenta, propter quem omnia detrimentum feci et arbitratus sum ut stercora.* Ecce nobilitatem suam dereliquit, divitias et honores que ex genere solent assequi, magisterium etiam legis,[7] uxorem etiam et filios,

---

[7] legis P4, V1] *om.* R1

12 Still, I see that fire comes from the stone and that the prepared wood is set on fire. Even though the pebble cannot burn, nor for that matter can I burn, still if you were prepared, you would burn all the same; one reads in Judges 6: *The angel of the Lord put forth the tip of the staff that he held in his hand and touched the meat and the unleavened bread, and fire sprang from the rock.* The *meat* [stands] for words of morality which are like sweets and nourish the inner person, the *bread* for words which strengthen the faith and make the inner person steadfast in faith. When someone suggests honestly to propose these words to others as best as he can, although he is like a *stone*, hard and without fire, then fire breaks out and inflames others through the touch of the *staff*, that is through God's help.

13 But it says in Psalms: *Who makes his angels spirits and his servants a flaming fire.* Who are these servants if not the clerics, who ought to burn before all others? Angels who live in contemplation closer to the Lord because of the heat are called seraphs, that is those who burn. So why do theologians burn less?

14 One reads in Revelation 21: *The city is laid out in a square, its length is as large as its breadth.* The saints say that there are four sides: faith, hope, charity and good works. One believes as much as one hopes, loves and does good works. Through faith one knows God, but it seems that knowledge and love do not match, because those who know better love less. This is because they do not really know or because they do not have hope, which must come in between.

15 Thus, as it has been said, we must not only love God, but we must be set on fire and burn with his love. If we loved him, we would renounce everything and love from the heart only because of him or in him, and if we burned with his love, we would altogether renounce everything, as Saint Paul, of whom we are talking, renounced everything because he burned, whence he was among those of whom the Lord says: *In truth I tell you who have left everything.*

16 But what did he renounce? He himself said in Philippians 3: *If anyone seems to put confidence in the flesh, I do even more: Circumcised on the eighth day, of the people of Israel and the tribe of Benjamin, a Hebrew of Hebrew [parents], Pharisee in the matter of the law; what once were my assets I now count as my losses through Christ, for whom I have suffered the loss of all things and count them as dung.* Thus he left behind his nobility, his wealth and honours which used to follow from his origins,

non quod ea habuerit sed ut non haberet quod⁸ propter Christum apud
se firmavit.

17 Unde [f. 139ra] dicit i Ad Cor. vii [7]: *Volo autem omnes homines
esse sicut meipsum.* Virgo enim erat et ad virginitatem alios exhortans
dicit: *Volo* etc., in hoc dans nobis formam que et qualia propter
Dominum derelinquere deberemus: genus enim suum et patriam dereliquit sicut et Abraham, Genesis xii [1]: *Dixit Dominus ad Abraham:
Egredere* etc. Quando ei locutus fuerit Dominus, utrum per seipsum vel
per angelum seu per hominem non dicitur, sed tantum quod ei locutus est
et ille obedivit ad innuendum, quod per quemcumque vel quocumque
modo nobis hoc Dominus dicat, ei obedire deberemus.

18 Olim dicebat Dominus [Gen. xii, 1]: *Egredere de terra et de
cognatione tua,* sed non dicebat: Veni in terram quam monstravero tibi.
Olim hortabatur homines ut mundum relinquerent, sed modo hortatur
ut veniant in terram quam ipse monstrabit eis et iam monstravit. Sed
posset quis dicere: Ad quid eduxit Dominus Abraham de terra sua?
Nonne in terra sua poterat ei benedicere? Certe ita, tamen causa innuitur
cum dicitur quod eduxit eos de Ur Caldeorum, ut irent in terram
Chanaam [cf. Gn. xi]. Sic Dominus si vellet, in patria nostra posset nobis
benedictionem suam dare et plenariam peccatorum remissionem, sed
ideo vult ut patriam vestram derelinquatis ut vos liberet de igne
demonum, cupiditatis, luxurie, invidie.

19 Beatus etiam Paulus dimisit magisterium, studium et scolas Gama-
lielis, sicut legitur de beato Benedicto: 'Recessit scienter inscius, pru-
denter indoctus.' Uxorem habere noluit. Ecclesie enim quodam modo
clericis desponsantur, sed potest dici multis ecclesiis quod quondam
Dominus dixit Samaritane, Io. iiii [18]: *Quinque vi-* [f. 139rb] *ros
habuisti, et hic quem modo habes non est tuus vir,* quia non gerunt vicem
sponsi sed predonis. Moyses uxorem suam dereliquit, ut iret quo
Dominus precipiebat, sed Dominus amplius facit modo. Sicut legimus
quod Iethro adduxit ad Moysen uxorem suam [cf. Ex. xviii], sic dominus
papa vult quod proventus ecclesiarum sequantur clericos in hac peregrinatione usque ad tres annos.

20 Sic ergo qui vere convertuntur ad Dominum omnia derelinqunt, ut

---

⁸ quod R1] *om.* P4, V1

his mastership in law, also his wife and children, not that he had them but he decided for himself never to have any for the sake of Christ.

17 Whence he said in 1 Corinthians 7: *I should like everyone to be like me.* He was a virgin and he encouraged others also to be virgins by saying: *I should like* etc., thus giving us a model as to what we ought to renounce for the sake of the Lord: he renounced his people and his country like Abraham, Genesis 12: *The Lord said to Abraham: Leave* etc. When the Lord spoke to him, it was not said whether this was himself or through an angel or a human being, but since the [Lord] spoke to him, he obeyed so as to tell us that we ought to obey the Lord no matter through whom or how he speaks to us.

18 The Lord then said: *Leave your country and your family*, but he did not say: Come to the country that I shall show you. Then he told people to leave the world, but now tells them to come to the country which he will show them and, in fact, has already shown them. But someone might say: Why did the Lord lead Abraham out of his country? Could he not have blessed him in his own country? This is of course true, but the reason for this is hinted at when it says that he led them out of Ur of the Chaldees in order to go to the land of Canaan. Thus, if he wanted, God could give us his blessing and a plenary remission of sins in our own country, but he also wants you to leave your country in order to liberate you from the fire of demons, desire, indulging and envy.

19 Saint Paul also left his mastership, his studies and the school of Gamaliel, as one reads of Saint Benedict: 'He withdrew knowledgeable yet ignorant, wise yet unlearned.'[2] He did not want to have a wife. In a certain way, churches are given in marriage to the clerics, but it can be said about many churches what the Lord once said to the Samaritan woman, John 4: *You have had five husbands, and the one you now have is not your husband*, because they do not treat them as a spouse but as a thief. Moses renounced his wife to go where the Lord told him, but now the Lord goes even further. Just as we read that Jethro brought his wife to Moses, so the lord pope wants the income of the churches to go to the clerics on this pilgrimage for up to three years.

20 Those who truly convert to the Lord thus leave everything, as has

---

[2] Cf. Gregorius Magnus, *Dialogues II*, ed. A. de Vogüé (Sources Chrétiennes 260; Paris, 1979), 126.

iam dictum est, quod fecit Paulus et amplius quia secutus est Dominum
de numero illorum quibus dicit Dominus: *Et secuti estis me*. Tota enim
vita beati Pauli non fuit nisi quedam sectatio Domini. Suum enim vivere
non fuit nisi quoddam sequi, unde dicit Ad Phil. iii [12]: *Sequor autem, si
quomodo comprehendam*. Sequebatur enim Dominum *si quomodo* posset
comprehendere, capere et habere, et de se quasi de cane currente post
predam loquitur i Ad Cor. ix [26]: *Ego igitur sic curro, non quasi in
incertum*. Directe enim currebat post illum, quem capere cupiebat.

21 Sic et nos facere deberemus iuxta consilium eiusdem, qui dicit ibidem
[24]: *Sic currite ut comprehendatis*, id est sic sequamini ut comprehendatis. Qui vult Christum capere [cf. Mt. xxii, 15] et habere oportet ut
eum sequatur. Iste secutus est eum usque ad mortem. Scitis quod canis
numquam predam comprehenderet fugientem per sentes, si aculeos
spinarum timeret, sed spinis se ingerit, laceratur, proprio sanguine
cruentatur. Sic qui Dominum vult comprehendere omni periculo et
labori se exponat. Quare? Quia tali via incedit preda sua, id est Dominus.

22 Deus, *in mari via tua et semite tue in aquis multis* [Ps. lxxvi, 20].
Oportet ergo eum sequi per mare. [f. 139va] Sed quia posset quis dubitare
per quod mare? Ideo determinatur modus, scilicet quia per amaritudinem
huius peregrinationis legitur Io. ultimo [xxi, 7–8]: *Symon autem Petrus,
cum audisset quia Dominus est, tunica succinxit se, erat enim nudus, et
misit se in mare; alii autem navigio venerunt*. Sic pauperes audientes,
quia Dominus est quem habebunt in premium, si propter ipsum tran-
sierint hoc mare, licet nudi et pauperes, mittunt *se in mare*, id est subeunt
onus istius peregrinationis. Divites vero *navigio veniunt* amminiculo
divitiarum suarum subvecti.

23 Utinam sic parati essent ad sequendum Dominum sicut ille qui
dicebat, Iob xxiii [11]: *Vestigia eius secutus est pes meus, viam eius
custodivi et non declinavi ex ea*. Multi volunt eum sequi, sed non per
viam per quam ipse ambulavit. Sed dicitur i Io. ii [6]: *Qui dicit se in
Christo manere debet sicut et ipse ambulavit ambulare*. Legitur i Re. xiiii
[13]: *Ascendit autem Ionathas repens manibus et pedibus et armiger post
eum*, et preponitur ibi [xiv, 4]: *Erat autem ascensus* ille valde difficillis.
'Ionathas filius columbe'; Christus de quo Pater mittendo columbam
testatus est: *Hic est Filius meus dilectus* [Mt. iii, 17].

24 Armigeri eius hii qui portant scutum eius, id est crucem, in qua *ex
utraque parte petre* [i Rg. xiv, 4] acute, ut ibi dicitur, quia et ex parte

already been said, just as Paul did to an even greater extent since he followed the Lord among those to whom the Lord said: *And you followed me.* Saint Paul's whole life consisted in nothing but following the Lord. His idea of life was always to follow something, as he said in Philippians 3: *I follow if I may catch it in whatever way.* He followed the Lord if he could catch the Lord *in whatever way*, hold and have him, and he speaks of himself as if of a dog running after its prey, 1 Corinthians 9: *This is how I run, not without a clear goal.* He ran directly after him whom he wanted to hold.

21 We also ought to do this, following his advice who said in the same passage: *Run so that you may catch*, meaning you should follow in the same way, so that you may also catch. He who wants to hold and have Christ must follow him. [Paul] followed him until his death. You know that a dog would never catch a prey fleeing through thornbushes if it were afraid of the spines of the thorns, rather it gets caught in the thorns, hurts itself and gets covered with its own blood. Thus, he who wants to catch the Lord needs to expose himself to every danger and labour. Why? Because on that journey he will come across his prey, that is the Lord.

22 God, *your way is in the sea and your paths in many waters.* Therefore it is right to follow him across the sea. But how could anyone doubt across which sea? The manner is determined in this way, so to speak by the bitterness of this pilgrimage, about which one reads in the last chapter of John: *When Simon Peter heard that it was the Lord, he tied his outer garment about him, for he was naked, and jumped into the water; but the others came in the boat.* So when the poor hear *that it is the Lord* whom they will have as their reward if they go across the sea for his sake, they jump into the water, naked and poor as it were, meaning that they take on the burden of this pilgrimage. The rich then *came in the boat* swept along by the stream of their wealth.

23 If they had only been prepared to follow the Lord in the same way as he who said, Job 23: *My foot has followed his steps, I have kept his path without swerving.* Many want to follow him, but not along the path on which he walked. It says in 1 John 2: *Whoever claims to remain in Christ must himself walk just as he walked.* One reads in 1 Kings 14: *Jonathan clambered up on his hands and feet and his armour-bearer after him*, and earlier it says: There *was a climb* which was rather difficult. 'Jonathan son of the dove';[3] Christ about whom the Father testified by sending the dove: *This is my beloved Son.*

24 His armour-bearers are those who carry his shield, meaning his cross, in which there are sharp *stones on either side*, as it says there,

---

[3] Cf. Hieronymus, 'Commentariorum in Matthaeum Libri iv', *CCSL*, LXXVII, 141.

cordis et ex parte corporis eis angustie imminent. Philistei vero de Ionathan et armigero eius dixerunt: *En Hebrei egrediuntur de cavernis, in quibus absconditi fuerant* [ibid. 11]. Sic pauperes et inermes accipientes crucem a sapientibus deridentur. [f. 139vb] Dicunt de eis: Isti vindicabunt forratum. Ionathas tamen et eius armiger fecerunt stragem magnam, et nisi ipsi precessissent, Saul et exercitus eius non congressi fuissent. Dicitur etiam ibi [ibid. 21] quod *Hebrei, qui ab heri et nudius tertius cum Philistiim fuerant, ascenderunt cum eis in castris et reversi sunt, ut essent cum Israel.* Hoc fortasse accidet de hiis qui modo favent Sarracenis: quod ab eis recedent.

25 Sed dicet quis: Sarraceni nichil michi nocuerunt. Ad quid ergo crucem accipiam contra eos? Sed si bene recogitaret, intelligeret quod Sarraceni magnam iniuriam faciunt cuilibet Christiano. Hoc bene intelligebat qui dicebat Mathatias, scilicet i Machab. ii [7]: *Ve michi, ut quid natus sum videre contritionem populi mei[9] et contritionem civitatis sancte! Ecce sancta nostra et pulchritudo nostra et claritas nostra desolata est, et coinquinaverunt eam gentes! Quid ergo nobis adhuc vivere?* Et sequitur [27]: *Exclamavit Mathatias voce magna in civitate dicens: Omnis qui zelum legis habet statuens testamentum exeat post me.* Quare dicit: *Statuens testamentum,* quod est morientium, nisi ad innuendum quod exire post ipsum erat ad mortem currere et se morti exponere?

26 Tales bene et recto itinere secuntur Dominum sicut et Paulus fecit, et sicut beatus Paulus ex hoc quod Christum est secutus premium habuit, sic illi qui Dominum secuntur. Sed quod premium? Subiungitur cum dicit: *In regeneratione* etc., quasi dicat: Non tantum sedebitis a dexteris, immo cum Domino iudicabitis, Iob xxxvi [6]: *Iudicium pauperibus* [f. 140ra] *tribuet.* Legitur Matheo xii [41–2] Dominum dixisse: *Regina austri surget in iudicio cum generatione ista et condempnabit eam, quia venit a finibus terre audire sapientiam Salomonis, et ecce plus quam Salomon hic. Viri Ninivite surgent in iudicio cum generatione ista et condempnabunt eam, quia penitentiam egerunt in predicatione Ione, et ecce plus quam Ionas hic.* Sic pauperes crucem accipientes et ad auxilium Domini properantes condempnabunt divites et magnates, qui hoc facere noluerunt.

[9] mei P4, V1] *om.* R1

because dangers threaten them on the side of the heart and on the side of the body. The Philistines said of Jonathan and his armour-bearer: *Look, the Hebrews are coming out of the holes where they have been hiding.* In the same way, the poor and unarmed who take the cross are ridiculed by the judicious. They say about them: They will use up the supplies. Still, Jonathan and his armour-bearer caused much damage, and had they not gone ahead, Saul and the army would not have followed them. It says there that *those Hebrews who had been with the Philistines for two days went up with them into the camp and returned to be with Israel.* This will perhaps happen to those who hold to the Saracens, namely that they will withdraw from them.

25 But someone will say: The Saracens have not done me any harm. Why should I take the cross against them? But if he thought about it well, he would realise that the Saracens greatly insult every Christian. Mattathias realised this well, who said in 1 Maccabees 2: *Alas, that I should have been born to see the ruin of my people and the ruin of the holy city! See how our holy one, our beauty and our glory is laid waste and how the gentiles have polluted her! What have we left to live for?* And later on: *Mattathias shouted at the top of his voice throughout the town: Let everyone who has any zeal for the law come out after me making his testament.* Why does he say: *Making his testament*, which is what the dying do, if not to indicate that coming out after him meant to march towards death and to expose oneself to death?

26 Such people follow the Lord well and on the right path as did Paul, and just as Saint Paul received a reward for following Christ, so they who follow the Lord will, too. But what reward? This is added where it says: *When everything will be made new again* etc., as if it were saying: You will not only sit on the right side, but you will also pass judgement with the Lord, Job 36: *He will give judgement to the poor.* One reads in Matthew 12 that the Lord said: *The queen of the south shall rise up in judgement on this generation and shall condemn it, because she came from the end of the world to hear the wisdom of Solomon, and look, there is something greater than Solomon here. The men of Nineveh shall rise in judgement on this generation and shall condemn it, because they repented at the preaching of Jonah, and look, there is something greater than Jonah here.* Thus the poor who take the cross and hasten to help the Lord will condemn the rich and powerful who do not want to do so.

27 Legitur i Re. xi [6–7]: *Insilivit spiritus Domini in Saul, cum audisset hec verba, et iratus est; furor eius nimis, et assumens utrumque bovem conscidit in frustra et misit in omnes terminos Israel per manum nuntiorum dicens: Quicumque non exierit et secutus non fuerit Saul et Samuel sic fiet bobus eius. Irruit ergo timor Domini super populum, et egressi sunt quasi vir unus.* Hoc idem comminatur Dominus eis qui nolunt eum in hoc articulo adiuvare. Duo boves, corpus et anima, qui sunt sub uno iugo parati[10], Ecc[co]. xl[11] [1]: *Grave iugum positum est super filios Ade.* Boves talium in *frustra* concidentur, id est diversis penis afficientur.

28 Egrediamur ergo et sequamur Christum, ut premium quod habebunt illi, qui eum secuti fuerint, habeamus et ut penam eternam quam incurrent illi, qui Christum nolunt sequi, caveamus. Et per intercessionem beati Pauli det nobis Dominus Noster Ihesus Christus ita eum sequi, et si a longe, ut eum assequi valeamus, qui vivit in secula seculorum. Amen.

[10] parati R1] positi P4, V1   [11] xl] xli R1, P4, V1

27 One reads in 1 Kings 11: *The spirit of the Lord seized on Saul, when he heard these words, and he was infuriated; his fury was great and he took a yoke of oxen, cut them into pieces and sent these by the hands of messengers throughout the territory of Israel saying: Anyone who will not go out and follow Saul and Samuel will have the same done to his oxen. The fear of the Lord swept on the people, and they marched out as one man.* The Lord threatens the same to those who do not want to help him in this situation. The two oxen [signify] the body and the soul that are put under one yoke, Ecclesiasticus 40: *A heavy yoke* is placed *on the sons of Adam.* The oxen of such people will be cut into *pieces*, meaning they will be given different punishments.

28 Let us, therefore, go out and follow Christ, so that we may gain the reward which those who follow him will gain and so that we ward off the eternal punishment which those who do not want to follow Christ will incur. May Our Lord Jesus Christ through the intercession of Saint Paul grant us to follow him, even if from afar, so that we may reach him, who lives for ever and ever. Amen.

Eudes of Châteauroux

SERMO II

R2 = Rome, Archivio Generale dell'Ordine dei Predicatori, XIV.35, ff. 21va–22vb

Additional manuscripts
P4 = Paris, Bibliothèque Nationale de France, lat. 15947, ff. 175vb–177ra
V1= Vatican, Biblioteca Apostolica, Pal. lat. 452, ff. 143vb–144vb

Reference
Schneyer, iv, 443, no. 602

Sermo de invitatione ad crucem[1]

1 ii Macha. xv [16]: *Accipe sanctum gladium, munus a Deo, in quo deicies adversarios populi mei Israel.* Hoc continetur in sompnio quod narravit Iudas Machabeus ad consolandum et ad animandum filios Israel, quos Nichanor extinguere et destruere moliebatur. Unde ibidem [11] dicitur de Iuda: *Singulos autem illorum armavit non clipeo et hasta et munitione sed sermonibus optimis et exhortationibus[2] exposito digno fide sompnio per quos universos letificavit.* Erat autem huius visus, quod Onias summus sacerdos Iude apparebat et Ieremias propheta, et Ieremias dabat Iude *aureum gladium* [ii Mcc. xv, 15].

2 Et dicebat ei: *Accipe sanctum gladium* etc. Simile facit Dominus hiis temporibus. Sicut enim tunc Nichanor et nationes gentium volebant

---

[1] sermo de invitatione ad crucem R2] de invitatione ad crucem accipiendum P4, de sancta cruce V1
[2] exhortationibus P4] exortationibus R2, hortationibus V1

Eudes of Châteauroux

SERMON II

Sermon about the invitation to the cross

1 2 Maccabees 15: *Take the holy sword as a gift from God, with which you will defeat the opponents of Israel, my people.* This [passage] is part of the dream which Judas Maccabaeus recounted in order to comfort and encourage the sons of Israel, when Nicanor was getting ready to extinguish and destroy them. In the same passage we read about Judas: *He armed each of them not with shield and lance for defence but with excellent words and exhortations by telling them a trustworthy dream, which cheered everybody up.* In his vision Onias, the highest priest, appeared to Judas together with the prophet Jeremiah, and Jeremiah gave Judas *the golden sword.*

2 And he said to him: *Take the holy sword* etc. The Lord does it in a similar way in our times. Just as at that time Nicanor and the heathen

populum Domini destruere, sic hodie Tartari intendunt et laborant, ut Christianos destruant et eos subiciant importabili servituti. Sed Dominus, volens populum suum de manibus Tartarorum liberare, porrigit Iude *gladium aureum, ut in eo deiciat adversarios populi* sui.

3 Ieremias interpretatur 'sublimis'. Quis est iste Ieremias nisi ille, de quo dicit Propheta [Ps. cxii, 4]: *Excelsus super omnes gentes Dominus et super celos gloria eius?* Et alibi [Ps. xlvi, 3]: *Quoniam Dominus excelsus, terribilis rex magnus* [f. 21vb] *super omnem terram.* Et Ysa. iiii [2]: *Et erit fructus terre sublimis.* Et Ysa. ii [22]: *Quiescite,* id est cessate, *ab homine, cuius spiritus in naribus eius, quia excelsus reputatus est ipse.* Et in Propheta [Ps. viii, 8]: *Omnia subiecisti sub pedibus eius.* Iste excelsus, attendens quod Tartari moliuntur destruere populum suum, porrigit *gladium aureum* Iude, ut in eo deiciat *adversarios populi* sui, id est porrigit crucem militibus precipue et ceteris fidelibus ad deiciendum Tartaros.

4 Crux enim gladius est, quo Dominus potestates aereas debellavit et membra earum et adhuc debellare non cessat. Iudas interpretatur 'confitens vel glorificans'. Et qui hodie melius et expressius confitentur Christum esse suum dominum quam milites? Ipsi enim ad vocationem ipsius veniunt, faciunt ei exercitum, Ysa. xlvi[3] [11]: *Vocans ab oriente avem et de terra longinca virum voluntatis mee.* Ipsi enim velut aves nobiles ad vocationem Domini veniunt, faciunt ei exercituum et equitationem, et in hoc confitentur esse dominum suum.

5 E contrario Christum negant qui nolunt venire in exercitu suo vel equitatione ut burgenses, immo intendunt ad exheredandum[4] eos qui vadunt. Qui etiam ita glorificant Dominum et honorant sicut nobiles, qui se et sua exponunt, ut nomen Domini magnificetur et laudetur et eius dominium dilatetur, et propter hoc a Domino honorabuntur iuxta verbum Domini, i Regum ii [30]: *Quicumque* [f. 22ra] *honorificaverit me glorificabo eum, qui autem contemnunt me erunt ignobiles,* id est viles, Iudas ergo, cui Dominus porrigit gladium et de quo vult ut pro eo accipiant gladium milites sui.[5]

6 Legimus in principio libri Iudicum [i, 1–2]: *Post mortem Iosue consuluerunt filii Israel Dominum dicentes: Quis ascendet ante nos contra*

---

[3] xlvi] xliiii R2, P4, V1
[4] exheredandum P4] exeredandum R2, V1
[5] sui] sunt R2, P4, V1

peoples wanted to destroy the people of the Lord, so today the Mongols intend and strive hard to destroy the Christians and to subject them to intolerable servitude. But since the Lord wants to free his people from the hands of the Mongols, he holds out the *golden sword* to Judas, so that he may defeat the *opponents of* his *people*.

3 Jeremiah is called 'sublime'.[1] Who is this Jeremiah if not the one about whom the Prophet says: *The Lord is high above all peoples and his glory above the heavens?* And elsewhere: *For the Lord most high is sublime, a fearsome and great king over all the earth.* And Isaiah 4: *And the fruit of the land shall be held high.* And Isaiah 2: *Have no more to do with*, that is renounce, *man, who has only the breath in his nostrils, because [the Lord] is reckoned to be sublime.* And in the Prophet: *You put all things in subjection beneath his feet.* This sublime one, noticing that the Mongols are getting ready to destroy his people, holds out *the golden sword* to Judas, so that with it he may defeat *the opponents of* his *people*, meaning he holds out the cross to the knights especially, but also to all other faithful, so that they may defeat the Mongols.

4 The cross is the sword with which the Lord fought the heavenly powers and their followers and up to now he has not stopped fighting them. Judas is interpreted 'the trusting or glorifying'.[2] And today, who but the knights more aptly and more evidently trust that Christ is their lord? They follow his call and form his army, Isaiah 46: *Calling a bird from the east and from a distant land a man of my will.* They follow the Lord's call like noble birds and they form his army and cavalry; thus they trust that he is their lord.

5 Conversely, those, like the townspeople, who do not want to join his army or cavalry reject Christ and what is more they aim to deprive those who join up of their inheritance. The latter glorify the Lord and honour him like the nobles, who risk their lives and goods in order to further and praise the name of the Lord and extend his reign; because of this they will be honoured by the Lord according to the word of the Lord, 1 Kings 2: *He who honours me I shall glorify, but those who despise me shall be unknown to me*, that is villains; thus Judas [will be glorified], to whom the Lord gave the sword and for whom he wanted his knights to take up the sword.

6 We read at the beginning of the book of Judges: *After the death of Joshua the Israelites consulted the Lord, asking him: Who will lead us*

---

[1] Hieronymus, 'Liber Interpretationis Hebraicarum Nominum', *CCSL*, LXXII, 59–161, here p. 136.
[2] Hieronymus, 'Liber Interpretationis', 152.

*Chananeum et erit dux belli? Dixit Dominus: Iudas ascendet. Ecce
tradidit terram in manu eius.* Cananeus terram occupaverat in qua nichil
iuris habebat; sic Tartari terram Christianorum,[6] et eos exheredare
intendunt. Et Dominus vult ut nobiles sint duces exercitus sui et quod
ipsi liberent populum Christianum de manibus Tartarorum.

7 De Iuda legitur, Gen. xlix [8–9]: *Iuda, te laudabunt fratres tui, manus
tue in cervicibus inimicorum tuorum, adorabunt te,* id est honorabunt,
filii patris tui, omnes enim sumus de eodem patre, *catulus leonis Iudas,* id
est audax et fortis. Et post [ibid. 10]: *Non auferetur ceptrum de Iuda et
dux de femore eius,* quia dominium semper remanebit penes nobiles,
velint[7] nolint feneratores, qui eos devorarent. Et quare hoc subiungit
[ibid. 11]: *Lavabit in vino stolam suam et in sanguinem uve pallium
suum,* id est corpora sua suo sanguine precioso, quo tota curia super-
celestis quasi vino optimo inebriata est, id est letificata, sicut quondam[8]
sanguine martyrum beatorum,[9] Iudicum ix [13]: *Vinum letificat Deum et
ho-* [f. 22rb] *mines.*

8 Et de Iuda dicitur Deut. xxxiii [7]: *Audi, Domine, vocem Iude,* id est
petitionem nobilium, *et ad populum suum introduc eum; manus eius
pugnabit[10] pro eo,* id est pro Domino, *et adiutor illius erit,* id est Domini,
contra adversarios eius. i Machabeorum iii [4] dicitur de Iuda bellatore:
Similis factus est leoni in operibus suis. Huic Iude Dominus porrigit
gladium crucis et dicit: *Accipe sanctum gladium.*

9 Crux Christi gladius est, quo Christus dyabolum debellavit. De quo in
Ps. [xliv, 4]: *Accingere gladio tuo super femur tuum, potentissime,* id est o
Christe! Ysa. xxvii [1]: *In die illa visitabit Dominus in gladio duro,
grandi et forti,* id est cruce, *super Leviatam, serpentem veterem.* De hoc
gladio, Ysa. xxxi [8]: *Cadet Assur in gladio non viri, et gladius non
hominis vorabit illum – non hominis* suple puri; et subiungit: *Et fugient[11]
tunc a facie gladii.* Et adhuc fugit dyabolus *a facie* huius *gladii,* id est
crucis, iuxta illud: 'Ecce crucem Domini, fugite, partes adverse!' De hoc
gladio dicit Christus nostro Iude: *Accipe sanctum gladium.*

10 Gladius iste sanctus est, quia omnia que sanctificantur per crucem

⁶ Christianorum] occupare *add.* P4
⁷ velint P4, V1] vel non R2
⁸ quondam P4, V1] condam R2
⁹ beatorumP4, V1] bonorum R2
¹⁰ pugnabit P4, V1] pugnabat R2
¹¹ fugient P4, V1] fugiant R2

against the Canaanites and be our war leader? And the Lord said: Judas will lead you. And so he delivered the country into his hand. The Canaanites occupied the land, for which they held no lawful title, and so do the Mongols the land of the Christians, and they aim to disinherit them. God wants the nobles to be the leaders of his army and to liberate the Christian people from the hands of the Mongols.

7 One reads about Judas, Genesis 49: *Judas, your brothers shall praise you, your hands on the necks of your enemies; your father's sons,* since we all have the same father, *shall worship you,* meaning honour you, *Judas, you lion's whelp,* which means bold and strong. And later: *The sceptre shall not pass from Judah nor the leadership from his thigh,* because the authority will always stay with the nobles, whether or not the usurers who devour them want it. Because of this it continues: *He will wash his cloak in wine and his robe in the blood of the grape,* meaning [they will wash] their bodies with his precious blood, on which the whole heavenly court is drunk, meaning merry, as on the best wine, just as once on the blood of the holy martyrs, Judges 9: *Wine which gladdens God and men.*

8 And in Deuteronomy 33 it is said of Judas: *Hear, O Lord, the voice of Judas,* that is the petition of the nobles, *and bring him to his people; his hand will fight for him,* that is the Lord, *and he will be his helper,* that is the Lord's, *against his enemies.* In 1 Maccabees 3 it says of Judas the warrior: *He was like a lion in his exploits.* To this Judas the Lord gave the sword of the cross and said: *Take the holy sword.*

9 The cross of Christ is the sword with which Christ fought against the devil. About this Psalms: *Gird your sword on your thigh, O most mighty,* meaning O Christ! Isaiah 27: *On that day the Lord will punish Leviathan, the old serpent, with an unyielding sword, massive and strong,* meaning the cross. About this sword, Isaiah 31: *Assyria shall not fall by the sword of a man, and a sword of no man shall devour it* – to *of no man* add: who is pure; and it goes on: *And they will then flee before the sword.* So far the devil has been fleeing *before* this *sword,* that is the cross, according to this: 'Behold the cross of the Lord, flee, you hostile elements!'[3] About this sword, Christ says to our Judas: *Take the holy sword.*

10 This sword is holy, because everything that is blessed is blessed with

---

[3] Gregorius Magnus, 'Liber Responsalis', *PL*, LXXVIII, 725–850, here col. 803D.

sanctificantur, et accipientes se sanctificat et mundat. Filiis enim Israel nolentibus transire Iordanem et accipere hereditatem sibi promissam dictum est Iosue iii [5]: *Sanctificamini* hodie, *cras* enim transibitis. Sic oportet ut qui nolunt habere hereditatem eternam sibi promissam sanctificentur, et hoc fit per crucem.

11 Crux enim figurata est per [f. 22va] mare, in quo lavabantur ingressuri templum, et bene per mare figurabatur, quia multum habet amaritudinis. De hoc dicit: *Accipe sanctum gladium, munus a Deo*, quia hoc est magnum donum Dei, ut homo crucem pro Christo accipiat. Nec potest hoc esse nisi ex gratia Dei, Ad Phylip. i[12] [29]: *Vobis datum est, non solum ut in eum credatis sed etiam ut pro eo patiamini.* Quot et quanti hoc donum desideraverunt et tamen habere non potuerunt! Et nota quod gladius iste erat aureus, quia crux aliis penitentiis prevalet et minus gravat, sicut incisio vel ustio facta auro.

12 Sequitur: *In quo deicies adversarios populi mei Israel.* Speramus quod ita fiet ad litteram; nichilominus tamen hoc spiritualiter fit in accipientibus crucem, quia debent deicere peccata. Ad litteram semper hoc fieret nisi peccata hominum impedirent. Per peccata enim separatur Deus ab hominibus et recedit ab eis, Osee vii [13]: *Ve eis, cum recessero ab eis.* Exo. xxxiii [15]: *Ait Moyses: Si non tu ipse precedis, ut educas nos de loco isto*, quasi dicat: Sine te nichil poterimus facere. Numeris xiiii [42]: *Nolite ascendere, non est enim Deus vobiscum, ne corruatis coram inimicis vestris!* ii Machab. xii [40]: *Invenerunt sub tunicis interfectorum de donariis idolorum,*[13] omnibus ergo manifestum est factum ob hanc causam eos coruisse.

13 Abiciatis ergo, karissimi, peccata, vos qui crucem accipistis vel assumere intenditis! Et dabit vobis Dominus victoriam de [f. 22vb] inimicis populi Christiani et post victoriam coronam inmarcescibilem,[14] quam nobis et vobis concedere dignetur Ihesus Christus Dominus Noster, qui vivit in secula seculorum. Amen.

[12] i] ii R2, P4, V1
[13] donariis idolorum P4, V1] doncrariis interfectorum R2
[14] inmarcescibilem P4] inmarcessibilem R2, V1

the cross, and it blesses and purges those who take it. In Joshua 3 the following was said to the sons of Israel who did not want to cross the Jordan and take up the inheritance that was promised to them: *You are blessed* today, *tomorrow* you will go across. Thus it is appropriate that those who do not want to have the eternal inheritance that is promised to them should be blessed, and this is done with the cross.

11 The cross was symbolised by the waters in which those who entered the temple were washed; it was well symbolised by the waters, because it holds much bitterness. About this it says: *Take the holy sword, the gift of God*, because it is a great present of God that man may take the cross for Christ. This can only happen by the grace of God, Philippians 1: *It is given to you not only to believe in him but also to suffer for him*. How many have how often desired this gift and still could not have it! And note that this sword was golden, because the cross stands above other penances and weighs less, just as engraving and smelting done with gold.

12 It follows: *With which you will defeat the opponents of Israel, my people*. Let us hope that it will happen like this literally; still, this happens spiritually with those who take the cross, since they must throw off their sins. This always happens literally unless people's sins stand in the way. Through sins God is separated from people and withdraws from them, Hosea 7: *Woe unto them, for I will have withdrawn from them*. In Exodus 33 *Moses says: If you yourself do not lead us to guide us away from this place*, as if saying: Without you we can do nothing. Numbers 14: *Go no further, since God is not with you, lest you fail before your enemies!* 2 Maccabees 12: *Under the tunics of the dead they found offerings to idols*; so it was clear to everybody that they had failed because of this.

13 Therefore, my dearest people, throw off your sins, you who take the cross or intend to take it! The Lord will grant you victory over the enemies of the Christian people and, after the victory, the everlasting crown, with which Our Lord Jesus Christ honours us and you, he who lives for ever and ever. Amen.

Eudes of Châteauroux

SERMO III

R2 = Rome, Archivio Generale dell'Ordine dei Predicatori, XIV.35, ff. 22vb-23vb

Additional manuscripts
P4 = Paris, Bibliothèque Nationale de France, lat. 15947, ff. 177ra-178ra
V1 = Vatican, Biblioteca Apostolica, Pal. lat. 452, ff. 144vb-145vb

Reference
Schneyer, IV, 443, no. 603

Sermo de invitatione ad crucem[1]

1 Gen. xlix [21]: *Neptalim cervus emissus dans eloquia pulchritudinis.* Sic benedixit Iacob filio suo Neptalim; sic et hodie benedicit Dominus illos, qui pro amore eius velut cervi spirituales lustra dimittunt propria, id est terram, in qua nati fuerunt et nutriti. Cervi enim tempore amoris propria cubilia et silvas sibi domesticas dimittunt, flumina transeunt et ad loca ignota se transferunt. Sic hiis temporibus amore Dei ardentes patriam derelinquunt et non tantum flumina transire immo maria festinant et adire barbaras regiones.

2 Hiis ergo quasi spiritualibus filiis Dominus benedicit dicens: *Neptalim cervus emissus. Neptalim* interpretatur 'comparatio vel dilatatio'. Legimus in Gen. xxix [31–5; xxx, 6–8] quod Lya quatuor filios genuit, Ruben, Symeon, Levi et Iudam, et quod Rachel Dam, filium Bala ancille

---

[1] sermo de invitatione ad crucem R2] ad invitandum ad accipiendum crucem et ad confortandum crucesignatos P4, de cruce signatis V1

Eudes of Châteauroux

SERMON III

Sermon about the invitation to the cross

1 Genesis 49: *Naphtali is a deer let loose, who speaks beautifully.* With this Jacob blessed his son Naphtali; in the same way, the Lord today blesses those who, like spiritual deer, for his love leave behind their own haunts, that is the land where they were born and raised. In the time of love, deer leave behind their own resting places and their familiar woods, cross rivers and take themselves to unknown places. In the same way nowadays, those burning with the love of God leave behind their fatherland and hasten to cross not only rivers but even seas and travel to foreign lands.

2 The Lord blesses them like spiritual sons when he says: *Naphtali is a deer let loose. Naphtali* is interpreted 'comparison or enlargement'.[1] We read in Genesis 29 that Leah gave birth to four sons, Reuben, Simeon, Levi and Judah, and that Rachel considered Dan, the son of Bilhah her

---

[1] Cf. Hieronymus, 'Liber Interpretationis', 70.

sue, suum proprium filium reputavit, similiter et Neptalim eiusdem filium, de quo dixit Rachel [Gn. xxx, 8]: *Comparavit me Dominus cum sorore mea, et invalui. Comparavit* dixit, quia Oolyab fuit de tribu Dam, qui cum Beseleel, qui de tribu Iuda, tabernaculum fabricavit [cf. Ex. xxxv, xxxvi]. Yram vero, qui templum Salomonis fecit, fuit filius cuiusdam mulieris de tribu Neptalim, et in magisterio isto nullum socium legitur habuisse [cf. iii Rg. vii]. Et ita Rachel invaluit [f. 23ra] Lye sorori sue, id est eam superavit.

3 Sic potest dici de hiis, qui modo iter arripiunt transmarinum: *comparabit* eos Dominus et equabit illos antiquis nobilibus, qui de regno Francie exeuntes Antyochiam et terram Ierosolimitanam acquisierunt. Sic et ministerio istius militie, prout confidimus de Dei misericordia, Terra Sancta evacuabitur a perfidis Sarracenis. Speramus etiam quod hec militia invalescet terras alias liberando a iugo Sarracenorum et restituendo populo et cultui Christiano. Unde recte hec militia Neptalim nominatur, quia illi antique militie non tantum modo comparabitur et equabitur immo etiam invalescet Domino concedente.

4 *Neptalim* etiam interpretatur 'dilatatio vel dilatavit me'. Vere corda istorum dilatavit Dominus per amorem, ut possint dicere cum Propheta [Ps. cxviii, 32]: *Viam mandatorum tuorum cucurri, quia dilatasti cor meum.* Ibi Augustinus: '*Viam mandatorum* Domini minime cucurisset, nisi Dominus *cor* eius dilatasset.' Ideo currit hec militia, ut impleat mandatum Domini, quia corda habent dilatata per amorem. Quod previdens Ysa. [lx, 8] admirando querit: *Qui sunt isti, qui ut nubes volant?* Et de hiis predicit, xl [31]: *Assument pennas sicut aquile, current et non laborabunt, ambulabunt et non deficient.*

5 Amor enim dilatat cor ut possit capere illum, quem *celi celorum capere non possunt,* sicut dicit Salomon in dedicatione templi, iii Re. viii [27]: *Si enim celum et celi celorum te capere non possunt, quanto magis domus hec, quam ego edificavi* tibi. Sed caritas dilatat cor, [f. 23rb] ut possit tantum Dominum capere. Crucesignati nostri possunt dicere: *Cor nostrum dilatatum est,* sicut dicit Apostolus ii Ad Corinth. vi [11].

6 Sed multorum corda coangustata sunt, ut Deum capere non possint, sed potius dicere illud, Ysa. [xxviii, 20]: *Coangustatum est stratum.* Et hoc facit peccatum: habent enim cor impeditum peccatis adeo, ut Dominum capere non possint. Sed deberent facere sicut Neemias fecit [ii] Hesdra ultimo [xiii, 8], qui vasa Thobie eicit de vestibulo templi.

servant, to be her own son, just as Naphtali, also [Bilhah's] son, about whom Rachel said: *The Lord has compared me with my sister, and I prevailed*. *He compared*, she said because Aholiab, who belonged to the tribe of Dan, constructed the tabernacle with Bezalel, who belonged to the tribe of Judah. Indeed, Hiram, who built the temple of Solomon, was the son of a certain woman of the tribe of Naphtali and it is written that he had no associate for this task. And in this sense Rachel prevailed over her sister Leah, that is she surpassed her.

3 The same can be said about those who will soon travel across the sea: the Lord will *compare* them and will put them on a par with those ancient nobles who left the Kingdom of Francia and conquered Antioch and the land of Jerusalem. In the same way, so we trust in God's mercy, the Holy Land will be emptied of the treacherous Saracens by the efforts of this army. We also hope that this army will prevail by liberating other countries from the yoke of the Saracens and giving them back to the Christian people and religion. And so this army is called Naphtali, because not only will it be compared and put on a par with this ancient army, but it will also prevail if God grants it.

4 *Naphtali* is also interpreted 'enlargement or he enlarged me'.[2] Indeed, the Lord enlarged their hearts with his love, so that they can say with the Prophet: *I run the way of your commandments, because you enlarged my heart*. For this Augustine: 'He would not have run *the way of* the Lord's *commandments*, had not the Lord enlarged his *heart*.'[3] And so this army runs to fulfil the commandments of the Lord, because their hearts are enlarged with love. Forseeing this Isaiah asked with astonishment: *Who are these flying like clouds?* And he made a prediction about them, [chapter] 40: *They will grow wings like eagles, they will run and not be weary, they will march and not faint*.

5 Love enlarges the heart so that it can contain him whom *the heavens could not contain*, as Solomon says when dedicating the temple in 3 Kings 8: *If heaven and the heaven of heavens cannot contain you, how much less this house, that I have built* for you? But charity enlarges the heart, so that it can contain even the Lord. Our crusaders can say: *Our heart is enlarged*, as the Apostle says in 2 Corinthians 6.

6 But the hearts of many have shrunk, so that they cannot contain God and instead say this, Isaiah: *The bed has shrunk*. This is what sin does: they have a heart which is so blocked by sins, that they cannot contain the Lord. They ought to do like Nehemiah in the last chapter of Ezra, who threw Tobiah's stuff out of the entrance to the temple.

---

[2] Hieronymus, 'Liber Interpretationis', 70.
[3] (Augustinus), 'Dialogus Quaestionum lxv', *PL*, XL, 733–52, here col. 749.

7 Crucesignati vero nostri evacuaverunt corda sua per veram penitentiam et deposuerunt onera peccatorum, dissolverunt *colligationes impie-
tatis* [Is. lviii, 6], reddiderunt et restituerunt ea que male habuerant vel
rapuerant, ut relinquant post se benedictionem et non maledictionem.
Isti sunt veri Neptalim et possunt vere dicere: Dilatavit me Dominus.

8 Et sunt sicut *cervus emissus,* quia tempus amoris in cordibus eorum
fervet. Ideo sicut cervi lustra propria derelinqunt,[2] et possunt dicere [Ct.
ii, 12]: *Vox turturis audita est in terra nostra.* Gemitum enim modo
habent pro cantu, tamen iste gemitus procedit ex amore. Possunt dicere
illud, Abachuc ultimo [iii, 19]: *Posuit pedes meos tanquam cervorum, et
super excelsa statuens me,* quia nec silve nec montes nec lutosa nec
flumina possunt eos retinere, nec possunt aliquibus retenaculis retineri.

9 Et hoc facit amor Dei: omnia enim vincula rumpunt amor Dei et
timor[3] gehenne. Iudicum xvi [9] legitur: *Qui rupit vincula quomodo si
rumpat quis filum de stupa tortum cum sputamine,* [f. 23va] *cum odorem
ignis acceperit.* Ita *ignis* Spiritus Sancti omnia *vincula* rumpit in istis, unde
in fine Canticorum [viii, 6]: *Fortis est ut mors dilectio,* que omnes
iuncturas dissolvit et maxime iuncturam corporis et anime. Dura ut
infernus emulatio quia, sicut illi qui in inferno sunt non curant de caris
suis, sic hii emulatione Dei accensi de caris suis curare non videntur,
uxores et filios propter Dominum dimittentes.

10 Hii sunt ergo *cervi emissi* et possunt dicere cum Abachuc [iii, 19]:
*Deus Dominus fortitudo mea et ponet pedes meos tanquam cervorum et
super excelsa statuens me deducet me quasi victor in psalmis canentem.*
Isti sicut cervi desiderant ad fontem aquarum viventium, ad fontem vite.
Vere ergo de hiis dicitur: *Neptalim cervus emissus.*

11 Sequitur: *Dans eloquia pulchritudinis.* Hoc erit quando *cantabunt
Domino canticum novum, quia mirabilia fecit* [Ps. xcvii, 1], quando
confitebuntur Domino, quoniam bonus, et maxime quando in domo
Domini in secula seculorum laudabunt Dominum. Modo turpiter lo-
quntur quia sunt balbi, sed tunc balbus velociter loquetur, sicut dicit Ysa.
xxxv [6]: *Aperta erit linga mutorum*; tunc loquentur linga Chananea.

---

2 derelinqunt P4, V1] delinqunt R2
3 et timor P4, V1] om. R2 *lacuna*

7 Indeed, our crusaders emptied their hearts through true penance and laid down the weight of their sins, they dissolved *the bands of wickedness*, they gave back and made restitution of what they possessed wrongly or had stolen, so that they would leave behind them blessing rather than curse. These are true Naphtalis and they can truly say: God enlarged me.

8 They are like *deer let loose,* because the time of love burns in their hearts. Like deer they leave behind their own haunts, and they can say: *The voice of the turtle dove is heard in our land.* Their song will soon be a sigh, but this sigh comes of love. They can say this, in the last chapter of Habakkuk: *He will make my feet like deer's feet and will put me on high places,* because no woods nor mountains nor swamps nor rivers can hold them back, nor can they be held back by any reins.

9 This is what the love of God does: the love of God and the fear of hell break all fetters. In Judges 16 one reads: *He broke the fetters as a strung strand of tow snaps, when it takes on the smell of fire.* In the same way the *fire* of the Holy Ghost breaks all *fetters* in them, whence at the end of the Song of Songs [it says]: *Love is as strong as death,* which severs all connections and in particular the connection between the body and the soul. Zealousness is as arduous as hell because, just as those who are in hell do not care about their loved ones, so these who are inflamed by the zealousness of God do not seem to care about their loved ones, leaving their spouses and sons behind for the sake of the Lord.

10 In this sense they are *deer let loose* and can say with Habakkuk: *The Lord God is my strength and he will make my feet like deer's feet and will put me on high places and lead me like a winner singing psalms.* Like deer they wish to go to the spring of the living waters, the spring of life. It is therefore right to say of them: *Naphtali the deer let loose.*

11 It follows: *Who speaks beautifully.* This will happen when *they will sing a new song to the Lord, for he has performed wonders,* when they will trust in the Lord, because he is great, and in particular when they will praise the Lord in the house of the Lord for ever and ever. They still speak in an ugly way, because they are stammerers, but then the stammerer will speak fluently, as Isaiah 35 says: *The tongue of the dumb will be loosened;* then they will speak the language of the Canaanites.

Modo loquuntur[4] ut parvuli [cf. i Cor. xiii, 11], sed tunc erunt evacuata que sunt parvuli.

12 Sed vos alii, quid deberetis facere? Deberetis facere sicut faciunt iuniores cervi: quando vident maiores cervos iter arripere, vadunt post eos et eos [f. 23vb] sequntur. Sic deberetis et vos facere, et si non vultis eos sequi corpore, saltem corde et oratione et subsidio debetis eos sequi, et si non modo saltem in alio passagio. Vale vobis dicimus: Rogate Dominum, ut vos conducat et, si ei placuerit, reducat sanos et incolumes, et nos et vos perducat ad gaudia sempiterna.

[4] loquuntur V1] locuntur R2, P4

They still speak like children, but what belongs to the child will soon be lost.

12 But you other ones, what ought you to do? You ought to do just as young deer do: when they see the older deer leave on their journey, they walk after them and follow them. You, too, ought to do this, and if you do not want to follow them in person, you must at least follow them with your heart, your prayer and your financial help, if not soon in another passage. We say good-bye to you: Pray to the Lord to lead you and, if he pleases, bring you back healthy and without injury, and to guide us and you to everlasting joys.

Eudes of Châteauroux

SERMO IV

R2 = Rome, Archivio Generale dell'Ordine dei Predicatori, XIV.35, ff. 27rb-28rb

Additional manuscripts
P4 = Paris, Bibliothèque Nationale de France, lat. 15947, ff. 178ra-178vb
V1 = Vatican, Biblioteca Apostolica, Pal. lat. 452, ff. 145vb-146va

Reference
Schneyer IV, 443, no. 604

Sermo de invitatione ad crucem[1]

1 Ecclesiastico xxxviii [5]: *Nonne a ligno indulcorata est aqua?* In hiis verbis breviter vobis ostenditur, quare crucem assumere debeatis: assumptione enim crucis quasi *a ligno* crucis omnis cordis amaritudo dulcoratur.

2 Legitur iiii Re. iiii [38–40] quod *filii* [f. 27va] *prophetarum* congesserant *colloquintidas in ollam*,[2] ut inde sibi pulmentum facerent. Sed postea volentes hanc decoctionem[3] pregustare, senserunt amaritudinem nimiam et dixerunt: *Mors in olla.* Quid per filios prophetarum nisi corda hominum vel ipsi homines designantur, qui, dum sibi volunt querere unde gaudeant, potius inveniunt unde tristentur?

---

[1] sermo de invitatione ad crucem R2] sermo de cruce et de invitatione ad crucem P4, de crucem assumentibus V1
[2] congesserant colloquintidas in ollam V1] comesserant colinquitidas in ollera R2, coniecerant colinquitidas in ollam P4
[3] decoctionem P4, V1] detectionem R2

Eudes of Châteauroux

SERMON IV

Sermon about the invitation to [take] the cross

1 Ecclesiasticus 38: *Was not the water sweetened by the wood?* In these words you are succinctly shown why you should take the cross: by the taking of the cross all the bitterness of the heart is sweetened *by the wood* of the cross.

2 One reads in 4 Kings 4 that the *sons of the prophets* threw some *wild vine into a pot* in order to prepare some soup for themselves. But later, when they wanted to try this concoction, they tasted the excessive bitterness and said: *There is death in the pot.* What is [represented] by the sons of the prophets if not people's hearts? Or, do they not stand for people who, when they want to ask themselves what makes them happy, rather find out what makes them sad?

3 Et unde credunt repleri letitia et delectatione, replentur amaritudine et tristitia, teste Salomone qui dicit in Ecclesiaste [vii, 27]: *Inveni amariorem morte mulierem.* Inter cetera maiorem delectationem reperit vir in muliere quam in vino vel cibo seu divitiis vel honoribus. Si ergo *mulierem*, que dulcissima reputatur, invenit *amariorem morte*, qua nichil est amarius, quid ergo de aliis?

4 Ecclesiaste i [17–8]: *Dedique cor meum, ut scirem prudentiam, et agnovi quoque quod in hiis esset labor et afflictio spiritus, eo quod in multa sapientia multa sit indignatio, et qui addit scientiam addit et dolorem*, quia hoc solum scit homo: se nichil scire, ut dicit Philosophus.

5 Ecc[ste]. v [9]: *Avarus non implebitur pecunia, et qui amat divitias fructum non capiet ex eis.* Hoc solum invenit: quod labor est in acquirendo, timor in custodiendo, dolor in amittendo.

6 Idem in dignitatibus, in quibus amaritudo nimia, reperitur periculum et timor, Eze- [f. 27vb] chiele iii[4] [14]: *Spiritus quoque levavit me et assumpsit me, et abii amarus in indignatione spiritus mei.*

7 Et gaudium de liberis sive de multitudine liberorum frequenter in amaritudinem conmutatur, et accidit eis quod legitur Ruth i [20–1]: *Nolite me vocare Noemy, quod est pulchra, sed vocate me Marath, quod est amara, quia amaritudine replevit me Omnipotens; egressa enim sum plena, et vacuam me reduxit Omnipotens.* Sic multe liberos suos amittunt non sine magno dolore.

8 Multi etiam possunt dicere cum Iob vii [2–3]: *Sicut mercennarius prestolatur finem operis sui, sic et ego habui menses vacuos et noctes laboriosas enumeravi michi.* Recogitat homo quod multum laboravit et nichil utile sibi fecit immo potius dampnum, et si etiam bonum fecit, hoc ignorat, Ecc[ste]. ix [1]: *Nescit homo an ira an odio dignus sit.*

9 Item, quando credit quod status Christianitatis melioretur vel status universalis, videt quod deterioratur et omnia convertuntur in malum, etiam ea que creduntur fieri bona intentione.

10 Sed *a ligno dulcoratur* hec *aqua*, quia dulcedine inestimabili debet respergi cor humanum et gaudio, quando considerat quod Deus tantum eum dilexit crucem pro eo ascendendo. Quid est quod pro nobis non faceret, qui hoc pro nobis fecit?

11 Ad Ro. v [10]: *Si enim cum inimici essemus, reconciliati sumus Deo*

---

[4] iii] ii R2, P4, V1

3 And when they think that they are filled with happiness and joy they are [in fact] filled with bitterness and sadness, according to the testimony of Solomon who says in Ecclesiastes: *I found woman more bitter than death*. On the whole a man finds more pleasure in a woman than in wine or food and wealth or honour. So if he finds a *woman*, who is considered to be the sweetest thing, *more bitter than death*, which is more bitter than anything else, what about other [pleasures]?

4 Ecclesiastes 1: *And I gave my heart to understand wisdom; and I also realised that [these] bring with them much hardship and grief, because there is much anger in much wisdom, and who adds knowledge also adds pain*, because man knows only this: that he knows nothing, as the Philosopher says.

5 Ecclesiastes 5: *The greedy will never have enough money, and he who loves riches will never reap any fruit from them*. He only finds this: that there is hard work involved in acquiring it, anxiety in keeping it safe, and pain in losing it.

6 In the same way there is danger and anxiety in honour, in which all too much bitterness is found, Ezekiel 3: *The spirit lifted me up and took me, and I went away bitter and angry within me*.

7 The joy of children or of a great number of children is often turned into bitterness, and it happens to them what one reads in Ruth 1: *Do not call me Naomi, which means beautiful, but call me Mara, which means bitter, because the Almighty has filled me with bitterness; I went out full, and the Almighty has brought me home empty*. Thus many [women] lose their children not without much pain.

8 Many can say with Job 7: *As a mercenary looks forward to the end of his work, so I had empty months and counted wearisome nights*. Man ponders that he has worked much and has not produced anything useful for himself but [has rather caused] damage, and even if he has done good, he does not know it, Ecclesiastes 9: *Man does not know whether he deserves anger* or hatred.

9 In the same way, when he believes that the state of Christendom or the state of the whole world might improve, he sees that it gets worse and everything is turned into evil, even that which people think is done with good intention.

10 But this *water* is *sweetened by wood*, because the human heart must be immersed in such unimaginable sweetness and joy, when he considers that God loves him so much that he went to the cross for him. What would he not do for us, who did this for us?

11 Romans 5: *For when we were enemies, we were reconciled to God by*

per mortem Filii eius; multo magis recon- [f. 28ra] *ciliati salvi erimus in vita ipsius*, item quando consideramus quod maior pars emende iam facta est pro nobis.

12 Item, quanto gaudio resperguntur qui lignum crucis ponunt in corde suo, quasi in aquis Marath [cf Ex. xv, 23], crucem pro Domino assumendo, crucem post Dominum baiulando [cf. Lc. xiv, 27], eius consilio aquiescendo, qui dicit [Lc. ix, 23]: *Qui vult venire post me, abneget semetipsum et tollat crucem suam et sequatur me!*

13 Quando videt, quod pro tam minimo ei tot et tanta debita dimittuntur et in tam minimum laborem, scilicet in laborem huius peregrinationis, commutantur; quando videt quod quasi alter latro pendens in cruce absolvitur in momento [cf. Lc. xxiii, 43]; quando considerat quod Deus eum fecit suum signiferum; quando considerat quod super equm regium positus est velut alter⁵ Mardocheus [cf. Est. vi, 11].

14 Honoravit Dominus Petrum et Andream in hoc quod appensi fuerunt in cruce, unde uterque gaudens et exultans venit ad crucem. Letitia etiam debet ei inesse, quod pro modulo suo vicem rependit Domino, quod etiam caros suos qui sunt in purgatorio iuvare potest, si crucem et hanc peregrinationem assumpserit pro eis, et quod per crucem acquirit sibi vitam eternam. Ipsa est enim *lignum vite hiis, qui apprehenderunt eam* [Prv. iii, 18].

15 Currite ergo ut comprehendatis eam, ascendite *in palmam* cum sponsa et apprehendite *fructus eius* [Ct. vii, 8], remissionem peccatorum [f. 28rb] et vitam eternam, que nobis patrare dignetur Dominus Noster Ihesus Christus, qui vivit in secula seculorum!

⁵ alter] alter *add.* R2

the death of his son; how much more will we be saved by his life now that we are reconciled, also when we consider that the major part of the amends have already been made for us.

12 Similarly, in how much joy are they immersed who put the wood of the cross into their hearts, into the waters of Marah so to speak, when they take the cross for the Lord, carry the cross after the Lord, and heeding his advice who says: *He who wants to come after me, let him renounce himself, take up his cross and follow me!*

13 [And] when he realises that for so little so many great debts are taken off him and are exchanged for such a small effort, namely the effort of this pilgrimage; when he realises that he will be absolved from his sins instantly like the second thief on the cross; when he considers that God makes him his standard-bearer; when he considers that he is seated on the royal horse like another Mordecai.

14 The Lord honoured Peter and Andrew in that they were hung on the cross, which is why both went to the cross happy and jubilant. He must also feel joyous because he pays the Lord back in his own measure, because he can also help his loved ones who are in purgatory if he takes up the cross and this pilgrimage for them, and that through the cross he gains for himself eternal life. Indeed, the [cross] is the *wood of life for those who hold on to it*.

15 Therefore hurry to take it, climb the *palm tree* with the spouse and hold on to *its fruit*, the remission of sins and eternal life, which Our Lord Jesus Christ has deigned to make for us, who lives for ever and ever!

Eudes of Châteauroux

SERMO V

Pa = Pisa, Biblioteca Cateriniana del Seminario, 21, ff. 42ra (79ra)-43rb (80rb)

Additional manuscripts
R2 = Rome, Archivio Generale dell'Ordine dei Predicatori, XIV.35, ff. 26ra-27rb
P1 = Paris, Bibliothèque Mazarine, 1010, ff. 45va-46vb[1]

Reference
Schneyer, IV, 451, no. 700; IV, 468, no. 909

Sermo ad invitandum ad crucem

1 Apo. vii[2] [2–3]: *Vidi alterum angelum ascendentem ab ortu solis, habentem signum Dei vivi; et clamavit voce magna quatuor angelis, quibus datum est nocere terre et mari dicens: Nolite nocere terre neque mari neque arboribus, quoadusque signemus servos Dei nostri in frontibus eorum.* In hac visione nobis ostenditur, quante auctoritatis et [f. 42rb] virtutis sit crux, que propter Dominum assumitur, ibi: *Signum Dei vivi*; secundo, quis primo eam predicavit[3] aperte, ibi: *Et clamavit voce magna*; tertio, quod virtute crucis arcentur demones, ne noceant hiis qui confidunt in cruce, ibi: *Nolite nocere terre*; quarto, quod habentes hoc

---

[1] The sermon is mentioned in a marginal note in P4 (= Paris, Bibliothèque Nationale de France, lat. 15947, f. 178) with a reference to the second edition of Eudes's sermons: 'Item sermo ad invitandum ad crucem, Apoc. vi: *Vidi alterum angelum*, sermo xlii voluminis quod incipit: Sobrii estote et vigilate.'
[2] vii] vi Pa, R2, P1
[3] predicavit] predicaverit Pa, R2, P1

Eudes of Châteauroux

SERMON V

Sermon for the invitation to [take] the cross

1 Apocalypse 7: *I saw another angel rising from the sunrise, carrying the sign of the living God; and he called in a powerful voice to the four angels whose duty was to devastate land and sea: Do not devastate land and sea nor the trees, until we have signed the servants of our God on their foreheads.* In this vision, it is shown to us [firstly] how much authority and virtue the cross has which is taken for the sake of the Lord, here: *The sign of the living God;* secondly, who first preached it openly, here: *And he called in a powerful voice;* thirdly, that through the virtue of the cross demons are warded off, so that they cannot hurt those who have confidence in the cross, here: *Do not devastate the land;* fourthly, that

signum seu signati hoc signo sunt servi Dei et salvabuntur, ibi: *Quousque signemus* etc.

2 Dicit itaque: *Vidi alterum angelum ascendentem ab ortu solis.* Angelus nuntius. Beatus Iohannes evangelista, antequam diceret se vidisse hunc angelum, narrat se vidisse ante plures angelos, quia, antequam mitteretur Filius Dei, premissi fuerunt multi alii nuntii. Iste angelus, de quo hic loquitur, Filius Dei fuit, quem Deus pater misit in mundum ut quemdam nuntium ad annuntiandum *pacem*, ad annuntiandum *bonum* [Is lii, 7]. Unde Ysa. ix [6] vocat eum magni consilii angelum, et ipse dicit, Ysa. lxi [1]: *Spiritus Domini super me, eo quod unxerit me ad annuntiandum mansuetis; misit me, ut mederer contritis corde et predicarem captivis indulgentiam et clausis apertionem.*

3 Hunc angelum vidit beatus Iohannes *ascendentem ab ortu solis.* Ortus solis locus est in quo oritur sol; hec est Beata Virgo, ex qua et in qua ortus est *sol* veritatis et *iustitie* [Mal. iv, 2]. *Ab* isto *ortu solis* ascendit quia, ut dicitur in Lu. ii [52], *et Ihesus proficiebat sapientia et etate et gratia apud Deum et homines.* Et sicut sol ab oriente ascendit, ut videatur ab hominibus, ut mundum illuminet, calefaciat et fructus crescere faciat, sic Christus natus est de Vir- [f. 42va] gine gloriosa, ut hominibus appareret visibilis, ut eos amore sui inflammaret, ut nos fructibus bonis faceret habundare.

4 *Habentem signum Dei vivi,* id est 'crucem qua suos signaret, vel potentiam Patri equalem – ut *sicut Pater habet vitam in semet ipso, sic et dedit Filio vitam habere in semet ipso* [Io. v, 26] – vel immunitatem a peccato, per quam Deus appareret,[4] quia omnis homo peccator.' Onmis enim rationalis creatura quantum est ex se peccare potuit, ipse solus peccare non potuit, quia enim ea fecit que solus Deus facere potest. Ea fuerunt signa, quod esset equalis Deo patri et Deus vivus: et per hoc quod peccare non potuit, et per hoc quod in cruce, in qua moriebantur homines et que erat instrumentum mortis, in quantum Deus sive quoad deitatem mori non potuit, sed potius ibi mortem superavit, secundum quod predixerat per prophetam Osee xiii[5] [14]: *Ero mors tua, o mors!*

5 Et primo crucem ascendit, ut se hominem et etiam alios vivificaret,

---

[4] appareret P1] apponeret Pa, R2   [5] xiii] xii Pa, P1, R2

those who have this sign or are signed with this sign are God's servants and will be saved, here: *Until we have signed* etc.

2 So it says: *I saw another angel rising from the sunrise.* Angel [means] messenger. Prior to saying that he saw this angel, Saint John the Evangelist recounts that he had previously seen several angels, because, before the Son of God was sent, many other messengers were dispatched. The angel of whom this is said was the Son of God, whom God the Father sent into the world as a messenger to announce *peace* [and] to announce *good*. This is why Isaiah 9 calls him the angel of great counsel, and he himself says, Isaiah 61: *The spirit of the Lord is on me, because he has anointed me to bring the news to the meek; he has sent me to heal those contrite of heart and to preach indulgence to the captives and liberty to the imprisoned.*

3 This is the angel that Saint John saw *rising from the sunrise.* The place of the sunrise is where the sun is born; it is the Holy Virgin, from whom and in whom the *sun of* truth and *justice* was born. He rose *from* this *sunrise,* because, as it is said in Luke 2, *Jesus also increased in wisdom, age and in favour with God and with people.* And as the sun rises in the East, so that people can see it, so that it illuminates and warms the world and makes fruits grow, so Christ was born of the glorious Virgin to be visible to people, inflame them with his love and ensure that we have good fruits in abundance.

4 *Carrying the sign of the living God,* which means 'the cross with which he will sign his people, or the power equal to that of the Father – so that, *as the Father has life in himself, so he has granted the Son also to have life in himself* – or the immunity from sin, through which he is God, because every human is a sinner'.[1] Every rational creature can sin in as much as it exists in itself, but he alone could not sin, because he did what only God can do. These were the signs that he was equal to God the Father and the living God: that he could not sin, and that in as much as he was God or on account of his divinity he could not die on the cross, on which humans used to die and which was an instrument of death, but that he rather overcame death on it, according to that which he had predicted through the prophet Hosea 13: *O death, I shall be your death!*

5 And he first of all went to the cross to make himself, the man, as well

---

[1] *Biblia Latina cum Glossa Ordinaria*, ed. A. Rusch 4 vols. [reprint] (Turnhout, 1992), IV, 558, col. b.

unde Ad Phillippen. ii [9]: *Propter quod et Deus* etc. Et tunc verificatum fuit quod antea predixerat Io. xii [32]: Cum autem *exaltatus fuero a terra, omnia traham ad me ipsum* a puteo mortis. Et in hoc magnam auctoritatem et dignitatem cruci contulit, ut que fuerat lignum et arbor mortis fieret lignum et arbor vite, ut sicut antea qui gustabant de fructu eius moriebantur, sic qui de cetero gustarent de fructu eius vivificarentur.

6 Hec enim tria, scilicet quia faciebat talia que non nisi Deus facere potest, [f. 42vb] in quo erat equalis Patri, et quia peccare non potuit, et quia per mortem suam vivificavit nos, signabant et demonstrabant eum esse Deum vivum. Hec tria sunt: equalitas, qua est equalis[6] Patri, et immunitas a peccato et crux, sicut dicit ibi Glosa.

7 Sequitur: *Et clamavit voce magna.* In hoc ostenditur, quod ipse aperte primo crucem predicavit. Licet enim ante ipsum alii crucem penitentie predicaverint, tamen ipse solus crucem primo predicavit, Lu. [ix: 23]: *Si quis vult venire post me, abneget semetipsum et tollat crucem suam et sequatur me.* Assumentes enim crucem se abnegant, id est abiurant, se mortis periculo exponendo, suos eos derelinquendo, sua ea consumendo, tollentes crucem suam, ut postmodum a cruce portentur in celum quasi quodam vehiculo,[7] ut quondam imperatores, quando fiebat eis triumphus revertentibus a victoria, in vehiculo deportabantur. Sic et Ioseph *super currum* delatus fuit [Gn. xli, 43] et Helyas in celum levatus [cf. iv Rg. ii, 1]. Hanc crucem Dominus Ihesus aperte predicavit.

8 Sed quia posset quis dicere: Ad quid valet hec crucis assumptio?, et respondet: Ad hoc ut *quatuor angeli, quibus datum est nocere terre et mari,* eis non noceant. Isti *quatuor angeli* sunt demones, *quibus datum est nocere* habitantibus in quatuor partibus mundi. Et ideo dicuntur quatuor, licet multa milia sint; vel etiam quatuor dicuntur, quia quatuor modis nocent amorem Dei et proximi in cordibus hominum extinguendo.

9 Et ideo aspis vocatur, cuius [f. 43ra] venenum calorem vitalem et naturalem extinguit; vocatus est basiliscus, quia mala cupiditate incendit, unde [Ps. lxxix, 17]: *Incensa igni et suffossa;* leo vocatur, cum per

---

⁶ equalis] equali R2, P1, *post corr.* Pa
⁷ vehiculo *post corr.* P1] vinculo Pa, viculo R2

as other people alive again, whence Philippians 2: *For this God* etc. And then it became true what John 12 had predicted before: When *I am lifted up from the earth, I shall draw everything to me* from the abyss of death. And in this he assigned great authority and dignity to the cross, so that what used to be the wood and tree of death would become the wood and tree of life, so that as those who tasted its fruit before died and those who since then have tasted its fruit have been made alive.

6 These three signal and demonstrate that he is the living God, namely that he did things that only God can do, in which he was equal to the Father, and that he could not sin, and that he made us alive through his death. These three are: equality, through which he is equal to the Father, immunity from sin and the cross, as it says in the Gloss.[2]

7 It follows: *And he called in a powerful voice*. In this it is shown that he was the first to preach the cross openly. Even though other people preached the cross of penitence before him, he alone first preached the cross, Luke: *If anyone wants to come after me, let him renounce himself and take up his cross and follow me*. Those who take the cross renounce, that is abjure, themselves by exposing themselves to mortal danger, leaving behind their loved ones, using up their belongings, carrying their cross, so that afterwards they may be carried to heaven by the cross as in some vehicle, just as once the emperors were carried in a vehicle, when a triumph took place for them after returning from a victory. In the same way, Joseph was carried away *in a chariot* and Elijah taken up to heaven. This is the cross that the Lord Jesus preached openly.

8 But since someone might say: What is taking the cross good for?, he answers: so that *the four angels whose duty was to devastate land and sea* do not devastate them. Those *four angels* are the demons *whose duty it is to devastate* the people who live in the four parts of the world. And therefore, they are called four, even though they are many thousands; and they are also called four because they devastate in four different ways by extinguishing the love of God and one's neighbour in people's hearts.

9 And therefore, it is called a snake, whose poison extinguishes the natural warmth of life; it is called a basilisk, because it ignites evil desire, whence: *It is burned with fire and cut down*; it is called a lion, because it

---

[2] See previous note.

violentiam efficientem, licet non sufficientem, ad malum inducit; draco, cum per insidias et occulte hominem ad malum inducit. Unde in Ps. [xc, 13] hiis quatuor nominibus nominatur, cum dicitur Christo: *Super aspidem et basiliscum ambulabis et conculcabis leonem et draconem*; intuit:[8] et maxime in hiis, qui crucem assumunt pro te.

10 Virtute enim crucis arcentur demones, ne noceant quantum vellent et possent; per terram: homines fixi et firmi in fide 'fructus bonorum operum proferentes'; per mare: homines instabiles, qui vento temptationum ducuntur, sese collidunt[9] pleni amaritudinibus peccatorum; per arbores: qui in parte fixi sunt, in fide scilicet, in parte mobiles sunt modo ad bonum modo ad malum. Ne his noceant, arcentur virtute crucis demones ut sanguis in postibus [cf. Ex. xii, 23] et fumus *iecoris super carbones* [Tb. viii, 2].

11 Sequitur: *Quoadusque signemus servos Dei in frontibus eorum.* Ad hoc enim nos huc venimus missi a summo pontifice, ut per assumptionem crucis signentur et distinguantur servi Dei a servis diaboli et ut stipendia recipiant Domini et ut a gladio pene eterne non occidantur, Eze. ix [6]: *Omnem autem super quem videritis thau ne occidatis!* Et Apo. ix [2–5] legitur, quod *ascendit fumus putei sicut fumus fornacis magne, et obscuratus* [f. 43rb] *est sol et aer de fumo putei, et de fumo putei exierunt locuste in terram, et data est illis potestas sicut habent potestatem scorpiones in terra, et preceptum est illis ne lederent fenum terre neque omne viride neque omnem arborem, nisi tantum homines qui non habent signum Dei in frontibus suis.*

12 Homines consueverunt accipere ordinem[10] Templariorum propter libertatem, inmunitatem et tuitionem. Sed signum crucis, si assumatur propter Deum et homo faciat quod crux exigit, fit servus Dei, stipendiarius ipsius, et liber et immunis ab omni peccato, et ab omni malo custoditur.

13 Sed nota quod Christus ascendit in crucem et aliena vestimenta non rapuit, sed propria dereliquit [cf. Lc. xxiii, 34]. Non recte ergo crucem accipiunt[11] qui aliena rapiunt et ea que debent non solvunt; et melius est

---

[8] intuit Pa] in tuis R2, P1
[9] collidunt Pa] colludunt R2, P1
[10] ordinem Pa] signum R2, P1
[11] accipiunt Pa] assumunt R2, P1

induces [people to do] evil by potent, though not adequate, violence; and a dragon, because it induces people to [do] evil deceitfully and secretly. This is why it is given those four names in Psalms, when Christ is told: *You will walk upon the snake and the basilisk and you will trample the lion and the dragon*; he does it especially with regard to those who take the cross for your sake.

10 The demons are warded off by the virtue of the cross, so that they may not devastate as much as they would and could; the earth [meaning] people who are strong and firm in their faith 'offering the fruits of their good works;'[3] the sea [meaning] unsteady people, who are driven by the wind of temptations, colliding with each other full of the bitterness of their sins; the trees [meaning] those who on the one hand are firm, namely in the faith, and on the other hand sometimes veer towards good, sometimes towards evil. The demons are warded off by the virtue of the cross, so that they may not devastate such people, just as the blood on the doorposts and the smoke of *the liver over the coals*.

11 It follows: *Until we will sign the servants of our God on their foreheads*. This is why we have come here, sent by the pope, so that the servants of God may be signed by the taking of the cross and distinguished from the servants of the devil and that they may receive God's payment and may not be killed by the sword of eternal pain, Ezekiel 9: *Do not kill anyone on whom you see the thau!* And one reads in Revelation 9 that *smoke arose from the abyss like the smoke from a huge furnace, and the sun and the air were darkened by the smoke of the abyss, and out of the smoke of the abyss locusts dropped onto the earth, and they were given the power that scorpions have on the earth, and they were told not to harm the grass of the earth nor anything green nor any tree, but only those people who do not have the sign of God on their foreheads.*

12 People used to join the order of the Templars because of its freedom, immunity and security. But, if the sign of the cross is taken for the sake of God and if a man does what the cross demands, it makes him God's servant, his mercenary, free and immune from all sin, and he is protected from all evil.

13 But note that Christ went to the cross and did not steal somebody else's clothes, but he left his own. This is why those who have stolen other people's things and do not pay what they owe do not take the cross

---

[3] Ambrosius Mediolanensis, 'De Ioseph', 75.

homini ut 'nudus Christum nudum sequatur' quam cum multa familia sequatur diabolum et cum cruce sua demergatur in infernum. Non enim vult Dominus ut de rapina vel furto vel de re aliena ei serviatur.

14 Karissimi, si vultis salubriter crucem assumere, peniteamini[12] de peccatis vestris et derelinquatis ea, debita vestra solvatis, et si aliquid iniuriose possidetis, reddatis et restituatis, ut possitis audire: A Domino *hodie facta est salus tibi et domui tue* [Lc. xix, 9], et ut ad salutem perpetuam venire[13] valeatis, ipso prestante, qui vivit in secula seculorum. Amen.

[12] peniteamini Pa, P1] peniteatis R2
[13] venire Pa] pervenire R2, P1

in the right manner; it is better for a man 'to follow the naked Christ naked'[4] than to follow the devil with a great following and sink with his cross into hell. The Lord does not want people serving him with absconded or stolen goods or other people's belongings.

14 My dearest people, if you want to take the cross in the proper way, repent your sins and leave them behind, pay your debts, and if you possess anything unlawfully, return it and make restitution, so that you can hear: *Today salvation has come to you and your house* from the Lord, and so that you may come to eternal salvation, with him granting it, who lives for ever and ever. Amen.

---

[4] Hieronymus, 'Epistula 125 ad Rusticum', in: 'Epistulae III', *CSEL*, LVI, 142

Gilbert of Tournai

SERMO I

P5 = Paris, Bibliothèque Nationale de France, lat. 15953, ff. 375r-376r

Additional manuscripts
C = Cambridge, University Library, Peterhouse 200, ff. 68ra-69va
M = Marseille, Bibliothèque Municipale, 392, ff. 98ra-100ra
P3 = Paris, Bibliothèque Nationale de France, lat. 15943, ff. 113ra-115rb

Reference
Schneyer, II, 303, no. 245

Ad crucesignatos et crucesignandos sermo primus

1 *Vidi alterum angelum ascendentem ab ortu solis, habentem signum Dei vivi* etc. Apoc. vii [2]. Verbum hoc competit cuilibet sancto et crucis negotio.

2 Notificatur ergo sanctus iste ex officio quod gessit, cum dicitur: *Angelum alterum*; ex virtutum exercitio in quo profecit, cum dicitur: *Ascendentem ab ortu solis*; ex signo deifico quod in se representavit, cum dicitur: *Habentem signum* etc.

3 Bene ergo notificatur ex officio, cum dicitur: *Vidi alterum angelum.* 'Angelus' enim est nomen officii, quod Latine dicitur 'nuntius'. Homo enim, qui vivit spiritualiter in opere et Christum credit fideliter in corde et ferventer annunciat ore, angelorum habet officium, Ps. [ciii, 4]: *Qui facit angelos suos spiritus et ministros suos ignem urentem*; vel *flammam*

Gilbert of Tournai

SERMON I

The first sermon to those who are or will become crusaders

1 *I saw another angel rising from the sunrise, carrying the sign of the living God* etc., Apocalypse 7. This passage is suitable for any saint and the business of the cross.

2 This saint is described by the office that he holds, since it says: *Another angel,* by the practice of virtues by which he advances, since it says: *Rising from the sunrise*; by the sacred sign which he represents in himself, since it says: *Carrying the sign* etc.

3 He is aptly described by his office, since it says: *I saw another angel.* 'Angelus' [i.e. angel] is the name for the office which in Latin is called 'nuntius' [i.e. messenger]. The man who lives spiritually in his works, faithfully in his heart believes in Christ and fervently announces him with his mouth holds the office of the angels, Psalm: *Who makes his*

ignis, ut dicitur He[b]. i [7]. Primus ergo angelus Christus, qui dicitur Ysa. ix [6] *magni consilii angelus*, quod sumptum est de translatione Septuaginta. Alter autem angelus iste sanctus missus ut nuntius ad preparandam viam salutis, Mal. iii [1]: *Ecce ego mittam angelum meum, qui preparabit viam ante faciem meam.*

4 Notificatur etiam ex virtutum exercitio, cum dicitur *ascendentem ab ortu solis*. Iste enim angelus est virtutum profectus, ut proficiamus in merito ascendentes de virtute in virtutem, 'donec videatur *Deus deorum in Syon*', ut dicitur in Ps. Et ad eius nuptias veniamus, qui nos[1] invitat dicens: *Amice, ascende superius*, Luc. xiiii [10]. Et bene *ab ortu solis*; ut sicut ab oriente sol ascendens crescit in lumine successive usque ad perfectum diem, ita circuit iste per virtutum merita usque ad perfectionem, Ysa. xli [2]: *Suscitavit ab oriente iustum, vocavit eum ut sequeretur se.*

5 Notificatur etiam ex signo deifico, cum dicitur: *Habentem signum Dei vivi*. Hoc signum est representatio passionis in corpore proprio, per quod vivimus in presenti vita gratie, in futuro vita glorie. In cuius figura Numeri xxi [8]: *Pone serpentem pro signo; qui percussus aspexerit vivet.* Qui enim Christum crucifixum in cruce pendentem, designatum per *serpentem eneum* [Nm. ix, 9] in palo fixum, corde contrito consideraverit et passionem ipsius et crucem in seipso expresserit, vivet et non peribit, Deut. xxviii [66]: *Erit vita tua quasi pendens ante te.*

6 Spiritualiter simus angeli puritate conversationis, ascendentes emulatione perfectionis, signati caractere et signo dominice passionis. Hoc enim signum habuit Christus ut signet milites suos, qui prior signari voluit, ut alios precederet[2] cum vexillo crucis. Io. vi [27]: *Hunc Pater signavit Deus*, cuius carni crux affixa fuit, que modo molli filo affigitur vestris vestibus.[3] Et sicut sagittatores et balistarii contendunt ut signum figerant, ita Iudei unanimiter ut crucifigerent Christum, Trenis iii [12–15]: *Posuit me quasi signum ad sagittam, misit in renibus meis filias*

---

[1] nos C] nobis P5, M, P3   [2] precederet M, C, *post corr.* P3] precedent P5
[3] vestibus C, M, P3] vestibulis P5

angels spirits and his servants burning fire; or *a flame of fire*, as it says in Hebrews 1. The first angel is Christ, who in Isaiah 9 is called *the angel of great counsel*, which is taken from the Septuaginta translation.[1] The second angel is this saint who was sent as a messenger to prepare the way of salvation, Malachi 3: *Look, I shall send my angel, who will prepare the way before me.*

4 He is also described by the practice of virtues since it says: *Rising from the sunrise.* This angel is accomplished in virtues, so that, rising in merit, we may advance from virtue to virtue, 'until *the God of gods* may be seen in Zion',[2] as is said in Psalms.[3] We may come to his wedding, he who invites us by saying: *My friend, move up higher*, Luke 14. It is well [said]: *From the sunrise*; just as the sun, rising in the east, grows slowly brighter until the middle of the day, so he passed to perfection by the merits of virtues, Isaiah 41: *He raised up the just person from the east [and] called him to follow him.*

5 He is also described by the sacred sign, when it says: *Carrying the sign of the living God.* This sign is the representation in his own body of the passion, through which we live in this present life of grace [and] in the future life of glory. For its prefiguration see Numbers 21: *Put a serpent as your sign; anyone who is struck and sees it will live.* For anyone who looks with a contrite heart at Christ crucified hanging on the cross, who is designated by the *serpent of bronze* attached to the pole, and expresses his passion and the cross in himself will live and not die, Deuteronomy 28: *Your life will, as it were, hang before you.*

6 Spiritually we are angels in terms of the purity of conduct, rising through the zeal of perfection, signed with the symbol and the sign of the Lord's passion. This is the sign which Christ had to sign his soldiers; he wanted to be signed first, so that he could precede all others with the banner of the cross. John 6: *God Father has signed him*, to whose flesh the cross was attached, which is now attached to your clothes with soft thread. And just as archers and balisters compete with each other to hit a sign, so the Jews [competed with each other] unanimously to crucify Christ, Lamentations 3: *He set me as a sign for the arrow, he sent the*

---

[1] *Septuaginta*, ed. A. Rahlfs, 2 vols. (Stuttgart, 1935), II, 578.
[2] Cf. Thomas de Chobham, 'Sermones', *CCCM*, LXXXII A, 244.
[3] This reference is unclear.

pharetre sue; factus sum in derisum omni populo, canticum eorum tota die
replevit me amaritudinibus.

7 Crux enim bene *signum* dicitur, quia se offert sensui et aliud representat intellectui. Est enim signum directivum, discretivum, rememorativum, remunerativum. Sic enim adhibentur signa quandoque in preliis,
quandoque in biviis, quandoque in amicitiis, quandoque in premiis.

8 Signum directivum ponitur in biviis sicut cruces, ut viam rectam
ostendant, et si erratum est ad crucem rectam viam resumant. Ysa. xi
[10]: *Radix Iesse, qui stat in signum populorum; ipsum gentes depreca-*
buntur, et erit sepulchrum eius gloriosum. Radix Iesse Christus, qui de
Iesse sumpsit originem secundum carnem et ex incendio amoris se in
holocaustum exhibuit. Unde et Iesse interpretatur incendium vel 'insule
holocaustum'. Ipse *stat in signum populorum*, id est in cruce, quod est
signum populi ad ostendendum viam rectam paradisi. Si enim rectum est
secundum Philosophum inter terminos spatium brevissimum, certum est
quod via assumendi crucem est via rectior ad salutem, quia quanto via
brevior tanto rectior. Crux autem citissime facit crucesignatos devotos,
immo martires veros, pro causa Christi de terra ad celum evolare, unde
Luc. [ix, 23]: *Qui vult venire post me, abneget semetipsum et tollat*
crucem suam et sequatur me.

9 Et sequitur: *Et erit sepulcrum eius gloriosum.* Glorificatur enim Christi
sepulcrum, quando ex amore et devotione crucem assumunt, ut videant
illud et honorent ipsum. Et vere magna gloria est sequi Dominum, *indui*
vestibus regiis [Est. vi, 8] et habere aliquid signum vel panniculum de
armis suis, quod vulgariter dicimus 'pannuncel'.

10 Est etiam signum discretivum, quo signantur milites in preliis,
Numeri ii⁴ [2]: *Singuli per turmas et signa atque* [f. 375v] *vexilla*
castrametati sunt. Hoc enim signo discernit Dominus suos [Ez. ix, 4, 6]:
Signa thau super frontes virorum gementium, parvulum⁵ et mulieres
interficite; omnem autem super quem videritis signum thau ne occidatis!
Soli enim *gementes et dolentes super abhominationibus, que fiunt in*
Ierusalem signo crucis muniti, quod signum pretendit, ista littera thau a

---

⁴ ii] iii P5, C, M, P3   ⁵ parvulum C] parvulorum P5, M, P3

shafts from his quiver into my loins; I became a joke to all people, their song filled me with bitterness all day long.

7 The cross is aptly called a *sign*, because it offers itself to the senses and represents something else to the mind. For it is a sign of direction, distinction, recollection [and] reward. So signs are sometimes used in battles, at crossroads, for friendship [and] as prizes.

8 A sign of direction is put at a crossroads, like crosses, to show the right way, and if one has taken a wrong turn, one can resume the right way at the cross. Isaiah 11: *The root of Jesse, standing as a sign for the peoples; the nations will beseech him, and his sepulchre will be glorious. The root of Jesse* [is] Christ, who descended from Jesse in the flesh and offered himself to a burnt-offering out of burning love. Hence, Jesse is also interpreted as fire or the 'island of the burnt-offering'.[4] He *stands as a sign for the peoples*, meaning on the cross, which is *the sign for the people* to show the right way to paradise. If it is right according to the Philosopher that between two lines [there is] a shortest distance, then it is certain that the way of taking the cross is the better way to salvation, because the shorter a way the better it is. The cross most quickly makes devout crusaders, real martyrs indeed, fly from earth up to heaven for the cause of Christ, whence Luke 9: *Who wants to come after me, let him renounce himself and carry his cross and follow me.*

9 And it follows: *And his sepulchre will be glorious.* The sepulchre of Christ is praised when people take the cross out of love and devotion, so that they may see it and honour him. It is indeed a great mark of esteem to follow the Lord, *to put on royal robes* and to have some sign or a piece of cloth of his arms, which we call 'pannuncel' in the vernacular.

10 It is also a sign of distinction, with which soldiers are signed in battle, Numbers 2: *All of them camped by unit, signs and standards.* By this sign the Lord knows his people: *Sign a thau on the foreheads of all men who grieve; slay children and women; but do not kill those on whom you see the sign of the thau!* Only those *grieving and lamenting over the abominations which took place in Jerusalem* who carry the sign of the cross are liberated from the demons by this letter thau, as the sign

---

[4] Hieronymus, 'Liber Interpretationis', 111.

demonibus liberantur. Pectus enim ferreum habet et non est dignus misericordia qui non dolet de obproprio patris sui et de hereditate sua perdita, Tren. v[6] [2]: *Hereditas nostra versa est ad alienos et domus nostra ad extraneos.*

11 Sed contigit aliquando milites formidolosos fugere, qui tamen, quando vident vexillum domini sui elevatum, revocantur ad pugnam et vincunt per Dei adiutorium et signum ostensum, Ysa. xi [12]: *Levabit Dominus signum in nationes et congregabit profugos Israel et dispersos Iuda colliget.* Crux enim signum revocatorium est eorum scilicet, qui diu erraverunt per devia peccatorum, Ysa. xlix [22]: *Ecce, levabo ad gentes manum meam et exaltabo ad populos signum meum; manum meam,* que est destructiva scelerum, reformativa operum, ostensiva vulnerum, collativa munerum; *et exaltabo* inquit *signum meum,* quia sicut habita victoria ponitur super muros regium signum, ita crucesignati congrediuntur contra dyabolum et vincunt per signum.

12 ii Mac. viii[7] [23–24]: *Dato signo adiutorii Dei commiserunt Iudei cum Nichanore et maiorem partem exercitus eius vulneribus debilem factam fugere compulerunt.* Nota ergo quod Iudeis in arcto constitutis apparuit signum de celo, quo viso sese recollegerunt et hostes vicerunt, sicut faciunt milites, quando vident signum regis: animantur et rege statuto in prelio et iusto existente bello fugere verentur. Bellum nunc iustum est, quia contra inimicos fidei, usurpatores nostri patrimonii, pro causa Dei, et fidei et nostre salutis res est. Stat rex noster in prelio vulneratus, ut viriliter dimicet Christianus et, si usque ad sanguinem sustineat, in vulnera sui regis aspicat et confidat.

13 Unde et tempore Constantini, cum deberet ingredi contra hostes suos iuxta Danubium, dicitur apparuisse signum crucis in celo et vox audita est: 'Constantine, in hoc vince!', quod et rei probavit eventus. Exo. xii [13]: *Erit sanguis vobis in signum, et videbunt sanguinem; nec erit in vobis plaga disperdens, quando percussio terram Egypti.* ii Mac. xv[8] [35]: *Suspenderunt caput Nichanoris in summa arce, ut esset evidens et manifestum signum auxilii Dei.* Hoc autem est signum regis Ierusalem, ad litteram scilicet crux rubea in albo panno, Christi scilicet passio in corde mundo, non draco cupiditatis vel aquila ambitionis, que sunt signa

---

[6] v] iiii P5, C, M, P3   [7] viii C, M] vii P5, P3   [8] xv] xvii P5, C, M, P3

suggests. He who does not lament over his father's disgrace and his lost inheritance has a chest of iron and is not worthy of pity, Lamentations 5: *Our inheritance has been turned over to strangers and our home to outsiders.*

11 It sometimes happens that frightened soldiers flee, but are called back to battle, when they see the raised standard of their lord, and achieve victory with the help of God and the sign that was shown, Isaiah 11: *The Lord will hoist a sign for the nations and assemble the outcasts of Israel and gather the scattered people of Judah.* The cross is a sign which calls back those who have long strayed on the detours of sins, Isaiah 49: *Look, I shall raise up my hand to the nations and hoist my sign to the peoples; my hand,* which destroys crime, reforms works, shows wounds, gives gifts; and it says: *I shall hoist my sign;* because as the royal sign is put on top of the walls after a victory, so the crusaders gather against the devil and defeat [him] with the sign.

12 2 Maccabees 8: *With the sign of God's help* the Jews attacked *Nicanor and they forced the major part of his army to flee, which was weakened by injuries.* Note that a sign from heaven appeared to the Jews, when they were in distress, and when they saw it, they rallied and defeated their enemies, as do soldiers, when they see the king's sign: they regain their spirit and they dare not flee as the king is on the battlefield and their war is just. This war is just, because [it is fought] against the enemies of the faith, the usurpers of our patrimony, and for the sake of God, and because it is a matter of the faith and our salvation. Our king stands wounded in battle, so that a Christian may fight manfully and that, if he fights to the blood, he may behold and have faith in his king's wounds.

13 When in the time of Constantine, he had to fight against his enemies on the Danube, it is said that the sign of the cross appeared in the heavens and a voice was heard: Constantine, win with this [sign]!,[5] which the outcome of the matter proved right. Exodus 12: *The blood will be a sign for you, and they will see the blood; you will escape the destructive plague, when I strike the land of Egypt.* 2 Maccabees 15: *They hung Nicanor's head from the highest arch, so it might be obvious and a manifest sign of the help of God.* This then is the sign of the king of Jerusalem, literally a red cross on white cloth, the passion of Christ in a pure heart, so to speak, not the dragon of cupidity or the eagle of

---

[5] Cf. Cassiodorus, 'Historia Ecclesiastica Tripartita', *CSEL*, LXXI, 17.

Romanorum, immo verius antichristi et bestie in Apo. [xiii], quibus signantur milites dyaboli.

14 Ergo, veri Christiani, Ysa. lxii [10]: *Preparate viam, planum facite iter, levate signum ad populos!* Hoc est dare aliis bonum exemplum: *Levate,* id est surgite, et sumite crucis signum. Quando homo fert baculum elevatum et erectum, tunc timet canis. Quando ponitur signum in prediis vel in vineis, tunc fugit avis. Quando vero homo baculum trahit per terram vel abscondit subtus capam, tunc canis mordet a posteriori. Sic crucis signum non est abscondendum sed aperte portandum et accipiendum contra canes infernales, qui multum timent baculum, quo gravissime verberati sunt et veri fideles consolati, Ps. [xxii, 4]: *Virga tua et baculus tuus ipsa me consolata sunt.* Ysa. xxx [31]: *A voce Domini pavebit Assur,* id est dyabolus, *virga percussus.*

15 Est etiam crux signum rememorativum sicut signum quod datur amicis in perpetuandis amicitiis, ut viso signo fiat amici absentis rememoratio. Hoc enim signum nobis[9] relinquit Dominus ad Patrem per crucem recessurus, Can. viii [6]: *Pone me ut signaculum super cor tuum, ut signaculum super brachium tuum, quia fortis est ut mors dilectio.* Ponamus ergo crucem Christi *super cor,* hoc est in corde per affectum amoris, et *super brachium* per effectum operis. Et si vere Christum diligis, pro Christo mori paratus eris. Nulla enim carnis illecebra, nulla prosperitas, nulla dignitas, non robur corporis, non quilibet elegantia seculi, nec hominum gratia, nichil denique ex omnibus, que in mundo vel concupisci vel diligi possunt, morti prevalet iminenti.
16 *Ut*[10] *signaculum*[11] inquit. Signaculum ponitur ad notitiam sicut circulus in taberna, ad custodiam sicut sigillum in carta, ad gratiam et decorem sicut in auribus sponse et aliquarum mulierum in aliquibus regionibus murenule auree vermiculate argento. Et tu hoc signo signeris, quod arceat adversarios, teipsum custodiat, proximum edificet et Christum letificet. Hanc crucem Christi in corde habeas et eius stigmata in corpore tuo feras, ut intus offerens victimam holocausti etiam foris habeas pellem eius. Debet enim qui se dicit per internam dilectionem in

---

[9] nobis C, M, P3] *om.* P5   [10] ut M, C] vel P5, P3
[11] signaculum] crucis *add.* C

ambition, which are the signs of the Romans, indeed of the antichrist and the beast in the Apocalypse, with which the soldiers of the devil are signed.

14 Therefore, true Christians, Isaiah 62: *Prepare the way, make the journey a smooth one, raise the sign to the peoples!* This means giving a good example to others: *Raise*, meaning stand up, and take the sign of the cross. When a man carries a stick and holds it up, then a dog is frightened. When a sign is put in fields and vineyards, then a bird flies away. But when a man drags the stick on the ground or hides it beneath his cloak, then the dog bites from behind. In the same way, the sign of the cross must not be hidden but carried openly and must be taken up against the dogs of hell, who are very frightened of the stick, with which they are beaten most severely but with which the true believers are comforted, Psalms: *Your rod and your stick have comforted me.* Isaiah 30: *At God's voice Assyria*, meaning the devil, *will be terrified, struck with his rod.*

15 The cross is also a sign of recollection like a sign which is given to friends to prolong friendship, so that a friend who is away remembers, when he sees the sign. The Lord left us this sign, when he returned to the Father by the cross, Song of Songs 8: *Set me like a sign in your heart, like a sign on your arm, for love is as strong as death.* Therefore, let us put the cross of Christ *in our heart*, that is in the heart through the affection of love, and *on our arm* through the effect of our deeds. If you truly love Christ, you will be ready to die for Christ. No allure of the flesh, no wealth, no honour, no bodily strength, no kind of worldly elegance, nor human grace, indeed nothing of all things that can be desired or loved in this world is stronger than imminent death.

16 *Like a sign* it says. The sign is set for attracting attention like a hoop outside a tavern, for safekeeping like a seal on a charter, for grace and decoration like the golden jewellery with silver inlay, which in some regions wives or other women [wear] in their ears. And you are signed with this sign, which keeps away enemies, guards you, edifies your neighbour and makes Christ happy. May you have this cross of Christ in your heart and carry his stigmata on your body so that, offering the sacrifice of a burnt-offering inside, you may have his skin on the outside. He who claims to remain in Christ through internal love must walk as he

Christo manere per apertam operum et passionum eius imitationem sicut ille ambulavit et ipse ambulare, Exo. xiii [9]: *Erit quasi signum in manu tua, et quasi appensum quod ob recordationem ante oculos tuos.*

17 Ergo, si amicus Dei es, recordare obprobriorum que fiunt [f. 376r] Christo, quando inimici crucis Christi extenderunt manus sacrilegas in civitatem sanctam Ierusalem, ubi Christiani in Saracenorum servitute sunt, ubi sacramenta Christi deficiunt, ubi nomen Christi blasphematur, ubi ydolum abhominationis, Machometi scilicet nomen, iugiter exaltatur et honoratur,[12] Iere. li [50]: *Nolite stare, recordamini procul Domini, et Ierusalem ascendat super cor vestrum.* Poterat Dominus Ierusalem liberare, sed voluit amicos probare suos; sicut enim lapidem ponderosum solent proicere iuvenes ad probandas vires, ita Dominus per terram illam probat, qui sunt animo fortes et qui pusillanimes, Za.[13] xii [3]: *Ponam Ierusalem lapidem oneris cunctis populis.*

18 Affligitur Dominus in sui patrimonii amissione et vult amicos suos probare, si sunt fideles vasalli eius. Qui enim a domino ligio tenet feodum, si desit ei dum impugnatur et hereditas sua illi aufertur, merito feodo privatur. Vos autem quicquid habetis a summo imperatore tenetis, qui vos hodie citari facit, ut ei succuratis; et licet iure feodi non teneremini, tamen tanta beneficia contulit vobis[14] et adhuc tanta offert stipendia, ut remissionem peccatorum etc., quod ad istud signum adcurrere deberetis, ut veri testes fidei essetis sicut filii eterne hereditatis, Iere. xxxii [44]: *Imprimetur signum, et testis apparebit in terra Beniamin*, qui interpretatur 'filius dextere'.

19 Crux etiam est signum remunerativum in premiis. Sic enim pauperes in conviviis introducuntur cum signis, sicut Templarii libere sine pedagio procedunt, quando eorum vestimentis signum crucis ostendunt, sic vere crucesignati sine repulsa ingrediuntur ianuam paradisy, Ysa. ultimo [lxvi, 18–19]: *Venient et videbunt gloriam meam, et ponam in eis signum et mittam ex eis, qui salvati fuerint ad gentes.* Ieronimus in originali: 'Quo signo qui fuerit impressus manus percutientis effugiet', sicut dicitur Eze. ix [4], 'et isto signo postes domorum in Egypto signabantur, quando pereunte Egypto solus Israel mansit illesus', sicut dicitur Exo. xii [22–3].

---

12 honoratur C, M, P3] oneratur P5   13 Za.] Eze. P5, M, P3, Exo. C
14 vobis C, M, P3] *om.* P5

walked by the open imitation of his deeds and passion, Exodus 13: *It will be a sign in your hand,* as if hung up for remembrance *in front of your eyes.*

17 Thus, if you are a friend of God, remember the disgrace which the enemies of the cross of Christ caused Christ, when they put their sacrilegious hands on the holy city of Jerusalem, where the Christians are slaves to the Saracens, where there are no more sacraments of Christ, where the name of Christ is blasphemed, where the idol of abomination, that is the name of Mohammed, continues to be exalted and honoured, Jeremiah 51: *Do not wait, remember God from afar, and Jerusalem will come into your heart.* The Lord could have liberated Jerusalem, but he wanted to test his friends; just as youths have the habit of throwing a heavy stone in order to test their strength, so the Lord tests through this land [of Jerusalem] who is strong in spirit and who is weak, Zechariah 12: *I shall place Jerusalem as a heavy stone for all peoples.*

18 The Lord is afflicted by the loss of his patrimony and wants to test his friends [and find out] if they are his faithful vassals. He who holds a fief from a liege lord and abandons him, when he is attacked and when his patrimony is taken away from him, is rightly deprived of his fief. You hold everything that you have from the highest emperor, who today has you called to his aid; and even if you are not bound by feudal law, he bestowed on you so many benefices and offers you so much pay, such as the remission of sins etc., that you must rush to this sign in order to be true witnesses of the faith like the sons of the eternal inheritance, Jeremiah 32: *The sign will be imprinted, and a witness will appear in the land of Benjamin*, who is interpreted 'son of the right hand'.[6]

19 The cross is also a sign of reward [as] in prizes. Thus the poor are admitted to a feast with signs, just as the Templars can move around freely without [having to pay] toll, when they display the sign of the cross on their garments, and so the crusaders truly walk through the gate of paradise without rejection, the last chapter of Isaiah: *They will come and see my glory, and I shall put a sign on them and send those who are saved to the nations.* Jerome in the original: 'He who is marked with the cross will escape from the killing hand', as it says in Ezekiel 9, 'and the doorposts in Egypt were signed with this sign, when Israel alone remained unhurt, while Egypt was destroyed',[7] as it says in Exodus 12.

---

[6] Hieronymus, 'Liber Interpretationis', 62, 79, 152, 155, 159.
[7] Hieronymus, 'Commentariorum in Esaiam Libri xii-xviii', *CCSL*, LXXIII A, 788.

20 Et Iosue ii [17–18]: *Innoxii erimus a iuramento, quo adiurasti nos, si ingredientibus nobis terram signum* non *fuerit funiculus iste coccineus, et eum ligaveris in fenestra.* Crux enim Christi *funiculus* est *coccineus,* per quem peccatores de cavernis suis, peccatorum scilicet latibulis, educuntur, per quem liberata est Raab aliis pereuntibus [cf. Ios. ii, 6]. Et dum duri et obstinati pereunt, crucesignati fideles hoc funicolo ad Christum trahuntur et eis terra promissionis *in funiculo distributionis* [Ps. lxxvii, 54] datur, quia veri crucesignati, qui vere contriti et confessi ad servitium Dei accinguntur et in ipso moriuntur, veri martires reputantur, liberati a peccatis mortalibus et venalibus et ab omni[15] penitentia sibi iniuncta, absoluti et a pena peccatorum in hoc seculo et a pena purgatorii in alio, a tormentis gehenne securi gloria eterna per hoc signum investientur.

21 Sic enim consuetudo est nobilium, quod per cyrothecam vel aliam rem vilem vasallos suos investiunt feodis pretiosis; sic Dominus per crucem, que est ex modico filo, vasallos suos investit de celesti regno. Quando enim bonum forum est rerum venalium, tunc sapientes necessariis, ut non indigeant, muniunt hospitium suum contra caristiam superventuram, quam metuunt; modo Dominus de regno suo optimum facit forum, dum crucesignatis exponit pro peregrinatione modici temporis regnum celorum.

22 Non simus sicut symia, que nucem abicit, dum exterius amaritudinem in cortice sentit, et numquam ad dulcedinem nuclei pervenit, non sicut asinus, qui in molendino commoratur, et quia recedere non vult ab eo, quando[16] molendinum inceditur et ipse cum eo; qui asinus est adeo piger, quod videns lupum venientem infigit caput suum dumeto vel spinis et permittit renes suos devorari a lupo usque ad pulmonem et, quia abscondit faciem suam, credit quod nullam sustineat lesionem.

23 Vos ergo, fratres, considerantes premia celestia non terreamini a laboribus itineris, quia omnes passus Dominus in libro suo scribit ad mercedem remunerationis, ut sicut *non peribit capillus de capite* [Lc. xxi, 18] nec momentum de tempore, ita nec passus de nostra peregrinatione.

24 Recitat magister Iacobus de Vitriaco, quod, cum semel predicaret de cruce suscipienda, aderat ibi vir quidam religiosus, conversus Cysterciensis dictus frater Symon, divinis visionibus assuetus, qui rogavit

---

[15] et ab omni C, M, P3] *om.* P5   [16] quando] *om.* P5, C, M, P3

20 And Joshua 2: *We will be blameless of the oath which you made us swear if, when we come into the land, the sign will* not *be this scarlet string, and you will tie it to the window.* The cross of Christ is the *scarlet string,* by which the sinners are led from their caves, meaning the hideouts of their sins, and by which Rahab was freed, while the others perished. So while the hardened and the obstinate are killed, the faithful crusaders are drawn to Christ by this string and the promised land is given to them *by the line of distribution,* because true crusaders, who are truely contrite, have confessed their sins and prepare for the service of God and then die, are considered true martyrs, freed from mortal and venial sins and absolved from all penance enjoined on them, the punishment for their sins in this world and the punishment of purgatory in the next, they are safe from the tortures of hell and will be invested by this sign with eternal glory.

21 Thus it is a custom among the nobility to invest their vassals with precious fiefs by a glove or another worthless object; in the same way the Lord invests his vassals with the heavenly kingdom by the cross which is made of ordinary thread. When there is good business for goods on sale, wise people stock their larder with necessary things – so they do not run out of them – for a future food shortage which they fear; now the Lord offers a very good business for his kingdom, when he gives the heavenly kingdom to crusaders for a short pilgrimage.

22 Let us not be like the monkey, that throws away the nut when it smells the bitterness of the skin on the outside and never gets to the sweetness of the core, and not like the donkey that stays at the mill when the mill burns down and [the donkey] with it, because it does not want to move away from [the mill]; the donkey is so lazy that, when it sees the wolf coming, it puts its head in a shrub or a thornbush and lets the wolf eat his loins down to the flesh and it thinks that it does not sustain any wounds, because it hides its face.

23 You, brothers, do not be afraid of the hardship of this journey when you consider the heavenly reward, because the Lord writes down in his book all the steps for the deal on the reward, so that as *not a hair of the head will be lost* nor a moment of time, so also not a step of our pilgrimage.

24 Master James of Vitry recounts[8] that, when he once preached about taking the cross, there was a certain religious man, a Cistercian lay brother called Brother Symon, who used to have divine visions, who

---

[8] Cf. James I, 21.

Dominum cum lacrimis, ut ostenderet ei quale meritum collaturus erat crucesignatis. Qui statim in spiritu vidit Beatam Virginem filium suum tenentem, et secundum quod uniusquisque signum crucis corde contrito recepiebat, filium suum illi dabat. Qui ergo ita signatus fuerit, sigillum regis secum portabit, nec dilationem introitus regni sustinebit.

25 Apoc. vii [2–3] vidit Iohannes *angelum habentem signum Dei vivi*, clamantem angelis percussoribus, ne nocerent signatis. Patet ergo, quomodo crux dicitur signum directivum, discretivum, rememorativum et remunerativum.

with tears asked the Lord to show him what kind of reward crusaders were given. At once he saw in his mind the Holy Virgin holding her son and that she gave her son to everybody who received the cross with a contrite heart. He who will be signed in this way, will carry with him the seal of the king and will suffer no delay when entering his kingdom.

25 In Apocalypse 7 John saw *an angel carrying the sign of the living God,* who called to the killing angels not to harm those who were signed. So it is obvious why the cross of God is called a sign of direction, distinction, recollection and reward.

Gilbert of Tournai

SERMO II

P5 = Paris, Bibliothèque Nationale de France, lat. 15953, ff. 376r-v

Additional manuscripts
C = Cambridge, University Library, Peterhouse 200, ff. 69va-70ra
M = Marseille, Bibliothèque Municipale, 392, ff. 100rb-100vb
P3= Paris, Bibliothèque Nationale de France, lat. 15943, ff. 115va-116ra

Reference
Schneyer, II, 303, no. 246

Ad crucesignatos et crucesignandos sermo secundus

1 [f. 376v] *Vidi alterum angelum* etc., *habentem signum Dei vivi* [Apc. vii, 2], crucem scilicet Christi, in qua invenitur vita, Prov. viii[1] [35]: *Qui me invenerit, inveniet vitam et hauriet salutem a Domino, vitam* gratie, *salutem* glorie.

2 Signat autem dyabolus suos signo mortis, Christus autem suos signo vite. Signo mortis signantur duplices et proditores similes Iude, qui dedit Christo osculum in signum pacis et perficiebat opus proditionis, Mt. xxvi [48–9]: *Qui tradidit eum dedit eis signum dicens: Quemcumque osculatus fuero, ipse est; tenete eum,* et sequitur: *Accedens ad Ihesum dicit: Ave, rabi!, et osculatus est eum.* Sic multi in facie ungunt et a tergo pungunt, ore se Christianos dicunt et opere Christum crucifigunt.

---

[1] viii] xiii P5, C, M, P3

Gilbert of Tournai

SERMON II

The second sermon to those who are or will become crusaders

1 *I saw another angel* etc., *carrying the sign of the living God*, meaning the cross of Christ, in which life is found, Proverbs 8: *He who finds me will find life and receive salvation from the Lord*, the *life* of grace and the *salvation* of glory.

2 The devil signs his followers with the sign of death, but Christ his followers with the sign of life. Deceivers and traitors are signed with the sign of death like Judas, who gave Christ a kiss as a sign of peace, fulfilling his work of treachery, Matthew 26: *He who betrayed him gave them a sign saying: The one I will kiss is the man; arrest him,* and it follows: *Approaching Jesus he said: Greetings, Rabbi!, and kissed him.* Thus many talk sweet words to your face and stab you from behind, calling themselves Christians and crucifying Christ with their works.

3 Signo autem dyaboli signantur carnales et incontinentes, Sap. ii [8–9]: *Nullum pratum sit quod non pertranseat luxuria nostra* – nemo nostrum exsors sit luxurie nostre[2] – *ubique relinquamus signa letitie.* Hec sunt signa mortis: Sicut, quando videntur ludere delfines in mari signa sunt proxime tempestatis, sed parvi pisces sub petris absconduntur et tempestatem evadunt nec cum fluctibus iactantur, sic amatoribus mundi multis turbinibus rerum secularium iactatis et ludentibus et pereuntibus in terra propria, crucesignati salvantur et quasi absconduntur in terra aliena et ignota. Sicut Abraham, cui facte sunt promissiones, postquam de terra sua et cognatione sua exivit, Gal. iii [16]: *Abrahe dicte sunt promissiones et semini eius*, id est eis qui de terra sua exeunt exemplo ipsius.

4 Signo etiam dyaboli signantur invidentes. Hoc est signum quod habuit Caym in capite, tremor scilicet et inquietudo[3] capitis, ut dicunt Gn. iv[4] [14–15]. Qui invidi sunt velut ursi semper inquieti; ursus enim ligatus ad stipitem numquam pene desinit vel in circuitum pergere vel pedibus suis caput suum modo in unam partem, modo in aliam iactare; ita invidia vix permittit cor aliquo momento requiescere. Et quia ex invidia detractio, ideo Dan. vii [5] dicitur illi *bestie,* que erat *similis urso: Surge, comede*[5] *carnes plurimas!*

5 Invidi enim vitam suam preferunt, alienam rodunt, proximorum infirmitates delectabiliter carpunt. Ergo *carnes* comedunt, sicut ursus plantas suas lambendo suggit et *carnes* alienas devorat et comedit; et utinam ita *carnes* lacerarent quod ossibus parcerent! Hii sunt, qui detrahunt crucesignatis et crucem suscipere paratis et sicut canes mordent in baculo crucis; sed crucesignati quasi boni peregrini pertranseunt et non immorantur cuilibet cani oblatranti. Canis enim nequam iacet super fenum et manducare nequit nec cetera animalia, que manducare possent, manducare sinit, Prov. iii [27]: *Noli prohibere benefacere eum qui potest; si vales et ipse benefac.*

6 Propter hoc Luc. ii [34] dicitur: Christus *positus in signum, cui contradicetur.* Sapientes enim mundi huic signo et divites detrahunt verbo et contradicunt facto similes truncis veteribus, qui nichil aliud quam fumigare faciunt et accendi non possunt, quia Iere. vi [29]: *Frustra*

---

[2] nemo . . . nostre P3, C, M] *om.* P5   [3] inquietudo C, M] inquirendo P5, P3
[4] iv] iii P5, C, M, P3   [5] comede C, M, P3] comedes P5

3 Those given to bodily lust and pleasures are also signed with the sign of the devil, Wisdom 2: *There is no meadow which our indulging does not walk on* – none of us is without indulging – *we leave signs of our enjoyment everywhere.* These are signs of death: just as small fish hide beneath rocks, so they escape the storm and are not swept away by the current, when dolphins are seen playing in the sea, which is a sign of an approaching storm, so crusaders are saved, so to speak hiding in a foreign and unknown land, whereas lovers of this world are swept away, while playing in the many eddies of worldy things, and die in their own country. In the same way, Abraham, to whom promises were made, left his own country and his people, Galatians 3: *Promises were addressed to Abraham and his progeny*, meaning to those who after his example leave their own country.

4 The envious are also signed with the sign of the devil. This is the sign which Cain had in his head, namely a trembling and restlessness of the head, as it says in Genesis 4. The envious are like bears, always restless, because a bear tied to a tree-trunk never stops either going round in a circle or throwing his head from one side to the other with its paws; in the same way, envy hardly ever allows the heart to rest for one moment. Because envy results in taking away things, in Daniel 7 the *beast* which was *like a bear* was told: *Get up and eat quantities of flesh.*

5 The envious prefer their own lives, gnaw at those of others and seize with delight on the weaknesses of their neighbours. They eat *flesh* as a bear sucks his plants while licking them and eats and devours the *flesh* of others; and if they would only hurt the *flesh* and save the bones! It is they who distract crusaders and those who are ready to take the cross and like dogs they bite the stick of the cross; but the crusaders persist like good pilgrims and do not bother about some barking dog. A dog is useless when it lies in the hay and cannot eat [it] and does not let other animals eat that could eat [it], Proverbs 3: *Do not prevent from doing good someone who can do it; if it is in your power, do good yourself.*

6 Because of this it says in Luke 2: Christ *is set as the sign that will be opposed.* The wise of the world draw the rich away from this sign by their words and contradict it by their deeds like old logs, that can only smoke but cannot be lighted, as Jeremiah 6: *In vain the blower of bellows*

conflavit conflator, id est Christus, qui[6] sufflatorium fecit ex pelle carnis sue et ligno crucis et clavis, ut ignem sue caritatis accenderet in cordibus nostris, quo faciliter accenduntur pauperes quasi stupa, sed non hii trunci veteres pleni luto et aqua.

7 Signo etiam dyaboli signantur notorii peccatores, Eze. xvi [25]: *Ad omne caput vie educasti signum prostitutionis tue et abhominabilem fecisti decorem tuum. Ad omne caput vie* signum hoc ponitur, quando aperte peccatur, quando culpa publicatur; ergo, sicut publice peccasti, publice accipe signum Christi, ut sicut alios exemplo tuo corrupisti ita exemplo tuo invites alios ad opus meriti. Iustum est enim, ut qui se Deo abstulit et perdidit cum aliorum destructione seipsum cum multorum edificatione restituat. Cur confundimini aperte accipere crucem? Non accipiebatis consilium ab uxoribus, a parentibus eundi ad dyabolum?

8 Cur ergo expectatis consilium eundi ad Deum? Impleatur in vobis quod dicit propheta [Ps. lxxxv, 17]: *Fac mecum signum in bono, ut videant qui oderunt me et confundantur, quoniam tu, Domine, adiuvisti me et consolatus es me. Ut videant qui oderunt me*, scilicet demones, *et confundantur* coram omnibus, sicut latro confunditur, quando in furto comprehenditur et in medio foro in pallori ponitur. Impletur autem in peccatoribus notoriis illud Sap. v [13]: *Nullum quidem signum virtutis valuimus ostendere; in malignitate autem nostra consumpti sumus.*

---

[6] qui C, M] *om.* P5, P3

blows, meaning Christ, who made a bellows from his skin, the wood of the cross and the nails, so that the fire of his charity would be lighted in our hearts; like flax the poor are more easily lit by this, but not these old logs full of mud and water.

7 Notorious sinners are also signed with the sign of the devil, Ezekiel 16: *You put up a sign of your prostitution at the entrance of every alley and made your beauty to be abhorred.* This sign is put up *at the entrance of every alley*, when someone openly commits a sin and when a wrong is made public; thus, as you sinned in public, take the sign of Christ in public, so that by your example you may invite others to [do] good works just as you corrupted them by your example. It is just that he who removed himself from God and ruined himself by pulling down others, should restore himself by edifying many. Why are you ashamed to take the cross publicly? Did you not take advice from your spouses [and] parents to go to the devil?

8 Why then are you expecting advice to go to God? What the prophet says will be fulfilled in you: *Show me a sign for good, so that they who hate me see it and are ashamed, because you, Lord, helped me and comforted me. So that they who hate me*, namely the demons, *see it and are ashamed* in front of everybody, just as a thief is ashamed, when he is caught in a robbery and put in pillory in the middle of the market place. This then is fulfilled in notorious sinners, Wisdom 5: *We can show no sign of virtue; we are consumed in our own wickedness.*

Gilbert of Tournai

SERMO III

P5 = Paris, Bibliothèque Nationale de France, lat. 15953, ff. 376v-378r

Additional manuscripts
C = Cambridge, University Library, Peterhouse 200, ff. 70ra-71rb
M = Marseille, Bibliothèque Municipale, 392, ff. 100vb-101ra
(includes ff. 100bis r+v)
P3 = Paris, Bibliothèque Nationale de France, lat. 15943, ff. 116ra-118ra

Reference
Schneyer, II, 303, no. 247

Ad crucesignatos et crucesignandos sermo tertius

1 *Vidi alterum angelum habentem signum* etc. [Apc. vii, 2]. Hoc signo crucis signat Dominus suos, unde electi in Apoc. vii dicuntur signati.

2 Est autem crux *signum* clementie quantum ad reos, victorie quantum ad dubios et formidolosos, iustitie quantum ad sanctos, glorie quantum ad perfectos.

3 De primo, Hester iiii [11]: *Cuncte noverunt provincie quod, si quis non vocatus atrium interius regis* assueti[1] *intraverit, statim interficiatur, nisi forte rex auream virgam ad eum extenderit pro signo clementie atque ita possit vivere.* Non audet pec- [f. 377r] cator accedere ad Deum videns se reum; porrigit ei *rex virgam*, crucem scilicet, per suam clementiam et sic impetrat veniam. Hec est virga de qua Levit. ultimo [xxvii, 32] dicitur,

---

[1] assueti] assueri P5, C, M, P3

198

Gilbert of Tournai

SERMON III

The third sermon to those who are or will become crusaders

1 *I saw another angel carrying the sign* etc. With this sign of the cross the Lord signs his followers, whence the elect in Apocalypse 7 are called those who are signed.

2 The cross is a *sign* of clemency for criminals, of victory for the doubtful and fearful, of righteousness for the holy and of glory for the perfect.

3 About the first, Esther 4: *All provinces knew that if someone who was not summoned, entered the private appartments of the king*, whom he knew, *he was to be killed immediately unless the king pointed his golden staff at him as a sign of clemency and he thus could live.* A sinner does not dare to approach God as a criminal, but because of his clemency *the king* holds *his staff* out to him, that is his cross, and he thus obtains forgiveness. This is the staff about which it says in the last chapter of

quod *quicquid sub pastoris virga transierit sanctificatum erit Domino.* Ad litteram enim, ut dicunt, pastor habebat virgam tinctam sanguine et *quicquid decimum* de grege transibat tangebat et sanguine signans[2] Domino sanctificabat.

4 Virga enim crucis et sanguine Christi sanctificamur et ab aliis signatis discernimur. Sed timeant rebelles et in peccatis suis perseverantes, ne signum clementie vertatur eis in signum iracundie, Numeri. xvii[3] [10]: *Refer virgam Aaron in tabernaculum testimonii, ut servetur ibi in signum rebellium[4] filiorum Israel,* ut tanto puniantur gravius, quanto potuerunt misericordiam invenire levius.

5 Quicquid enim sustinent crucesignati modicum est et quasi nichil respectu premii interminabilis: labor brevis, merces in ianuis, Ro. viii [18]: *Non sunt condigne passiones huius temporis ad futuram gloriam, que revelabitur in nobis.* Ergo ad hoc signum accedatis qui hactenus fuistis in tenebris et peccatis, Ysa. xiii [2]: *Super montem caliginosum levate signum,* id est super cor tenebrosum crucis vexillum.

6 Est etiam crux signum clementie. Sicut enim Christus in cruce per dilectionem inexpressibilem, quam ad nos habuit, per quinque canales corporis quinque fluvios sanguinis patefecit sufficiens diluvium ad lotionem totius mundi, ita et nunc per viscera misericordie sue se totum crucesignatis diluendis exponit, quia Can. iiii [15] *fons* prius erat signatus, sed nunc *fons ille parvus crevit in fluvium* magnum *et in aquas plurimas redundavit,* Hest. x [6].

7 Est enim crux signum victorie. Per hoc enim signum homo vincit seipsum et omnem carnalem affectum, diabolum et mundum. Propter hoc Apoc. vii [9] dicitur de electis crucesignatis quod ipsi sunt *in conspectu agni, amicti stolis albis et palme in manibus eorum. Amicti stolis albis,* quia venerunt de tribulatione et laverunt stolas suas et dealbaverunt eas in sanguine *agni.* Et *palme in manibus eorum*[5] in signum quod victores sunt effecti. Palma enim arbor est victorie. Hoc signo armavit se beatus Martinus, cum barbari[6] minarentur obiciendum eum. 'Ergo, inquit, signo crucis non clipeo protectus aut galea hostium cuneos penetrabo securus.' Et in Tripartita Historia l[ib]. ix c[ap]. ix legitur,

---

[2] signans P5] signatis C, M, P3   [3] xvii] xvi P5, C, M, P3
[4] rebellium C, M, P3] rebellionum P5   [5] amicti . . . eorum C, M, P3] *om.* P5
[6] barbari M] barbaris P5, C, P3

Leviticus that *all that passes under the shepherd's staff will be consecrated to the Lord*. In the literal sense, so they say, the shepherd had a staff dipped in blood and he touched *every tenth* [animal] of the flock that passed and consecrated it to the Lord by signing it with blood.

4 By the staff of the cross and the blood of Christ we are consecrated and distinguished from those who are signed otherwise. But rebels who persist in their own sins must fear that for them the sign of clemency be turned into a sign of anger, Numbers 17: *Put Aaron's staff back in the tabernacle of the testimony, so that it should serve as a sign for the rebellious sons of Israel*; thus the more easily they could have found mercy, the harder they may be punished.

5 All that the crusaders suffer is little, indeed nothing, compared to the immeasurable reward: there is little labour [and] the wages are in front of the door, Romans 8: *The sufferings of this present time are nothing compared to the future glory which will be disclosed for us*. Therefore, proceed to this sign, you who until now have lived in darkness and sins, Isaiah 13: *Raise a sign on the cloudy mountain*, meaning the banner of the cross in your dark heart.

6 The cross is also a sign of clemency. Just as on the cross Christ opened five rivers of blood through the five channels of his body – a flood sufficient to cleanse the whole world – because of the inexpressible love which he had for us, so he now shows his whole self to the crusaders to cleanse them through the inmost parts of his compassion, because in Song of Songs 4 he was once designated as a *spring*, but now this *little spring has grown into a* big *river and has overflown into many waters*, Esther 10.

7 The cross is also a sign of victory. By this sign man wins over himself and all bodily feelings, the devil and the world. Because of this it says in Apocalypse 7 about the elect crusaders that they are *in front of the lamb, dressed in white robes with palms in their hands. Dressed in white robes,* because they have suffered hardship and washed their robes and daubed them with the blood of the *lamb. With palms in their hands* as a sign that they turned out to be victorious. The palm is the tree of victory. Saint Martin armed himself with this sign, when the barbarians threatened to kill him. He said: 'I will go towards the troops of the enemies, safely protected not by a shield or a helmet but by the sign of the cross.'[1] And in the Historia Tripartita book nine chapter nine one reads that

---

[1] Sulpicius Severus, *Vita S. Martini*, ed. J. Fontaine (Sources Chrétiennes 133; Paris, 1967), 260.

quod statuit Constantinus ut imprimeretur crux in monetis Christianis; et hoc signo signarentur arma militum suorum.

8 Hoc autem signo non tantum vincuntur hostes infernales vel materiales sed etiam affectus carnales. Unde legimus de quodam nobili milite, quod iturus ultra mare fecit adduci ad se filios parvulos, quos valde diligebat. Et cum eos diu aspiciens amplecteretur, dixerunt ei famuli eius: Dimitte pueros istos et recedatis, quia multi vos expectant, ut vos deducant. Quibus ille: Ideo coram me filios meos adduci feci, ut excitato affectu ad eos cum maiori angustia mentis reliquam eos pro Christo et ita magis merear apud Deum. Profecto enim patria, propria, parentes, uxor et filii vincula sunt retinentia.

9 Sed teste Ieronimi: 'Facile rumpit hec vincula amor Christi et timor gehenne', pro cuius amore cum magno glaudio sancti labores sustinent et in laboribus delectantur, sicut ursus ictibus impinguatur, sicut aque Marath per immissionem ligni dulcorantur [cf. Ex. xv, 23], per farinam Helysei coloquintide agri, illa scilicet silvestria holuscula, de quibus clamabant filii prophetarum: *Mors in olla, vir Dei* [iv Rg. iv, 40], sua amaritudine privantur.

10 Hoc figuratum est in signo Ione, Mat. xii [39–41] et Ione i [15]: Misso enim Iona in mari *stetit mare a fervore suo,* quia quod prius videbatur importabile[7] exemplo Crucifixi fit leve, qui se *exinanivit* usque ad carnem, usque ad crucem, *usque ad mortem* [Phil. ii, 7–8]. Sicut enim tigris rabido cursu insequitur venatorem et tanto affectu prosequitur fetum, ut se mittat in venatoris spiculum, ita Christus, ut nos eriperet de manu venatoris, id est dyaboli, in spiculum[8] mortis se misit.

11 Et ideo teste Augustini, cum Christus per alia beneficia ad amorem suum nos incitaret, per mortis beneficium nos coegit. Huius victorie signum in figura eorum, qui nolunt[9] crucem accipere: nolebat[10] Achaz, rex impius, petere, quia nolebat[11] Deum glorificare, Ysa. vii [11–12]: *Pete tibi signum a Domino Deo tuo; et dixit: Non petam et non temptabo Dominum,* alia littera est: non exaltabo Dominum. Sciebat enim rex impius quod si peteret accepturus esset et glorificaretur Dominus.

---

[7] importabile C, M, P3] *om.* P5   [8] spiculum C, M, P3] speculum P5
[9] nolunt C, M, P3] volebat P5   [10] nolebat C, M, P3] volebat P5
[11] nolebat C, M, P3] volebat P5

Constantine decreed that the cross be imprinted on Christian coins; and with this sign the weapons of his soldiers were signed.[2]

8 Not only the infernal and material enemies are beaten with this sign, but also bodily feelings. Thus we read about a certain noble knight that, when he was about to go across the sea, he had his small sons, whom he loved very much, brought to him.[3] And when he embraced them and looked at them for a long time, his servants said to him: Send those boys away and leave, because many people are waiting for you to take you away. He [told] them: I had my sons brought before me so that, by exciting my feelings towards them, I would leave them behind for Christ's sake with greater anguish of the mind, so that I would count for more with God. When one leaves one's country, one's belongings, parents, spouse and children are bands which hold one back.

9 But according to the testimony of Jerome, 'the love of Christ and the fear of hell easily break these bands';[4] for his love the saints suffer much hardship with great joy, just as a bear is patted with strokes, the waters of Marah are made sweet by throwing in wood, and the wild vine was deprived of its bitterness by Elisha's flour, this woodland weed about which the sons of the prophets cried out: *Man of God, there is death in the pot!*

10 This is symbolised by the sign of Jonah, Matthew 12 and Jonah 1: When Jonah was thrown into the sea, *the sea stopped raging*, because what earlier seemed unbearable was made easy by the example of the Crucified, who *emptied himself* unto the flesh, unto the cross, *unto death*. Just as the tiger follows the hunter in a wild chase and follows its cub with such affection that it throws itself into the hunter's spear, so Christ threw himself into the spear of death to snatch us from the hand of the hunter, that is the devil.

11 And likewise, according to Augustine's testimony,[5] while Christ encourages us to love him by other favours, he forces us to it by the favour of his death. The sign of this victory also stands for those who do not want to take the cross: Ahaz, the heathen king, did not want to ask [for a sign], because he did not want to glorify God, Isaiah 7: *Ask for a sign for yourself from the Lord, your God; and he said: I shall not ask and I shall not tempt the Lord*, which in other words means: I shall not praise the Lord. The heathen king knew that if he asked he would be accepted and the Lord would be praised.

---

[2] Cassiodorus, 'Historia Ecclesiastica', 27.
[3] Crane, no. cxxxiv. Tubach, no. 1392. This is taken from James of Vitry's 'sermo ad peregrinos'; see also Appendix.
[4] Hieronymus, 'Epistulae I', *CSEL*, LIV, 48.
[5] I have not been able to identify this reference. Cf. James II, 14.

12 Crux etiam signum iustitie. Iustitia enim est,[12] ut conformemur Christo, qui pro nobis tribulationem sustinuit a principio nativitatis sue usque ad finem vite, Luc. ii [12]: *Hoc vobis signum: Invenietis infantem pannis involutum et positum in presepio.* *Pannis involutum* in quo paupertas; non enim erat ornatus sericis sed involutus panniculis. *Positus in presepio,* in quo vilitas. *Infantem* expositum scilicet frigori hyemis illo tempore in quo asperitas.

13 Que est iustitia ista vel satisfactio, ut per hiis tribus queras: divitias, delicias et honores? Christus in presepio, tu in palatio; Christus [f. 377v] in vilibus pannis, tu in sericis et ornamentis; Christus in asino, tu in equis et phaleris; Christus in cruce, tu in balneis; Christus in sepulcro, tu in lectis eburneis et superstitiosis; Christus nudus in cruce, tu in mutatoriis que pendent in perticis; Christus confixus manus, tu in manicis consuticiis et cyrothecis et anulis; Christus confixus pedes, tu in calceis rostratis, laqueatis, lunulatis, perforatis; Christus in corona spinea, tu in discriminalibus mitris, vittis et collitergiis[13] et sertis; Christus aceto potatus, tu vino inebriatus; Christus cucurrit ad clavos ferreos, tu ad gariophilos; Christus ligatus ad columpnam, tu dissolutus evagaris per camporum et platearum licentiam effrenatam; Christus perforatum habuit latus lancea et tu cinctum aurea zona vel argentea; Christus pretioso sanguine animam tuam[14] redemit, tu illam vili pretio dyabolo vendis; semel crucifixus est a Iudeis, tu eum pluries crucifigis in membris et super dolorem vulnerum addis; conspuis eum in facie, dum bonis detrahis;[15] acetum ei porrigis, dum malitia et rancoris corruptione in proximum exardescis.

14 Sed verum signum iustitie apparet in crucesignatis, qui corde, ore et opere se exercent in servitio Dei: corde per devotionem, ore per gratiarum actionem, corpore et opere per laboris satisfactionem. Et hee sunt tres sagitte quas iecit Ionatas, filius regis, in agro *quasi exercens se ad signum,* i Reg. xx [20].

15 Efficax enim satisfactio est labor peregrinationis, quia sicut omnibus membris homo peccavit, ita in cunctis membris laborando satisfacit. Et si peccavit nimio affectu ad uxorem et filios, satisfacit dimittendo eos; et licet hec satisfactio sit multum meritoria, magis tamen est consolatoria

---

[12] est C, M, P3] *om.* P5   [13] collitergiis C, M, P3] colltergiis P5
[14] tuam C, M, P3] suam P5   [15] detrahis C, M, P3] detrahes P5

12 The cross is also a sign of righteousness. Righteousness means that we conform to Christ, who suffered tribulations for us from the beginning at his birth to the end of his life, Luke 2: *This [is] a sign for you: You will find a baby wrapped in swaddling cloths and lying in a manger. Wrapped in swaddling cloths* which [reflects] poverty; he was not adorned with silk but wrapped in rags. *Lying in a manger* which [reflects] baseness. *A baby*, exposed to the cold of winter in this rough season.

13 What kind of righteousness or satisfaction are you looking for through these three: riches, luxuries and honours? Christ was in a manger, you [live] in a palace;[6] Christ [was dressed] in poor cloth, you [wear] silk and finery; Christ [rode] on a donkey, you [ride] on horses with rich trappings; Christ [hung] on the cross, you [slouch] in the baths: Christ [lay] in the tomb, you in sumptuous ivory beds; Christ [was] naked on the cross, you [dress in] stately dresses [that hang] on your clothes-rails; Christ had his hand transfixed, you [wear] stitched sleeves, gloves and rings [on your hands]; Christ had his foot transfixed, you [wear] pointed, laced, turned up and pierced shoes [on your feet]; Christ [wore] a crown of thorns, you [wear] hairpins, hats, bands, ribbons and garlands; Christ drank vinegar, you get drunk on wine; Christ hurried towards the iron nails, you run after cloves; Christ was tied to a column, you wander negligently with unbridled freedom across squares and streets; Christ had his side pierced by a lance and you gird yourselves with a gold or silver belt; Christ redeemed your soul with his precious blood, you sell it to the devil for a cheap price; he was crucified once by the Jews, you again and again crucify him in his limbs and increase the pain of his wounds; you spit in his face while taking away his belongings; you offer him vinegar, while you burn with evil and bitter corruption against your neighbours.

14 But the true sign of righteousness appears in the crusaders, who practise the service of God with their heart, mouth and works: with the heart by devotion, with their mouth by giving thanks and with their body and works by the labours of satisfaction. These are the three arrows which Jonathan, the king's son, shot in the field *as if practising at a sign*, 1 Kings 20.

15 The labour of the pilgrimage is efficient satisfaction, because as a man has sinned with all his limbs, so he does satisfaction by [using] all his limbs. And if he has sinned by too much affection for his spouse and sons, he does satisfaction by leaving them; and even if this kind of

---

[6] The pattern of the following comparisons was probably taken from Ambrosius Mediolanensis, 'Expositio Evangelii Secundum Lucam', *CCSL*, XIV, 49. A similar passage is found in one of Pope Innocent III's letters, see *PL*, CCXV, col. 1340.

quam afflictiva: *Petra enim fundit rivos olei*, Iob xxix [6], quo unguntur contra asperitatem vie pedes peregrini. Si ergo in duro[16] lecto iaceas, attende quod Christus tener et parvulus reclinatus est in duro[17] presepio et duriorem lectum habuit in patibulo. Si dolent pedes ex itinere, cogita quod pedes Christi clavis confixi sunt pro tua liberatione. Si doles caput, quia forte pulvinar non habuisti, cogita quod Christus habuit durum cervical, quando spinis voluit coronari.

16 De hoc signo Iud. vi [37–40], quando expressus est ros de vellere et remansit vellus incorruptum; quia mittitur a Deo ros dulcedinis et gratia consolationis celestis in cor crucesignati, quod non est per impatientiam fractum sed celitus confortatum.

17 Crux etiam est signum glorie. Mt. xxiv [29–30]: *Tunc apparebit signum Filii Hominis in celo*, tunc quando *sol obturabitur*[18] *et luna non dabit lumen suum*; tunc *apparebit*, tunc radiabit et lucebit lumen crucis, unde Crisostomus, omelia prima de cruce et latrone. Sicut imperatorem regalis pompa precedit et militaris ordo preeundo vexilla humeris portare consueverunt[19] et hiis eius declaratur adventus, sic Domino de celo veniente angelorum cetus et archangelorum multitudo illud signum humeris portant excelsis et regalem nobis adventum nunciant.

18 Patet ergo quod crux, que primitus fuit signum ignominie, signum est glorie, Ecc[us]. xxxvi [6–7]: *Innova signa et immuta mirabilia, glorifica manum et brachium dexterum, excita furorem et effunde iram.* Bene dicit *glorifica manum et brachium dextrum*, id est crucesignatum pro Christo pugnantem et in modum manus dextere ictus suscipientem et caput suum defendentem. *Excita furorem* et cetera, quantum ad eos, qui sunt cruci rebelles et Christum crucifigunt in membris suis. Propter hoc enim veniet Christus cum cruce, ut hii qui eum crucifixerunt sue sentiant damnationis cecitatem; et ideo impudientie eorum signum portat et tunc vulnera corporis demonstrabit.

19 Hoc est quod[20] cantatur in ecclesia, hoc signum crucis erit in celo cum Dominus ad iudicandum venerit et illa claritas glorie radiabit in crucesignatis, Gn. ix [13]: *Arcum meum ponam in nubibus, et erit signum federis inter me et terram.* Quia sicut arcus creatur in nubibus ex solari

---

16 duro C, M, P3] tuo P5   17 duro C, M, P3] tuo *del. et suppl.* duro P5
18 obturabitur P5] obscurabitur C, M. P3
19 consueverunt C, M, P3] consuerunt P5   20 quod C, M, P3] quid P5

satisfaction is very meritorious, it is more comforting than damaging: *The rock poured out rivers of oil*, Job 29, with which the pilgrim's feet are anointed against the roughness of the road. So if you are lying on a hard bed, be aware that the tender little Christ was put in a hard manger and had an even harder bed in the form of the rood. When your feet are sore from travelling, consider that Christ's feet were pierced by nails for your liberation. If your head hurts because you do not have a pillow, consider that Christ had a hard cushion when he wanted to be crowned with thorns.

16 About this sign [see] Judges 6, where the dew was squeezed from the fleece and the fleece stayed untainted; thus the dew of sweetness and the grace of heavenly consolation are sent by God into the heart of the crusader, which is not broken by impatience but comforted from heaven.

17 The cross is also a sign of glory. Matthew 24: *Then the sign of the Son of Man will appear in heaven*, when *the sun will be darkened and the moon will not give its light*; then the light of the cross *will appear*, radiate and shine, whence Chrysostomus, homily 1 about the cross and the thief.[7] Just as the imperial pomp precedes the emperor and the ranks of the military who walked before him used to carry the standards on their shoulders and with these announced his arrival, so, when the Lord descends from heaven, the host of the angels and the multitude of the archangels carry this sign on their elevated shoulders and announce to us the royal arrival.

18 It is obvious, therefore, that the cross, which first was a sign of shame, now is a sign of glory, Ecclesiasticus 36: *Renew the signs and make new wonders, glorify your hand and your right arm, rouse your fury and pour out your rage*. It says fittingly *glorify your hand and your right arm*, meaning the crusader who fights for Christ and receives the blows with his right hand and defends his head. *Rouse your fury* etc., with regard to those who are the rebels of the cross and crucify Christ in his limbs. Because of this Christ will come with the cross, so that those who crucified him feel the blindness of their damnation; he thus carries the sign of their impudence and will show the wounds of his body.

19 This is what is sung in church, this sign of the cross will be in the sky when the Lord comes to judge and the radiance of glory will shine on the crusaders, Genesis 9: *I shall set my bow in the clouds, and this will be the sign of the covenant between me and the earth*. Because, as a bow in the clouds is created by sunbeams penetrating the clouds – and it was the

---

[7] Iohannes Chrysostomus, 'De Cruce et de Latrone Homilia i', *PG*, XLIX, cols. 399–408.

radio penetrante nubes et fuit signum cessationis diluvii et serenitatis, ita in cordibus crucesignatorum et corporibus relucebit divina claritas et cessatio iracundie Dei et manifestatio eterne felicitatis. Ipsi enim fuerunt quasi nubes elevati ad celestia, discurrentes ad exequenda divina precepta, summi regis signiferi, domus eius clavigeri.

20 Crux enim clavis est celi, que[21] portas paradisi quinque milibus annorum clausas aperuit crucesignato et crucifixo bono latroni [cf. Lc. xxiii, 42–3]. Et eodem tempore duo beneficia immo tria Dominus exhibuit: nam paradisum patefecit, latronem primum ante omnes homines in ipsum introduxit et crucesignatis maximam spem dedit, quando cherubin custodientibus paradisum cum flammeo gladio latro paradysum intravit.

21 De hac clave Ysa. xxii [22]: *Ponam clavem domus David super humerum eius.* Hinc est quod hodie aperitur thesaurus glorie celestis, et ipse dominus papa, qui sponsus est ecclesie, obligat bona sponse sue [f. 378r] et ex plenitudine potestatis, quam habet sicut Christi vicarius, offert tam largas indulgentias accipientibus crucem et succurentibus Terre Sancte.

22 Dicitur quod bonum forum trahit argentum de bursa. Non ergo surdam aurem faciatis[22] Domino clamanti et offerenti nobis paradisum. Ipse enim quasi ebrius et crapulatus a vino modo bonum forum facit et quasi pro nichilo dat regnum suum. Ps. [xxxv, 7]: Pro nichilo *salvos facies* illos, quia moriuntur et salvantur multi crucesignati, antequam tempus veniat peregrinandi. Multi hodie currunt et properant, dum modica pecunia offertur eis, et non currunt ad regnum celorum, quod offertur eis. Et, ut vulgariter loquimur, multi accurrerent si clamaretur: 'Gaaigne maile, gaaigne denier!' Et nos clamamus: 'Hauot a paradis!', et accurrunt pauci. Et timent, Domine, *qui habitant terminos terrenorum a signis tuis* [Ps. lxiv, 9]!

---

[21] que C, M, P3] qui P5   [22] faciatis C, M, P3] facitis P5

sign of the end of the deluge and good weather –, so the divine radiance, the end of the wrath of God and the manifestation of eternal happiness will be reflected in the hearts and bodies of the crusaders. They are as clouds raised up to the heavens, running to and fro carrying out the divine precepts, the standard-bearers of the highest king, the keepers of the keys to his house.

20 The cross is in fact the key to heaven, that opened the gates of paradise, which were closed for five thousand years, to the crusader and the good thief who was crucified [with Christ]. At that time God offered two or even three favours: he opened up paradise, he brought the thief into it first before all other people and he gave the greatest hope to crusaders when, while the cherubs guarded paradise with the sword of flames, the thief entered paradise.

21 About this key see Isaiah 22: *I shall place the key of David's house on his shoulder.* Because of this, the treasure of heavenly glory is today opened up, and the lord pope himself, who is the spouse of the church, pledges the goods of his spouse and, by the plenipotentiary powers which he holds as vicar of Christ, he offers such great indulgences to those who take the cross and come to the aid of the Holy Land.

22 It is said that a good business draws money from [people's] purses. So you should not close your ears to the Lord, who calls out and offers us paradise. As if he were inebriated and drunk on wine, he now makes good business and gives his kingdom away for just about nothing. The Psalm [says]: for nothing *you will save* them, since many crusaders will die and be saved, before the time to go on the pilgrimage arrives. Today many run and rush when they are offered a little money and they do not run to the kingdom of heaven which is offered to them. And, as we say in the vernacular, many run when someone calls: 'Gaaigne maile, gaaigne denier!' [Have a halfpenny, have a penny!]. We shout: 'Hauot a paradis!' [Hurry up to paradise!], and only few run. O Lord, may they *who live at the ends of the earth fear your signs!*

Humbert of Romans

SERMO I

A = Avignon, Bibliothèque Municipale, Musée Calvet 327, ff. 135r-136r

Additional manuscripts

F = Frankfurt a. M., Stadt- und Universitätsbibliothek, Praed. 29, ff. 139rb-vb
Re = Reims, Bibliothèque Municipale, 612, ff. 29rb-vb
S = Segovia, Catedral, Estanceria B 331, ff. 90rb-vb

Ad peregrinos crucesignatos

1 Notandum quod est quedam peregrinatio generalis, secundum quam omnes, qui sunt in mundo isto, dicuntur peregrini, ii Co. v [6]: *Quamdiu sumus in corpore, peregrinamur a Domino.* Quod recognoscens David dicit [Ps. xxxviii, 13]: *Advena ego sum apud te et peregrinus.*
2 Sed sunt quidam, immo multi, qui invenientes in ista peregrinatione aliqua placentia adherent eis, ita quod non curant redire ad celum unde venerunt, sicut multi filiorum Israel peregrinantes in Babylonia remanserunt ibi nec curaverunt redire in Iherusalem cum aliis, detenti aliquibus delectablibus ibidem. Quod contra dicitur, [i] Pe. ii [11]: *Obsecro vos tamquam advenas et peregrinos abstinere vos a carnalibus desideriis, que militant adversus animam,* eam scilicet detinendo et impediendo, ne revertatur ad locum unde venit.

3 Alia est[1] peregrinatio specialis[2] Christianorum illorum, qui conversi ad aliquem sanctorum visitant limina ipsius ex causis predictis in titulo

---

[1] est F, Re, S] *om.* A   [2] specialis A, Re] spiritualis F, *om.* S

Humbert of Romans

SERMON I

To crusader pilgrims

1 It must be noted that there is a general pilgrimage, according to which all who are in this world are called pilgrims, 2 Corinthians 5: *While we are in the body, we are on a pilgrimage far from God.* Realising this David said: *I am a stranger with you and a pilgrim.*

2 But there are those, indeed many, who, when they find something pleasant on this pilgrimage, stay with that, thus not caring to return to heaven where they came from, just as many sons of Israel remained in Babylon on their pilgrimage there and, detained by something enjoyable, did not care to return to Jerusalem with the others. Against this it says, 1 Peter 2: *I urge you as strangers and pilgrims to abstain from carnal desires which rage against the soul*, keeping it back, so to speak, and stopping it from returning to the place where it came from.

3 Then there is a special pilgrimage of those Christians who, as devotees of one of the saints, visit his shrine for the reasons named under the previous heading.[1] But since many of them break their fasts and [do not

---

[1] This refers to the previous model sermon in the collection which is entitled 'Ad Peregrinos Quoscumque'.

precedenti. Sed quia multi istorum in huiusmodi peregrinatione frangunt ieiunia et festa et defraudant socios vel hospites vel theolonarios[3] vel exponunt se mulieribus vel alia illicita committunt sub habitu peregrini, dicit Dominus, Sopho. i [8]: *Visitabo super omnes, qui induti sunt veste peregrina*, que scilicet vestis exterior apparet in pera et baculo et clavina[4] et huiusmodi signis. *Visitabo*, inquit, ad videndum scilicet, utrum sint boni peregrini vel falsi, sicut sunt quidam trutanni [f. 135v] qui simulant se peregrinos et non sunt. Propter quod dicitur in vulgari: 'Deus scit qui est bonus peregrinus.'

4 Alia est peregrinatio prerogative excellentie, scillicet crucesignatorum, que in multis precellit alias peregrinationes Christianas. Alie enim fiunt propter aliquem sanctum, ista autem propter sanctum sanctorum, scilicet Christum, specialiter.

5 Item in aliis exponunt se homines labori, in ista autem exponunt se morti, et hoc in casibus multis. Item in aliis cito revertuntur homines ad domum et patriam suam, in ista autem vadunt longe ad peregrinandum diu. Item secundum hanc subvenitur communi bono Christianitatis, per alias autem soli proprio commodo. Item peregrinis aliis non datur aliqua indulgentia, istis vero datur plenaria[5] indulgentia peccatorum. Item in istis relucet clare exemplar Christi, qui baiulans sibi crucem exivit in locum Calvarie. Sic et isti Christum sequentes crucem eius deferunt, quod non alii faciunt, sed alia signa peregrinationis.

6 Notandum autem quod quanto peregrinatio ista est maioris prerogative, tanto peregrini isti maiorem curam debent apponere, ut eam debito modo et digno faciant. Proinde debent eam facere sancte, ut impleatur in eorum via illud quod dicitur Ysa. xxxv [8]: *Via sancta vocabitur*; iterum lete, Ps.[6] [cxviii, 54]: *Cantabiles michi erant iustificationes tue in loco peregrinationis mee*; et illud [Ps. cxxxvii, 5]: *Et cantent in viis Domini, quoniam magna est gloria Domini*. Et notantur in hiis duobus due esse letitie, quarum una surgit a presenti gratia, cum dicit: *Iustificationes*, alia a futura gloria, cum dicit: *Quoniam magna est gloria Domini*. Item perseveranter, ut nec levitate nec adversitate nec aliis causis retrahantur

---

[3] theolonarios F, S] theleonearios A, thelonarios Re
[4] clavina A, Re] vinia F, clavia S
[5] plenaria A] plena F, Re, S   [6] Ps. Re, F] sper. A, *om.* S

observe] feasts in such a pilgrimage and cheat on their companions, their hosts or the toll-gatherers, or associate with women or commit other illicit acts in the pilgrim's habit, the Lord says, Zephaniah 1: *I shall visit all who wear pilgrim's clothes*, that is the exterior attire which consists in the purse, the staff, the cloak and such signs. *I shall visit*, he says, in order to see whether they are good or false pilgrims, as there are some vagabonds who pretend to be pilgrims but are not. Because of this one says in the vernacular: 'God knows who is a good pilgrim.'

4 Then there is a pilgrimage of outstanding excellence, namely the one of the crusaders, which surpasses other Christian pilgrimages in many ways. Other [pilgrimages] take place because of some saint, but this one because of the saint of saints, namely Christ, especially.

5 Thus on the other [pilgrimages] people expose themselves to hardship, but on this one they expose themselves to death, and this in many instances. Thus on other [pilgrimages] people quickly return to their home and fatherland, but on this one they go far for a long pilgrimage. Thus by this [pilgrimage] the common good of Christendom is assisted, by other ones only personal well-being. Thus other pilgrims are not given an indulgence, but these ones are given a plenary indulgence of their sins. Thus in these [pilgrims] the example of Christ, who went to Calvary carrying his own cross, shines forth clearly. Thus these [pilgrims] who follow Christ carry his cross, which others do not do, as they carry other pilgrimage signs.

6 It must be noted that just as this pilgrimage is of greater standing, these pilgrims must also take greater care to carry it out as they should and in a dignified manner. Above all they must perform it in a sacred manner, so as to fulfil in their journey what is said in Isaiah 35: *It shall be called a sacred journey*; also [it should be performed] joyfully, [as it says in] Psalms: *Your judgements were my songs in the place of my pilgrimage*; and [also] this: *And they will sing on the journeys of the Lord, because the Lord's glory is great*. And it is noted in these two [passages] that there are two [kinds of] joy, one of which originates in the present [time of] grace, as it says: *Judgements*, the other in the future [time of] glory, as it says: *Because the Lord's glory is great*. Also [this pilgrimage should be performed] with perseverance, so that [the pilgrims] do not out of fickleness, adversity or other reasons withdraw from what they have begun until they have completed it, because: *Woe to those who stray from the right paths*, as it says in Ecclesiasticus 2. Job 17: *The just will keep to his path*.

ab incepto quousque compleverint, quia: *Ve illis qui dereliquerunt vias rectas*, sicut dicitur Ecc[us]. ii [16]. Iob xvii [9]: *Tenebit iustus viam suam.*

7 Materia de predictis. Thema: He[b]. ultimo [xiii, 13–14]: *Exeamus ad Christum extra castra improperium*, scilicet crucem, *eius portantes; non enim habemus hic manentem civitatem, sed futuram inquirimus.* Notandum quod hoc verbum impletur in peregrinis crucesignatis. Ad pleniorem autem intelligentiam [f. 136r] eorum, que ad eos[7] pertinet, notandum est quod quedam est peregrinatio generalis etc. ut supra.

---

[7] que ad eos F, S] quod ad eos Re, *om.* A

7 Subject matter for the above. Theme: The last chapter of Hebrews: *Let us go to Christ outside the camp carrying his shame*, meaning the cross; *we have no permanent city here, but we are looking for the future one*. It must be noted that this word is fulfilled in the crusader pilgrims. For a better knowledge of what pertains to them, it must be noted that there is a general pilgrimage etc. as above.

Humbert of Romans

SERMO II

A = Avignon, Bibliothèque Municipale, Musée Calvet, 327, ff. 217v-219r

Additional manuscripts
F = Frankfurt a. M., Stadt- und Universitätsbibliothek, Praed. 29, ff. 66rb-67ra
Re = Reims, Bibliothèque Municipale, 612, ff. 70va-71ra
S = Segovia, Catedral, Estanceria B 331, ff. 131ra-rb

De predicatione crucis in genere quocumque

1 [f. 218r] Notandum quod sicut reges in magnis negotiis guerrarum insurgentium solent congregare militiam magnam et aperire thesauros suos ad dandum larga donaria, ita Rex Glorie per vicarium suum in terris pro negotiis fidei et ei annexis, que sunt maiora negotia que possint esse in ecclesia, congregat fideles suos ad militandum contra infideles et eorum fautores et de thesauris suis profert largissima dona indulgentiarum ad elargiendum istis[1] militaturis.

2 Et ideo talibus datur signum crucis in signum quod pro fide Crucifixi[2] assumunt huiusmodi certamen, et in signum quod sint milites Crucifixi eius signum portantes, et in signum quod larga indulgentia, que datur eis, tota assumitur de thesauro passionis Christi in cruce complete. Sunt ergo tria, que debent movere ad huiusmodi crucem sumendam, scilicet zelus fidei et fidelitas ad Deum, verum universorum dominum, et largitas indulgentiarum.

---

[1] istis F, Re, S] suis A   [2] Crucifixi A, F, S] Christi Re

Humbert of Romans

SERMON II

About the preaching of the cross of whatever kind

1 It must be noted that, as kings usually gather a large force in great matters of impending war and open their treasures to give large gifts, so in the matters of faith and that which pertains to it, which are the major matters within the church, the King of Glory gathers his faithful through his vicar on earth to fight against the infidels and their supporters and offers a very large gift of indulgences from his treasures to bestow on those who will fight.

2 And so such people are given the sign of the cross as a sign that they take up this war for the faith of the Crucified, and as a sign that they are soldiers of the Crucified carrying his sign, and as a sign that the large indulgence which is granted them is taken entirely from the treasure of Christ's passion, which was filled up on the cross. Thus there are three [reasons] which should cause [people] to take the cross, namely the zeal for the faith and faithfulness to God, the true lord of all, and the generosity of the indulgences.

3 Circa primum notandum quod nichil est in terris ita magnum sicut fides. Unde Augustinus de verbis Domini: 'Nulle maiores divitie, nulli thesauri, nulli honores, nulla huius mundi[3] maior substantia quam fides catholica, que peccatores homines salvat, cecos illuminat, infirmos curat, cathecuminos baptizat, fideles iustificat, penitentes reparat,[4] iustos augmentat et martires coronat.'

4 Item infideles pro sua fide, immo pro[5] infidelitate, ita zelant quod se tradunt igni et mortibus acerbis pro ea, ut patet in hereticis. Ita etiam zelant quod semper impugnant alios pro sua fide dilatanda, ut patet in Sarracenis. Item sancti tam Veteris Testamenti, ut patet in Machabeis, quam Novi, ut patet in apostolis et martiribus, mirabilia passi sunt pro zelo fidei, de quo loquitur Apostolus, He[b]. xi.[6]

5 Cum ergo homines interdum zelent in immensum pro re modica temporali, et infideles pro sua fide perversa, et sanci tot et tanta exempla zelandi pro fide nobis reliquerint, quantum debent zelare fideles pro sua fide, que est res tam pretiosa et fides tam verissima exemplo sanctorum precedentium!

6 Circa secundum notandum quod inter dominos terrenos et Dominum[7] Deum multa est differentia. A dominis enim terrenis tenentur res temporales, a Deo vero tenetur ipsum corpus. Unde ii[8] Ma. vii [11] unus de septem fratribus [f. 218v] positus in agone martirii respiciens membra sua dixit: *E celo ista possideo.* Item propter culpam dominorum terrenorum homines eorum frequenter male tractantur. Hic vero accidit e contario, Tre. iiii [20]: *Christus Dominus captus est in peccatis nostris*, id est pro peccatis nostris. Item domini terreni fideles suos pro se decertantes interdum aut parum aut in nullo remunerant. Dominus vero Deus non sic, immo promittit septem valde magnas promissiones, Apo. ii et iii, fideliter pro se decertantibus.

7 Si ergo homines propter fidelitatem servandam domino terreno, a quo non habent nisi temporalia et pro quo frequenter multa mala sustinent et a quo modicam vel nullam remunerationem expectant, sic pugnant viriliter, quanto magis debent[9] hoc pro Domino celesti facere, a quo

---

[3] huius mundi] huiusmodi A, F, Re, *om.* S   [4] reparat F, Re, S] revocat A
[5] pro F, Re, S] *om.* A   [6] xi F, Re, S] ix A
[7] Dominum F, Re, S] verum A   [8] ii] i A, *om.* F, Re, S
[9] debent F, Re, S] *om.* A

3 About the first it must be noted that there is nothing in the world as great as faith. Hence Augustine about the words of the Lord: '[There are] no greater riches or treasures or honours, no substance of this world greater than the catholic faith, which brings salvation to sinners, makes the blind see, heals the sick, gives baptism to catechumens and justification to the faithful, restores penitents, strengthens the just and crowns martyrs.'[1]

4 Thus the infidels burn with such zeal for their faith, even though it is faithlessness, that they commit themselves to fire and bitter death for it, as is evident with the heretics. They also burn with such zeal that they always fight against others to spread their faith, as is evident with the Saracens. Thus the saints of the Old Testament, as is evident with the Maccabees, as well as the New Testament, as is evident with the apostles and martyrs, took upon themselves extraordinary suffering for their faith, about which the Apostle talks in Hebrews 11.

5 Since at times people burn with enormous zeal for a small temporal matter, and the infidels for their perverted faith, and since the saints left us so many great examples of fighting for the faith, how much more should the faithful fight for their faith, which is such a precious thing and such a true faith, according to the example of past saints!

6 About the second it must be noted that there is a great difference between wordly lords and the Lord God. From worldly lords temporal things are held, but from God the body itself is held. Whence in 2 Maccabees 7 one of the seven brothers in the agony of martyrdom said about his limbs: *I have these from heaven.* Thus people are often treated badly because of their worldly lord's fault. Here it happens the other way around, Lamentations 4: *Christ the Lord was captured in our sins*, that is for our sins. Thus worldly lords sometimes reward their followers who fight for them with little or nothing. But not the Lord God: he makes seven very large promises, [in] Apocalypse 2 and 3, to those who fight for him faithfully.

7 So if people fight manfully to keep the faith to a worldly lord, from whom they only hold temporal things and for whom they often suffer much evil and from whom they expect little or no reward, how much more should they do this for the heavenly Lord, from whom they hold

---

[1] Augustinus , 'Sermones dubii', *PL*, XXXIX, cols. 1639–720, here col. 1690.

habent corpus et animam et qui tot pro eis passus est et tam gloriose remunerat pugnantes[10] pro se!

8 Circa tertium notandum quod sunt quedam terre que habent aquarum penuriam, ut Egiptus, et ideo Egiptii, quando excrescit Nilus et est aquarum habundatia, cum magna cura satagunt implere cisternas suas aqua. Item, quando fit alia dona, quanto maior est tanto pauperes plures tunc ardentius currunt ad eam. Item, quando magnus aliquis est in statu benigno, tanto indigentes gratia accedunt tunc ad eum pro gratia obtinenda.

9 Porro tempore crucis predicante cataracte celi aperte sunt in habundantia indulgentiarum, sancta mater ecclesia manus suas aperit et palmas suas extendit ad pauperes. In eodem annus benignitatis divine et iubileus Christianorum, quo non debita denariorum sed peccatorum relaxantur, instat. Verum finitur cito ista pluvia et cito cessabit ista dona et cito transibit ista benignitas, et ideo ve illis, qui non currunt[11] ad istas indulgentias largas!

10 Conclusio: Ecce, karissimi, sancta mater ecclesia auctoritate divina suffulta movet bellum contra tales propter tales et tales causas[12] fidei. Moveat vos zelus fidei, moveat vos fidelitas quam debetis Domino, cuius est bellum,[13] moveat vos et largitas indulgentiarum, que datur crucem sumentibus, et venite ad beatum istud signum sumendum!

11 Cantus. Materia de predictis. Thema. [i] Thi. vi [12]: *Certa bonum certamen fidei, apprehende vitam eternam!* Notandum quod sunt quidam inertie dediti, qui semper quiescunt et numquam decertant. Alii vero sunt qui [f. 219r] decertant interdum, sed malo certamine. Et hii omnes tendunt ad mortem eternam. Alii vero sunt qui pugnant optimo certamine, scilicet fidei, et sic tendunt ad vitam eternam, ut hic dicitur. Notandum autem quod sicut reges etc. ut supra.

---

10 pugnantes F, Re, S] pugnant A   11 currunt] *add.* modo F, Re, S
12 causas F, Re, S] causa A
13 moveat vos . . . est bellum F, S]

their body and soul and who has suffered so greatly for them and rewards those who fight for him so gloriously!

8 About the third it must be noted that there are lands which have a shortage of water, like Egypt, and thus the Egyptians take great care to fill their cisterns with water when the Nile grows and there is an abundance of water. Thus, if there is some other kind of gift [on offer], the bigger it is the more eagerly more poor people come rushing for it. Thus, the more generous someone is, the more those who lack favour come to him in order to obtain favour.

9 During the time when the cross is preached the flood-gates of heaven stand open for an abundance of indulgences, mother church opens her arms and extends her hands to the poor. At the same [time], it is a year of divine generosity and a jubilee for the Christians, in which not the debt of money but that of sins is cancelled. But these rains will stop quickly and these gifts will cease quickly and this generosity will pass quickly, so woe to them who do not hasten towards these great indulgences!

10 Conclusion: See, my dearest people, the holy mother church supported by divine authority goes to war against such [and such] people because of such and such matters of the faith. May the zeal of faith move you, may the faithfulness which you owe to the Lord, whose war it is, move you and may the greatness of the indulgences which is given to those who take the cross move you; come and take this holy sign.

11 Chant. Subject matter for the above. Theme: [1] Timothy 6: *Fight the good war of the faith, win eternal life!* It must be noted that there are people given to idleness, who always rest and never fight. There are others who fight sometimes, but in a bad war. All those strive towards eternal death. But there are others who fight in the best war, namely that of the faith, and they thus strive towards eternal life, as it says here. It must be noted that, as kings etc. as above.

Humbert of Romans

SERMO III

A = Avignon, Bibliothèque Municipale, Musée Calvet 327, ff. 219r-220r

Additional manuscripts
F = Frankfurt a. M., Stadt- und Universitätsbibliothek, Praed. 29, ff. 67ra-67va
Re = Reims, Bibliothèque Municipale, 612, ff. 71ra-rb
S = Segovia, Catedral, Estanceria B 331, ff. 131rb-132ra

In predicatione crucis contra hereticos

1 Notandum quod inter omnia genera peccatorum heresis quaod multa est peior. Alia enim peccata multa non habent obstinationem, sed heresis habet hoc, quia secundum Augustinum error non facit hereticum sed obstinatio. Unde dicit: 'Errare potero, hereticus non ero.'
2 Preterea multa sunt alia peccata, que remanent in solo subiecto. Istud vero transit in alios, quia est infectivum. Propter quod significatur multotiens in scriptura per lepram. Beda: 'Leprosi non absurde intelligi possunt, qui vere fidei scientiam non habentes varias doctrinas profitentur errorum.'
3 Preterea multa sunt alia peccata, que non cooperiunt se, unde et illa perpetrantes bene recognoscunt se male facere. Istud vero se cooperit sub similitudine[1] boni, unde nullus hereticus dicit se male credere sed bene. Et ideo dicitur de hereticis Mt. vii [15]: *Veniunt ad vos in vestimentis ovium, intrinsecus autem sunt lupi rapaces.*

4 Iterum notandum quod inter omnia peccata hoc est valde nocivum.

---

[1] similitudine A, F, S] simulatione Re

222

Humbert of Romans

SERMON III

For the preaching of the cross against heretics

1 It must be noted that amongst all kinds of sins heresy is by far the worst. Many other sins do not involve obstinacy, but heresy does, because according to Augustine it is not the error that makes a heretic but his obstinacy. Whence he says: 'I will be able to err, but I will not be a heretic.'[1]

2 In addition, many other sins only concern one individual. This one, however, passes to other people since it is infectious. Because of this it is often referred to in the scriptures as leprosy. Bede: 'Lepers cannot be judged harshly, who without having the real knowledge of the faith confess to various doctrines of errors.'[2]

3 In addition, there are many other sins that do not cover themselves up, so that those who perpetrate them know full well that they do evil. But this one covers itself up under the guise of good, thence no heretic says that he thinks of himself as bad, but good. And so it is said about heretics in Matthew 7: *They come to you disguised as sheep, but underneath they are ravenous wolves.*

4 It must also be noted that among all sins this one is particularly

---

[1] I have not been able to identify this reference.
[2] Beda Venerabilis, 'In Lucae Euangelium Expositio', *CCSL*, CXX, 5–425, here p. 312.

Alia enim peccata nocent vel soli committenti illa[2] vel paucis aliis, istud vero intendit destruere totam ecclesiam. Propter quod signantur heretici, Iud. xv [4], per vulpes Sampsonis que caudas habebant colligatas, sed facies diversas, quia heretici, licet in se sint divisi, tamen omnes sunt alligati in intentione destruendi ecclesiam.

5 Preterea ipsi vias descendendi ad infernum multiplicant, dum novas adveniunt sectas errorum, per quas[3] illuc descenditur. ii Pe. ii [1]: *Erunt in vobis magistri mendaces, qui introducent hereses perditionis.*

6 Preterea ipsi gradientes per viam bonam fidei ad celum divertunt, sicut latrones divertunt peregrinos de via bona sub spe melioris vie. Et ideo dicitur de eis ii[4] Io. [7]: *Multi seductores exierunt in mundum.* Que est enim maior seductio quam sic bene ambulantes divertere? Ecce gravia nocumenta conari destruere totam [f. 219v] ecclesiam, facere novas vias ad infernum, divertere homines a via celi recta.

7 Iterum notandum quod ecclesia utitur multis remediis contra hereticos. Utitur enim doctrina predicando, disputando, conferendo. Sed hoc non prodest apud multos, quia ipsi perverse exponunt auctoritates et[5] magis credunt sensui suo, licet pauci sint et idiote, quam omni multitudini sanctorum et magistrorum sapientum qui fuerunt et sunt in ecclesia.

8 Item utitur remedio excommunicationis, quia heretici ipso facto sunt excommunicati. Sed ipsi de hoc non curant, quia non reputant quod prelati ecclesie habeant huiusmodi potestatem.

9 Item utitur penis contra eos, ubi habet[6] potestatem. Nam puniuntur quoad honores per depositionem, quoad temporalia per confiscationem, quoad corpus per carceres,[7] modo per mortem, cum relinquuntur curie seculari.

10 Sed contra hec interdum se defendunt per potentiam secularem, quam in se vel in suis fautoribus habent; et tunc, quando alia remedia minora non proficiunt, utitur ecclesia contra eos persecutione militari, sicut sapiens medicus ferro utitur ad prescindendum membrum putridum corruptivum aliorum, quando remedia leviora non prosunt. Melius est enim membrum ferro vel igne destrui, quam sana membra corrumpi.

---

[2] illa F, Re, S] illis A   [3] quas Re, S] quos, A, F
[4] ii] iii A, *om.* F, Re, S   [5] et F, Re, S] *om.* A
[6] habet A, F, S] habent Re   [7] carceres S] caracteres A, F, Re

harmful. Other sins do harm to the one who commits them or to a few others, but this one aims to destroy the whole church. Because of this the heretics are signified in Judges 15 by the foxes of Samson whose tails were tied together but whose faces were turned away from each other, because the heretics are united in their intention to destroy the church, although they are divided amongst themselves.

5 In addition, they multiply the ways for descending into hell, since they invent new sects of errors through which one descends there. 2 Peter 2: *There will be false teachers among you who introduce heresies of perdition.*

6 In addition, they will divert those who walk to heaven on the right path of faith, as thieves divert pilgrims from the right path in the hope of a better path. And thus it is said about these in 2 John: *Many deceivers will come into the world.* What is a greater deception than to divert those who are on the right path? Thus, trying to destroy the whole church, to make new ways to hell, to divert people from the right path to heaven [causes] great harm.

7 It must also be noted that the church uses many remedies against heretics. She uses doctrine through preaching, disputing and discussing. But with many this does not help because they quote perverse authorities and rather believe in their [own] judgements, although they are few and foolish, than in the whole multitude of the saints and wise masters who were and are in the church.

8 She also uses the remedy of excommunication because all heretics are automatically excommunicated. But they do not care about this, because they deny that the prelates of the church have this power.

9 She also uses punishments against them where she has power. Thus they are punished by deposition with regard to honours, by confiscation with regard to temporal belongings, with incarceration with regard to the body, and sometimes by death, when they are handed over to the secular court.

10 But they sometimes defend themselves against this by the secular power that they themselves or their supporters hold; and then, when other minor remedies do not work, the church uses against them armed persecution, just as a wise physician uses a blade to cut off a putrid limb which infects other parts, when lighter remedies do not work. It is better to let a limb be destroyed with a blade or with fire than to let the healthy parts be infected.

11 Et nota quod secundum legem veterem tria sunt genera hominum, qui digni sunt morte. Unum est blasphemi.[8] Le. xxiiii [16]: *Qui blasphemaverit nomen Domini moriatur morte.* Aliud est delinquentes in rem publicam. Exo. xxii [18]: *Maleficos non patieris vivere.* Isti enim vocantur malefici, qui alios ledunt. Aliud est phitonici, qui scilicet habent phitonem in ventre, Le. xx[9] [27]: *Vir sive mulier, in quibus phitonicus vel divinationis fuerit spiritus, morte morietur.*

12 Cum ergo heretici sint summe blasphemi, quia multa inconvenientia dicunt de Deo, et[10] summe noceant rei publice, scilicet ecclesia, ut preostensum est, et spiritum divinationis vel malum habeant, quo actore proculdubio multa divinant et sompniant de scripturis, quid faciendum est de eis in nova lege, in qua debet pro fide et omni veritate et ho- [f. 220r] nestate zelari magis?

13 Conclusio: Ecce videtis, karissimi, quanta est malitia hereticorum, videtis etiam quantum nocent in mundo, videtis iterum quam pie et modis multis piis laborat ecclesia eos revocare. Sed apud tales et tales nichil ista potuerunt proficere, immo per potentiam secularem se defendunt, et ideo sancta mater ecclesia, licet invita et cum dolore, contra eos convocat exercitum Christianum.

14 Quicumque ergo habet zelum fidei, quicumque diligit bonum commune Christianitatis, quicumque est quem tangit honor divinus, quicumque est qui vult habere istam magnam indulgentiam, veniat et accipiens signum crucis adiungat se militie Crucifixi![11]

15 Materia de predictis. Thema in Ps. [cf. v, 6–7]: Quis[12] consurget michi adversus malignantes aut quis stabit mecum adversus *operantes iniquitatem*? Et nota quod istud olim dictum a David rege modo dicitur a nostro David Ihesu Christo. Heretici siquidem sunt malignantes illi, de quibus dicitur [Ps. xxv, 5]: *Odivi ecclesiam malignantium.* Operantes autem *iniquitatem* sunt eorum credentes, qui in spe venie facilis, quam eis promittunt heresiarche, exponunt se audacter omni iniquitati. Notandum autem quod inter omnia genera etc. ut supra.

---

8 blasphemi F, Re] blasphemia A, S   9 xx F, S] xix A, xxvii Re
10 et F, Re, S] *om.* A   11 Crucifixi A, F, S] Christi Re
12 quis F, S] qui A, Re

11 And note that according to the old law there are three kinds of people who deserve death. One kind are blasphemers, Leviticus 24: *He who blasphemes the name of the Lord will be put to death.* Another kind are those who commit a crime against the community, Exodus 22: *Do not suffer the evil-doer to live.* They are called evil-doers who do harm to others. Another kind are the sorcerers, who so to speak have a snake in their stomach, Leviticus 20: *Any man or woman in whom there is a spirit of the sorcerer or of divination shall be put to death.*

12 Since heretics are the worst blasphemers, because they say many unfitting things about God, and since they do very great damage to the community, that is the church, as has been shown, and since they have the spirit of divination or evil, with the help of which they no doubt divine many things and dream up things about the scriptures, what then must be done about them under the new law, in which one must display even more zeal for the faith and all truth and honesty?

13 Conclusion: Now you see, my dearest people, how great the evil of the heretics is, you see how much damage they cause in the world [and] you see how the church piously strives to call them back, employing many pious means. But with such and such none of these could achieve anything, since they defend themselves with the secular power, and thus the holy mother church, though against her will and with pain, calls the Christian army against them.

14 Everybody who has zeal for the faith, who loves the common good of Christianity, who bothers about divine honour, who wants to have this great indulgence, shall come and take the sign of the cross and join the militia of the Crucified!

15 Subject matter for the above. Theme in Psalms: Who will stand up with me against the wicked or who will stand with me against the *evil-doers*? Note that this which was once said by King David is now said by our David, Jesus Christ. Heretics are indeed the wicked people about whom it says: *I hated the church of the wicked. The evil-doers* are their believers, who in the hope of easy forgiveness, which the heresiarchs promise them, boldly expose themselves to all wicked things. It must be noted that among all kinds etc. as above.

Humbert of Romans

SERMO IV

A = Avignon, Bibliothèque Municipale, Musée Calvet 327, f. 220r

Additional manuscripts
F = Frankfurt a. M., Stadt- und Universitätsbibliothek, Praed. 29, f. 67va
Re = Reims, Bibliothèque Municipale, 612, ff. 71rb-va
S = Segovia, Catedral, Estanceria B 331, f. 132ra

In predicatione crucis contra Sarracenos

1 Notandum quod ad sumendum crucem contra Sarracenos sunt sex que
debent movere: primum est zelus honoris divini, secundum est zelus
Christiane legis, tertium est fraterna caritas, quartum est devotio ad
Terram Sanctam, quintum est exempla precedentium, sextum conditio
belli.

2 Materia de predictis. Thema: Ysa. vi [3]: *Sanctus, sanctus, sanctus
Dominus Deus exercituum.* Require in opusculo 'De predicatione crucis
contra Sarracenos'.[1]

---

[1] require . . . Sarracenos A, F, Re] *om.* S

Humbert of Romans

SERMON IV

For the preaching of the cross against the Saracens

1 It must be noted that there are six [reasons] which should cause [people] to take the cross against the Saracens: the first is zeal for divine honour, the second is zeal for the Christian law, the third is brotherly love, the fourth is devotion to the Holy Land, the fifth is the example of those who went before, the sixth is the status of this war.

2 Subject matter for the above. Theme: Isaiah 6: *Holy, holy, holy is the Lord God of hosts.* See the work 'About the Preaching of the Cross against the Saracens'.[1]

---

[1] Humbertus de Romanis, *De Predicatione Sancte Crucis.*

Bertrand de la Tour

SERMO I

B = Barcelona, Archivo de la Corona de Aragon, Ripoll 187, ff. 82ra-va

Additional manuscripts
N = Naples, Biblioteca Nazionale, VIII.A.36, ff. 116ra-va
T2= Troyes, Bibliothèque Municipale, 2001, ff. 19va-20rb
V2= Vatican, Biblioteca Apostolica, Archivio Capitolare di S. Pietro, G.48, ff. 24va-25ra

Reference
Schneyer I, 572, no. 979; VII, 147, no. 56 and 453, no. 3; IX, 823, no. 55

Si euntibus ad bellum vel pugnam vel accipientibus crucem contra infideles.[1]

1 *Non timebis eos, quoniam Dominus Deus tuus tecum est*, Deut. xx[2] [1]. Quia varius est eventus belli, ut dicitur ii Rg., occurit etiam quam sepe robustus adversarius, sed obest maxime[3] bellantis pavens animus. Que tria, quia solent accidere plerumque non inmerito, administrant[4] materiam formidandi; ad que resecanda de cordibus pu-[f. 82rb] gnatorum totum exercitum propheta alloquitur[5] dicens: *Non enim* etc., ubi repellit pavorem ignavie,[6] contempnit timorem[7] superbie, ostendit datorem[8] victorie.

---

[1] si . . . infideles B] si euntibus ad bellum et accipientibus crucem V2, *om.* N, T2
[2] xx N, T2, V2] ii B   [3] maxime B] quam maxime N, V2, quam plurrimum T2
[4] administrant N, T2, V2] administrat B   [5] alloquitur] *add.* in voce Dei T2
[6] ignavie B, N, T2] ignorantie V2   [7] timorem B] tumorem N, T2, V2
[8] datorem B, T2, V2] actorem N

Bertrand de la Tour

SERMON I

If [you preach] to those going to war or into battle or those taking the cross against the infidels.

1 *You will not be afraid of them, because the Lord your God is with you*, Deuteronomy 20. Because the outcome of war is variable, as it says in 2 Kings, often a strong enemy attacks, but the greatest obstacle is the timid spirit of the fighter. These three things, since they usually do not happen undeservedly, provide the cause of fear; in order to cut them out of the hearts of the fighters, the prophet addressed the whole army by saying: *You will not* etc., with which he drove away the timidity of cowardice, scorned the fear of pride, and showed the giver of victory.

2 Quia pavor cordis[9] a nobis est elongandus, ait: *Non timebis.*[10] Ad pugnandum requiritur fervor audacie, vigor potentie,[11] rigor constantie. Hec tria dissipat timor: extinguit enim fervorem et ex hoc fit pugnans tepidus, disolvit vigorem et ex hoc fit pugnans languidus, prescidit rigorem et ex hoc fit pugnans marcidus. Deponenda enim sunt hec tanquam contraria probitati,[12] unde ibi subiungitur [Dt. xx, 3]: *Vos hodie pugnabitis contra inimicos vestros; non pertimescat cor vestrum.*

3 Quia timor hostium non[13] est a vobis formidandus[14] [cf. Dt. xx, 4], ait: *Eos.* In hoc pronomine sunt tres[15] littere,[16] per quas casus hostium figuratur. Erunt hodie hostes[17] vestri, favente Domino, sine discretione ideo dispositi ad moriendum, quod habet per 'e', que est littera clausa post et ante aperta: stultus enim est pugnans qui tergum munit et pectus immune[18] relinquit;[19] sine[20] impugnatione quia dispositi ad fugiendum, quod habetur per 'o', que est littera sperica[21] et ad motum apta: plus enim in pedibus quam in lacertis[22] confidunt; sine[23] rebellione[24] dispositi ad obediendum quod habetur per 's', que est littera huius caput depressum: humiliabuntur enim hostes[25] coram vobis; unde est hec littera que a vocali incipit et sine voce finitur.[26] Ideo ibi subiungitur [Dt. xx, 3]: *Non timeatis neque*[27] *formidetis eos.* Sap. iiii [19]: disperdet eos[28] *sine voce.*

---

[9] cordis B] cordium N, T2, V2   [10] non timebis N, T2, V2] nonne B

[11] potentie B, N, T2] persone V2

[12] contraria probitati B, T2, V2] bellanti contraria N   [13] non B] *om.* N, T2, V2

[14] formidandus B] superandus N, T2, V2   [15] sunt tres V2] *transp.* N, T2, sunt B

[16] littere] due vocales et una semivocalis *add.* T2   [17] hostes B, T2, V2] inimici N

[18] immune B] nudum T2, inherme N, V2

[19] relinquit] ideo hec littera unum habet oculum *add.* T2

[20] sine] erunt *praem.* N, T2, V2, *add.* vestra T2, vestri N, V2

[21] que . . . sperica B, N, V2] *om.* T2

[22] lacertis B, V2] lanceis N, in armis hostes vestri T2

[23] sine] erunt *praem.* N, T2, V2, vestri *add.* V2

[24] rebellione B, T2, V2] bellatione N, ideo *add.* N, T2, V2

[25] humiliabuntur enim hostes B] humiliabuntur enim hostes demisso capite N, hostes enim vestri demisso capiti humiliabuntur T2, humiliabuntur enim hostes capiti demisso V2

[26] finitur B] desinit seu finit N, finit T2, V2

[27] non timeatis neque B] nolite credere neque N, nolite metuere et nolite cedere neque T2, nolite cedere ne V2

[28] disperdet eos] disrumpet eos inflatos N, dissipet eos inflatos T2, disperdet et eos V2

2 Because the timidity of the heart must be kept away from us, it says: *You will not be afraid.* In order to fight, one requires the fervour of courage, the vigour of power, the rigour of firmness. Fear destroys these three: it extinguishes fervour and this makes the fighter lukewarm, it dissolves vigour and this makes the fighter feeble, and it destroys rigour which makes the fighter weak. These must be got rid of as [they are] opposed to uprightness, whence it follows in this passage: *Today you will fight against your enemies; do not be faint-hearted.*

3 Because you must not be afraid of the fear of the enemies, it says: *Them.* In this pronoun there are three letters which symbolise the fall of the enemies. With the Lord's consent, today your enemies will be without prudence, apt to die, which is signified by 'e', which is a letter closed in front and open in the back; thus a fighter who protects his back and leaves his breast unprotected is stupid. [They will be] without resistance because they are apt to flee, indicated by 'o', which is a round letter and can move; thus they rather trust their feet than the strength of their arms. [They will be] without rebellion apt to obey, indicated by 's', which is a letter whose head is bent down; thus your enemies will be humiliated in front of you; whence this letter begins with a vowel and ends voiceless. Thus it is added in this passage: *Do not be afraid of them nor fear them.* Wisdom 4: *He* will ruin them *without voice.*

4 Quia actor fortunii[29] est in nobis,[30] ait: *Dominus tecum est; tecum*[31] ut ductor qui debet ducere,[32] ultor qui debet affligere,[33] tutor qui debet reducere. Iud. vi [16]: *Ego ero tecum, percutietisque Madian quasi* [f. 82va] *virum unum*. Ideo habendus est iste Dominus maxime tempore belli.[34]

5 Fertur quod erat quoddam parve potente castrum, contra quod potentissima civitas ivit.[35] Illi timentes[36] dixerunt: Quid faciemus, quia nec unus remanebit ex nobis?[37] Eratque inter eos vir prudens, et dixit: Habeamus Deum nobiscum et prevalebimus. Quomodo, inquirunt,[38] habere poterimus? Ibo, inquid, ad illos et loquar in humilitate Domini. Et cum eivisset,[39] optulit pacem et quod haberent eos quasi servos; qui audire contempserunt.[40] Reversus autem ad suos ait: Confidite, quia Dominus nobiscum est! Et veniunt[41] ad certamen in nomine Domini et superata est a paucioribus multitudo.[42]

---

[29] fortunii B] fortium N, fortuni T2, fortius V2

[30] in nobis] a nobis est imitandus N, in vobis nudandusT2, in nobis iuvandus V2

[31] tecum B] *om.* N, T2, V2   [32] ducere B] educere N, T2, V2

[33] affligere B] confligere N, T2, V2

[34] Iud. . . . belli B, V2] ad hunc habendum debetis conari T2

[35] ivit B, N, V2] processit T2   [36] illi timentes B, N, V2] pauci ante timidi T2

[37] remanebit ex nobis B] resondebit ad centum N, T2, respondet ad centum V2

[38] inquirunt B, T2, V2] inqunt N   [39] eivisset B] exisset T2, exivisset N, V2

[40] audire contempserunt B, N] noluerunt eum audire T2, audientes contempserunt V2

[41] et veniunt B] et venientibus illi T2, venerunt ergo N, V2

[42] multitudo] Sic pugnat aliquando Dominus pro suis *add.* N, Hinc Iud. vi [16]: *Ego ergo tecum percutietisque Madian quasi vir unum*. Petendus est et habendus Dominus in tempore belli. Legitur in Historia Romanorum quod, cum Eugenius et Arbogastes cum instructa acie militum Alpium transitus retinuissent contra Theodosium imperatorem, Theodosius expers cibi et sompni omnino incumbens tota nocte pervigil extitit, cum tantum se a suis destitutum sciret et ab hostibus circumsceptum nesciret. Fiducialiter tamen mane arma arripiens signum crucis prelio dedit sicque se in bellum, ac si eum sui sequerentur, immisit. Et ecce veniens turba a parte Theodosii in hostium aciem ruit et missa ab hostibus spicula valenter in eos refixit. Et sic hostilis exercitus prostratus est ibique Eugenius inaptus atque intersectus est armorum vero sua propria manu percussus, per quem patet quod homo non pugnavit sed Deus. Ordinate his sicut materia requirit. *add.* T2

4 Because the maker of our fortune is in us, it says: *The Lord is with you*; *with you* like a leader who must lead, an avenger who must do injury, a protector who must lead home. Judges 6: *I shall be with you, and you will crush Midian as though it were one man*. Therefore this Lord must be held on to in particular in time of war.

5 The story goes that there was some weak town, which a very powerful city attacked. The people there were afraid and said: What shall we do, since none of us will be spared? Among them there was a prudent man who said: Let us have God with us and we shall prevail. How can we have [him with us]?, they asked. I shall go to them, he said, and speak with the humility of the Lord. And when he went out, he offered them peace and that they could have them as slaves; [but] they refused to hear [him]. Having returned to his people he said: Have faith, because the Lord is with us! And they went into battle in the name of the Lord and the many were beaten by the few.[1]

---

[1] I have not been able to trace the source of this story.

Bertrand de la Tour

SERMO II

B = Barcelona, Archivo de la Corona de Aragon, Ripoll 187, ff. 82va-83ra

Additional manuscripts
N = Naples, Biblioteca Nazionale, VIII.A.36, ff. 116va-vb
T2 = Troyes, Bibliothèque Municipale, 2001, ff. 20va-21rb
V2 = Vatican, Biblioteca Apostolica, Archivio Capitolare di S. Pietro, G.48, ff. 25ra-va

Reference
Schneyer I, 572, no. 980; VII, 147, no. 57 and 453, no. 4; IX, 823, no. 56

De eodem[1]

1 *Non est vestra[2] pugna sed Domini*, ii Pal. xx[3] [15]. Quia secundum leges civiles[4] licitum est pro patria pugnare[5] et pro servitute vitanda,[6] quorum pugna, et si aliquo modo posset Dei dici, potius tamen est hominum quam Dei. Lex enim evangelica credere iubet istis. Sed ubi cadit status ecclesie ibi[7] perit[8] cultus divine latrie, et ubi movet zelus iustitie, ibi puto pugnam Dei fore, quia ibi agitur eius principale negotium et causa.[9] Cum[10] ergo

---

[1] de eodem B, V2] *om.* N, T2   [2] vestra B] nostra N, T2, V2
[3] xx] xiv B, xix N, T2, V2   [4] civiles B, N, V2] militibus T2
[5] pro patria pugnare B] pugnare pro patria N, T2, V2, pro re propria *add.* N, T2
[6] vitanda] pro re propria *add.* V2   [7] ibi B] et ubi N, ubi T2, V2
[8] perit B, T2, V2] perditur N
[9] quia ibi . . . causa B, V2] quia agitur principalis ibi Dei negotium et causa N, non enim nostrum negotium tunc sed suum agitur T2
[10] cum N, T2, V2] causa B

Bertrand de la Tour

SERMON II

About the same

1 *It is not your war, but the Lord's*, 2 Chronicles 20. Because according to civil law one is allowed to fight for the fatherland and in order to avoid servitude, such a fight, even if it can somehow be called God's [fight], is still that of men rather than God. The law of the gospels demands to believe in it. But where the stature of the church collapses, there the cult of divine worship perishes, and where the zeal for justice is at work, there I think it will be God's fight, because there his principal business and cause is pursued. Because in this time these evils are

hec mala in presenti pateant, debemus nos arma sumere.[11] Sed suum est pugnare ait sacra scriptura: *Non est vestra*[12] *pugna* etc., ubi proponitur campus certaminis, apponitur[13] manus iuvaminis,[14] ostenditur[15] modus conanimis.

2 Quia ergo patet campus ad congrediendum[16] viriliter, ait: *Pugna*, in qua debet homo agere sapienter ne circumveniatur, confidenter ne commoveatur, potenter ne deiciatur. Perniciosum est enim pugnare sine bono consilio, presumptuosum sine Dei auxiilio [f. 82vb], periculosum sine forti brachio. Valet enim sapientia contra primum, confidentia contra secundum, perseverantia contra tertium. Deut. xx [3]: *Vos ergo*[17] *contra inimicos vestros pugnam committitis, nec pertimescet*[18] *cor vestrum.*

3 Quia adest manus ad agrediendum fideliter, ait: *Dei.* Cum enim affligitur Dei ecclesia, cum dicitur divina iustitia, cum confunditur Dei familia, *Domini est pugna*,[19] quia debet stare pro sua ecclesia ne dissipetur, iustitia ne enervetur, familia ne desoletur; pro hiis omnibus assumit Deus pugnam.[20] Ps. [lxxxviii, 19]: *Domini est assumptio nostra.*[21]

4 Quia[22] claret[23] modus ad aggrediendum[24] feliciter, ait: *Non est vestra,*[25] alterius enim est ictus suscipere, hostes impellere, nosque deffendere, unde neque vestra est causa neque victoria,[26] unde ubi multitudo a paucis superata[27] est. Mirantibus responsum est quod per divinum auxilium,[28]

---

[11] arma sumere] arma sumere *add.* B   [12] vestra B] nostra N, T2, V2

[13] apponitur B, T2, V2] preponitur N   [14] iuvaminis N, T2, V2] unanimis B

[15] ostenditur N, T2, V2] *om.* B   [16] congrediendum B, T2, V2] aggrediendum N

[17] ergo B] hodie N, *om.* T2, V2   [18] pertimescat N, T2, V2] pertimescet B

[19] Domini est pugna B, N, T2] Dei est potentia V2

[20] assumit Deus pugnam N, V2] Deus pugnam B, assumit enim Dominus pugnam pro ecclesia tamquam pro sue mansionis cella, pro iustitia tamquam pro sue sessionis sella, pro familia tamquam pro sue irradiationis stella *add.* T2

[21] nostra] et sanci Israel regis nostri *add.* T2, V2   [22] quia N, T2, V2] qui B

[23] claret N, T2, V2] daret B   [24] aggrediendum B, N, T2] ingrediendum V2

[25] vestra B, N] nostra T2, V2

[26] ictus . . . victoria N] suscipere istud hostis B, ictus suscipere hostes repellere nosque defendere unde nec est nostra causa nec nostra pugna nec nostra victoria T2, ictus suscipere hostes impellere nosque defendere ut nec est nostra causa nec victoria V2

[27] superata N, V2] separata B

[28] auxilium B, V2] oraculum N, V2, hoc factum est *add.* V2

apparent, we must take up arms. But his is the fight, say the holy scriptures: *It is not your war* etc., where the battlefield is proposed, the hand of help is added and the manner of support is shown.

2 Because the field of manly combat is prepared, it says: *War*, in which man must proceed wisely in order not to be encircled, confidently in order not to be shaken, powerfully in order not to be brought down. It is ruinous to fight without good advice, presumptuous without God's help, dangerous without a strong arm. Wisdom is good for the first, confidence for the second, perseverance for the third. Deuteronomy 20: So *you shall begin the war against your enemies; do not be faint-hearted.*

3 Because the hand is there to attack with trust, it says: *God's.* When the church of God is attacked, when divine justice is pronounced, when the family of God is troubled, *it is the Lord's war,* since he needs to stand up for his church so that it is not destroyed, for justice so that it is not weakened, for his family so that it is not abandoned; for all these God assumes the fight. Psalm: *God is our assumption.*

4 Because the manner to attack successfully is evident, it says: *It is not your,* but somebody else's, task to receive blows, to strike the enemies and to defend ourselves, whence it is neither our cause nor our victory [and] whence the many are overcome by the few. To those who are

quoniam in multis pugnat[29] homo, in paucis pugnat Deus, nec resistere poterit homo Deo, ii Pal. xx[30] [17]: *Non eritis vos qui dimicabitis;*[31] *sed tantummodo confidenter state!* Propter quod oportet ut cor nostrum sit rectum cum Deo; aliter est[32] periculum.[33]

5 Legitur in Hystoria Tripartita quod[34] Constantius, Constantini pater, quosdam[35] Christianos in palatio suo haberet milites. Eos probare voluit, si cum Deo essent et solidi in fide.[36] Deditque edictum publice,[37] quod si qui venirent ad sacrificandum diis suis hii essent circa eum in palatio, si qui vero sacrificare nollent de palatio exirent. Tunc aliqui fuerunt preponentes religionem Christianam promissis[38] regis, dicentes ullis promissis vel flagris ad sacrificandum se posse induci. Alii vero fuerunt prompti[39] ad sacrificandum diis[40] sperantes[41] amicitiam regis. Tunc rex illos deliberavit amicos[42] et consiliarios qui constantes[43] et solidi erant in fide; [f. 83ra] ille sed tamquam fideles publice[44] promotores et pugnatores elegit.[45] Alios autem inter effeminatos et miseros a se expulit, dicens numquam eos circa principem esse fideles, qui fuerunt Dei sui aptissimi[46] proditores.[47]

---

[29] pugnat N, V2] pugitur B
[30] xx] xix B, N, V2   [31] dimicabitis N, V2] dimittatis B
[32] cum Deo aliter est N] non Deo alias est B, cum eo aliter enim est magnum V2
[33] unde ubi . . . periculum B, N, V2] magnum *add.* N, Dei est totum, unde enim est victoria in bellis nisi a Deo, qui suos fideles protegit, infideles deicit, invincibiles vincit. Hinc legitur in Historia Romanorum quod victa et prostrata maxima multitudine infidelium a paucis fidelibus mirabantur infideles quid cause fuit; quibus per oraculum repsonsum est quod quando per multis pugnavit homo, per paucis pugnavit Deus, nec resistere potuit homo Deo. Ideo firmi, fixi et stabiles cum Deo, in Deo et pro Deo, ii Para. xxix [rather xx, 17]: *Non enim eritis vos qui pugnabitis sed tantummodo confidenter state.* T2
[34] quod] cum *add.* B   [35] quosdam T2] quo scientia B
[36] essent . . . fide B] erant solidi et in fide firmi T2
[37] edictum publice B] *transp. et add.* inter Christianos sicut T2
[38] promissis T2] permissis B   [39] fuerunt prompti B] preparati fuerunt T2
[40] diis B] *om.* T2   [41] sperantes B] proponentes T2
[42] amicos B, T2] *praem.* habere T2,   [43] constantes B, T2] *praem.* cum Deo T2
[44] publice T2] publica B   [45] ille . . . elegit B] *om.* T2
[46] aptissimi B] paratissimi T2
[47] legitur . . . proditores B, T2] ordinate ut debet etc. *add.* T2, *om.* N, V2

astonished [by this] it is answered that [this happens] through divine help, because man fights with many, [but] God fights with few, so that man cannot resist God. 2 Chronicles 20: *It will not be you who fight; but just stand firm!* Because of this your heart ought to be upright with God; otherwise there is danger.

5 One reads in the Historia Tripartita that Constantius, the father of Constantine, had some Christians knights in his palace.[1] He wanted to test them [to see] if they were with God and firm in their faith. He publicly gave an order that if they came to sacrifice to his gods they could stay with him in the palace, but if they did not want to sacrifice, they should leave the palace. In the event, there were some who put the Christian religion before the king's promises, saying that they could not be induced to sacrifice by any promises or whippings. Others were, however, ready to sacrifice to the gods hoping for the king's friendship. So the king considered as friends and cousellors those who were steadfast and firm in their faith; he publicly chose them as his followers, special confidants and champions. The others, however, he chased away as weaklings and miserable people, saying that those who were the most blatant traitors to their God, could never remain with their prince as his followers.

[1] Cassiodorus, 'Historia Ecclesiastica', 21.

Bertrand de la Tour

SERMO III

B = Barcelona, Archivo de la Corona de Aragon, Ripoll 187, ff. 83ra-rb

Additional manuscripts
N = Naples, Biblioteca Nazionale, VIII.A.36, ff. 116vb-117rb
T2= Troyes, Bibliothèque Municipale, 2001, ff. 21va-22rb
V2= Vatican, Biblioteca Apostolica, Archivio Capitolare di S. Pietro, G. 48,
ff. 25va-vb

Reference
Schneyer I, 572, no. 981; VII, 147, no. 58 and 453, no. 5; IX, 823, no. 57

Item alia de eodem[1]

1 *Leva clipeum contra Hay,*[2] Ios. 8 [18]. Hay[3] civitas infesta contra Dominum, molesta contra Dei populum, exusta per incendium, representat infidelem populum,[4] qui est armatus contra Dominum, preparatus contra[5] Dei cuneum, deputatus in obrobrium, contra quod iubet Dominus levare *clipeum*. Ait ergo: *Leva clipeum* etc., ubi sub methaphora Iosue principem vel vexillarium huius exercitus alloquitur sub[6] hiis

---

[1] item alia de eodem B] has tres poteris predicare pro crucis assumptione V2, *om.* N, T2
[2] Hay B, T2] Nay N, Chaym V2   [3] Hay B, T2] Nay N, Chaym V2
[4] representat infidelem populum B] hunc infidelem populum representat N, T2, V2 contra qua iubet Dominus levare clipeum *add.* T2
[5] contra N, T2, V2] *om.* B   [6] sub B, T2, V2] dominus N

Bertrand de la Tour

SERMON III

Another one about the same

1 *Raise the shield against Ai*, Joshua 8. Ai, a city hostile to the Lord, a nuisance to God's people, burned down by fire, represents a faithless people armed against the Lord, standing ready against God's troops, destined for disgrace, against whom the Lord orders the *shield* to be raised. Thus it says: *Raise the shield* etc., where using a metaphor he addresses Joshua, the prince or standard-bearer of the army, with these

verbis, que sub spiritu sumpta continent[7] ducis animationem, crucis exaltationem, hostis comminationem.[8]

2 Quia ergo animatur dux, qui debet vos[9] precedere, ait: *Leva!* Duci dicitur, qui debet[10] esse alter Iosue: corde[11] devotissimus,[12] mente constantissimus,[13] in plebe amantissimus. Si hec tria princeps habet, beatus est,[14] quia si[15] est fidelissimus auxiliabitur[16] a Domino, constantissimus[17] confortabitur ab eo,[18] amantissimus convallabitur[19] a populo. Que enim potentia[20] stabit contra Dominum, que audacia contra probum animum, que superbia contra unum populum?[21] Psalmus [lxxiii, 3]: *Leva manus tuas in superbias.*[22]

3 Quia nominatur crux, que debet vos[23] protegere, ait: *Clipeum*, qui est corporis protectio, generis distinctio, militis ornatio. Crux enim est que[24] debet[25] protegere ab insultibus, distinguere ab infidelibus, componere[26] in celestibus. Ideo querenda, assumenda et retinenda est[27] saltem propter vestram[28] utilitatem. Nam ex protectione defendimur inter noxios, distinctione cognoscimur[29] inter filios, compositione admittimur inter angelos. Unde [Ios. viii, 26] *Iosue* virtutem huius clipei sentiens *non*

---

7 que sub . . . continent B] que sub spirituali sensu sumpta continent N, que sumptis sub spiritu continent V2, leva etc. quod verbum continet T2
8 comminationem B, N, V2] dominationem T2
9 debet vos T2, V2] debet nos N, vox debet B
10 duci . . . debet B] dicitur hoc duci qui debet N, seu dux qui debes T2, duci quodam dicitur qui debet V2
11 corde B] in fide T2, fide N, V2
12 devotissimus B, T2, V2] constantissimus N
13 constantissimus B, T2, V2] devotissimus N
14 si . . . est B] si hec tria princeps habet bonus est N, si tria hec princeps habet beatus est V2, hec tria si habet dux nec est quod sibi posset obsistere T2
15 quia si N, T2, V2] sin B   16 auxiliabitur B, T2, V2] roborabitur N
17 constantissimus B, N] potentissimus T2, V2   18 ab eo B, N, V2] in animo T2
19 convallabitur B, N, V2] defensabitur vel cassabitur T2
20 que enim potentia B, N, T2] quia est persona V2
21 populum] quin immo quorumque superbia adest cadet cor eo *add.* T2
22 superbias] eorum *add.* V2, eorum in finem N, T2   23 vos B] nos N, T2, V2
24 crux enim est que V2] crux enim est B, ipse est crux Christi que T2
25 protegere . . . debet B, T2, V2] *om.* N   26 componere B, T2, V2] et ponere N
27 assumenda et retinenda est B, T2, V2] est et retinenda N, quia est similiter fabricata *add.* T2
28 vestram B] nostram N, T2, V2   29 cognoscimur N, T2, V2] connoscimur B

words, which taken in the spiritual sense contain the encouragement of the leader, the exaltation of the cross and the threat to the enemy.

2 Because the leader, who must go before you, is encouraged, it says: *Raise!* This is said to a leader who must be another Joshua: very devout of heart, very steadfast in his mind, and very much loved by the people. If a prince has these three, he is fortunate, because if he is very faithful he will be helped by the Lord, [if he is] very steadfast, he will be comforted by him, [and if he is] very much loved, he will be supported by the people. What power will stand against the Lord, what daring against an upright soul, what arrogance against one entire people? Psalm: *Raise up your hands against arrogance.*

3 Because the cross is said to protect you, it says: *Shield,* which is the protection of the body, the sign of one's people, the ornament of the soldier. It is the cross that must protect from insults, distinguish from infidels, make good in heaven. This is why it must be sought after, taken and kept at all events because of its usefulness to you. Thus, by way of protection we are defended among the harmful, by way of distinction we are recognised among the sons, by way of making good we are admitted among the angels. Hence *Joshua,* perceiving the virtue of this shield,

contraxit manum tenens [f. 83rb] *clipeum, donec interficeret omnes habitatores Hay.*[30]

4 Quia comminatur urbs, que debet iam cadere, ait: *Hay.*[31] Civitas est que ex precepto Domini decipitur per paratas[32] insidias, inpetitur per armatas familias, percutitur usque ad parvas reliquias. Sic favente Domino triumphabitis hodie.[33] Debent[34] decipi propter Dei mandatum, impeti[35] propter vestrum conatum, destrui[36] propter suum peccatum. Unde bene interpretatur Hay[37] 'questio[38] vite', quia, cum sit certum aput Deum de eorum morte, apud ipsos dubium est si vivant. Ideo ibi premittitur [Ios. viii, 4–5]: *Ponite insidias post civitatem; ego autem et reliqua multitudo ascendemus ex adverso.* Multum enim in bello facit audacia, multum electa familia multumque[39] auxilii[40] Dei clementia.[41]

5 Legitur,[42] post mortem Theodosii filiis Archadio et Honorio regnantibus, Guido[43] comes Affrice in parvulorum[44] necessitate armans Affricam proprio iure cepit usurpare. Cuius frater Maszelel[45] illius invidiam[46] perhorrescens rediit in Ytaliam paratus pro parvulis se exponere. Missus est igitur cum alia militia ad illum insequendum hostem. Qui sciens quantum in rebus desperatissimis[47] oratio ex clementia Dei valeat, per fidem Domini[48] Campaniam provinciam[49] adiit. Videlicet[50] sanctos viros secum adducens, cum eis aliquot dies continuavit et noctes[51] in orationibus pervigilavit. Ante triduum quoque quam contiguus hostibus fieret, vidit nocte[52] beatum Ambrosium paulo ante

---

[30] Hay B, N, T2] Chaym V2   [31] Hay B, T2] Nay N, Chaym V2

[32] per paratas B, N] contra paratas T2, preparatas V2

[33] hodie] de inimicis *add.* N, de inimicis Domini *add.* T2

[34] debent N, T2, V2] debet B   [35] impeti N, T2, V2] imperavitur B

[36] destrui N, T2, V2] destruitur B   [37] Hay B, T2, V2] Nay N

[38] questio T2] quis B, N, V2

[39] multumque B] sed quamplurrimum T2, *om.* N, V2

[40] auxilii B, T2] *om.* N, auxilium V2

[41] clementia B, T2, V2] penitentia N, et *praem.* V2

[42] legitur B, T2] in Hystoria Romanorum quod *add.* T2   [43] Guido T2] Silo B

[44] parvulorum B] parvulos T2   [45] Maszelel T2] Manael B

[46] invidiam] perfidiam T2   [47] desperatissimis T2] desperatissimi B

[48] perfidere B] per fidem Domini T2

[49] Campaniam provinciam B] Capuam insulam T2   [50] videlicet B] indeque T2

[51] noctes] aliquot *add.* T2   [52] nocte B] per sompnium T2

did not draw back the hand holding the shield, until he had killed all the inhabitants of Ai.

4 Because a city is threatened which still has to fall, it says: *Ai*. It is a city that is betrayed by a prepared ambush on the command of the Lord, attacked by armed families and destroyed down to small remains. So with God's favour you will triumph today. They will have to be betrayed on account of God's command, attacked on account of your effort, destroyed on account of their sin. Whence Ai is well interpreted 'question of life',[1] because, although it is certain with God that they will die, they are not sure if they will live. Before this passage it therefore says: *Put an ambush behind the city; I and the rest of the crowd shall come from the opposite side*. Daring counts greatly in war, as does a select family and the mercy of God's aid.

5 One reads[2] that, after Theodosius's death, in the reign of his sons Arcadius and Honorius Guido, count of Africa, took up arms to the detriment of the children and began to usurp Africa in his own right. His brother Mascezel, fearing his envy, returned to Italy ready to stand up for the children. He was sent with another army to fight against [Guido] as an enemy. Knowing how much in the most desperate matters a prayer out of God's clemency can mean, he went to the province of Campania trusting the Lord. He took with him holy men [and] spent several days and nights with them in prayer. Before the end of the third day, when he was also very near the enemy, he saw St Ambrose at night, who had died

[1] Hieronymus, 'Liber Interpretationis', 126.
[2] I have not been able to identify this reference.

defunctum,[53] quomodo et quando victoriam reciperet diem sibi assignantem[54] et locum. Que tertio denique die orationibus ymnis et psalmis
pervigilavit.[55] Cum quinque solum milibus adversus octingenta[56] milia
hostium pergens Dei[57] nutu sine bello in direptionem accepit.[58] Guido[59]
comes fugit et post[60] strangulatus[61] fuit.[62]

[53] defunctum T2] defectum B
[54] assignantem B] indicantem T2
[55] ymnis . . . pervigilavit B] ipsius per iugum montis T2
[56] octingenta B] octoginta T2   [57] Dei] eos *praem.* T2
[58] accepit] sed si nobilis miles veniat ad fratres et *add.* B   [59] Guido T2] Sildo B
[60] fugit et post B] fugam arripuit et post aliquos dies T2
[61] legitur post . . . strangulatus B, T2] *om.* N, V2
[62] fuit B] interiit. Ordinare hic ut decet T2, *om.* N, V2

shortly before, [telling him] how and when he would carry victory, [also giving] the day and place. All the same, he spent the third day with prayers, chants and psalms. With only five thousand soldiers he advanced against eight hundred thousand enemies and according to God's will he accepted [their surrender] for plunder without battle; the Count Guido fled and was later strangulated.

APPENDIX: THE RELATIONSHIP BETWEEN THE CRUSADE MODEL SERMONS OF GILBERT OF TOURNAI AND JAMES OF VITRY

THE DEPENDENCE of Gilbert of Tournai's *ad status* sermon models on those of James of Vitry has been noted before. In his study of Gilbert's *Collectio de scandalis ecclesiae*, Autbert Stroick for the first time clearly showed that Gilbert must have used James of Vitry's *ad status* collection for the *Collectio* as well as for his own *ad status* models.[1] David d'Avray and Martin Tausche described in some detail Gilbert's reliance on James for his marriage sermons.[2] Nicole Bériou did the same for the *ad leprosos* sermons.[3] While he sometimes took over entire passages word for word, Gilbert was far from simply copying James's text. There is agreement that Gilbert used James's material very imaginatively. He usually designed his own model sermon with regard to both content and structure. He was fairly selective in choosing passages from James and often re-arranged them in a new order. In contrast to James of Vitry, Gilbert generally used a rigid scheme for ordering his argument. Bériou rightly pointed out that this was probably due to the influence of the mid-thirteenth-century university environment in which Gilbert wrote.[4] With their clear structure and systematic use of distinctions, Gilbert's models certainly have a 'scholastic' feel to them.

The judgements pronounced on the resulting sermon texts vary. Studying the marriage sermons, d'Avray and Tausche were cautious

---

[1] A. Stroick, 'Verfasser und Quellen der Collectio de Scandalis Ecclesiae (Reformschrift des Fr. Gilbert von Tournay, O.F.M., zum II. Konzil von Lyon, 1274)', *Archivum Franciscanum Historicum*, 23 (1930), 3–41, 273–99, 433–66, here pp. 280–92, 445–59. See also E. Longpré in the preface to his edition of Gilbert's *Tractatus de Pace*, xxiii, n. 1.

[2] D'Avray and Tausche, 'Marriage Sermons', 85–117.

[3] Bériou and Touati, *Voluntate Dei Leprosus*, 33–80, esp. 43–8.

[4] Bériou and Touati, *Voluntate Dei Leprosus*, 48.

about the merits of the more systematic arrangement of Gilbert's models. They came to the conclusion that his choice of a rigid formal structure allowed him less flexibility and originality than James of Vitry for exploring the various aspects of a topic.[5] With regard to the *ad status* sermons generally, d'Avray even suggested that Gilbert's models lacked intellectual substance and thematical coherence, perhaps because he worked too fast.[6] Bériou, on the other hand, rather stressed Gilbert's skill in choosing his own thematic approaches despite his dependence on James of Vitry's text. She also praised Gilbert's models for their clear structural arrangements, arguing that this made them easy to use and popular with generations of preachers.[7]

Here we shall look at the precise relationship between the crusade model sermons of Gilbert of Tournai and James of Vitry in the hope of better understanding how Gilbert proceeded in his work. Below, the texts of Gilbert's three models are printed with the passages marked which he took over from James. **Bold** print indicates a borrowing from James's first model, underlined from his second. At the end of each passage a number in brackets gives the paragraph (of the above edition) where it appears in James's models. Only those passages in which Gilbert took over James's text word for word are marked. Some very minor alterations or omissions in these copied passages have been neglected for clarity's sake. Unmarked is also the *exemplum* about the knight and his sons in Gilbert III, 8, which is borrowed not from James's *ad cruce-signatos* models but from one of his *ad peregrinos* models, which in the collection directly follows the crusade model sermons.

A number of general observations can be made. Firstly, Gilbert must have found the initial Bible verse of James's first model, Revelation 7: 2, very useful since he adopted it for all three models. Secondly, for his first model he borrowed passages from both James's sermon texts; in contrast, in his second and third models, the borrowings are only from James I, as well as the *ad peregrinos* model. Thirdly, most of the text of Gilbert's models is his own; in fact, there are large sections in all three models in which Gilbert did not use any of James's material at all. Fourthly, in some instances Gilbert took over only a quotation from the Bible or elsewhere, which he used for his own argument in a way entirely different from James.[8]

When we consider the individual passages which Gilbert borrowed, and where they appear in his models, we gain a fairly clear idea of his

[5] D'Avray and Tausche, 'Marriage Sermons', 86, 117–18.
[6] D'Avray, *The Preaching of the Friars*, 144–6.
[7] Bériou and Touati, *Voluntate Dei Leprosus*, 46–8.
[8] Gilbert I, 8, 10, 11; III, 10, 11.

method, at least for the *ad crucesignatos* models. This may well be how
he proceeded. He first read James's models and let himself be inspired by
them. Then he thought of his own themes and arguments and designed a
formal structure to develop them. In doing so, Gilbert included passages
from James's models where they fitted his own argument. He often
seems to have chosen passages which provided him with appropriate
biblical authorities or which were suited as illustrative material, that is,
exempla, similes, metaphorical expressions, etc.

In his first model, Gilbert developed his text on Revelation 7: 2, the
initial Bible passage of James's first model.[9] He mainly borrowed
material from James's interpretation of the first part of the verse (*I saw
an angel rising from the sunrise, carrying the sign of the living God*),
which is the section that Gilbert himself chose as the basis of his model.[10]
Gilbert did not take over material from James's interpretation of the
second part of the Bible verse (*And he called in a powerful voice to the
four angels* etc.), nor any of the additional material, except for an
exemplum and a passage in which the crusade was presented allegorically
in terms of feudal practice.[11] From James's second model, Gilbert choose
two biblical authorities, another illustration of crusading in terms of
feudal practice and a number of short passages with language of strong
visual quality, such as the image of sinners being drawn from the cave of
their sins with a red string.[12] In addition, he copied out one part of
James's explanation of the indulgence.[13] All in all, the passages borrowed
from James were short and in no way dominated Gilbert's text.

In his second model, Gilbert took over even less from James, in fact
only three passages. One of them, James II, 38, seems to have inspired
him with the theme on which he constructed the entire argument. In this
passage, James warned his audience not to follow 'the advice of their
spouses and parents to go to the devil'. From this, Gilbert took the idea
of sinners who refuse to go on crusade being signed by the devil, in
contrast to crusaders who were signed by Christ. This idea formed the
core theme of Gilbert's second model.[14] The other two passages Gilbert
selected from James II were chosen for their illustrative quality: the

---

[9] See above pp. 46–7.   [10] James I, 1, 5, 6, 7, 8.   [11] James I, 20, 21.

[12] James II, 5, 6, 7, 26, 31, 46.

[13] James II, 18. It is interesting to note in this context that Gilbert ignored James's
remarks about the possibility of acquiring an indulgence for one's family and dead
parents. (See James II, 19. Eudes IV, 14, incidentally, makes the same point.) Gilbert
probably wanted to avoid controversy because this was a point about which canon
lawyers of the thirteenth century had not reached agreement. See B. Poschmann,
Penance and Anointing of the Sick, trans. and revised by F. Courtney (Freiburg
i.Br. and London, 1964), 227–8. Maier, *Preaching the Crusades*, 118–19.

[14] See also above p. 43.

image of a dog stopping other animals from eating and that of a thief being put in pillory. Gilbert's second *ad crucesignatos* model is thus a good example of how he looked for and found inspiration in James's sermon models, but then proceeded with his own plan and, in actual fact, borrowed very little from James.

In Gilbert's third model practically all the passages taken from James are biblical or other authorities, *exempla* or other illustrative material as, for example, the metaphor of the key to heaven used for describing the cross and the comparison of God with a drunken tradesman.[15] Here, as in the other two models, Gilbert obviously found it convenient to use James of Vitry's authorities where they fitted his own argument and appreciated his gift of illustrating his models with powerful visual imagery and striking comparisons. But also, in his third model, Gilbert composed a model which was largely nourished by his own ideas and which used biblical references and illustrative material that were not borrowed from James.

It seems that Gilbert of Tournai depended less on James's material for his *ad crucesignatos* sermon models than for his *ad coniugatos* and *ad leprosos* models. It is, therefore, certainly not possible to draw general conclusions about Gilbert's use of James's *ad status* sermon models from the study of the three *ad crucesignatos* models. However, it becomes clear that on the whole Gilbert of Tournai followed his own agenda when writing his *ad status* model sermons and used James of Vitry's models merely as a point of departure.

Gilbert of Tournai's *ad crucesignatos* sermon models with passages from James I marked in **bold** and James II <u>underlined</u>:

Ad crucesignatos et crucesignandos sermo primus

1 *Vidi alterum angelum ascendentem ab ortu solis, habentem signum Dei vivi* **etc. (1)** Apoc. vii [2]. Verbum hoc competit cuilibet sancto et crucis negotio.

2 Notificatur ergo sanctus iste ex officio quod gessit, cum dicitur: *Angelum alterum*; ex virtutum exercitio in quo profecit, cum dicitur: *Ascendentem ab ortu solis*; ex signo deifico quod in se representavit, cum dicitur: *Habentem signum* etc.

3 Bene ergo notificatur ex officio, cum dicitur: *Vidi alterum angelum*. 'Angelus' enim est nomen officii, quod Latine dicitur **'nuntius' (5)**. Homo enim, qui vivit spiritualiter in opere et Christum credit fideliter in corde et ferventer annunciat ore, angelorum habet officium, Ps. [ciii, 4]: *Qui facit angelos suos spiritus et ministros suos ignem urentem*; vel *flammam ignis*, ut dicitur He[b]. i [7]. Primus

---

[15] James II, 7, 10, 12, 13, 14, 30, 31.

ergo angelus Christus, qui dicitur Ysa. ix [6] *magni consilii angelus*, quod sumptum est de translatione Septuaginta. Alter autem angelus iste sanctus missus ut nuntius ad preparandam viam salutis, Mal. iii [1]: *Ecce ego mittam angelum meum, qui preparabit viam ante faciem meam.*

4 Notificatur etiam ex virtutum exercitio, cum dicitur *ascendentem ab ortu solis*. Iste enim angelus est virtutum profectus, ut proficiamus in merito ascendentes de virtute in virtutem, 'donec videatur *Deus deorum* in Syon', ut dicitur in Ps. Et ad eius nuptias veniamus qui nos invitat dicens: *Amice, ascende superius*, Luc. xiiii [10]. Et bene *ab ortu solis*; ut sicut ab oriente sol ascendens crescit in lumine successive usque ad perfectum diem, ita circuit iste per virtutum merita usque ad perfectionem, Ysa. xli [2]: *Suscitavit ab oriente iustum, vocavit eum ut sequeretur se.*

5 Notificatur etiam ex signo deifico, cum dicitur: *Habentem signum Dei vivi*. Hoc signum est representatio passionis in corpore proprio, per quod vivimus in presenti vita gratie, in futuro vita glorie. In cuius figura Numeri xxi [8]: *Pone serpentem pro signo; qui percussus aspexerit vivet.* Qui enim Christum crucifixum in cruce pendentem, designatum per *serpentem eneum* [Nm. ix, 9] in palo fixum, corde contrito consideraverit et passionem ipsius et crucem in seipso expresserit, vivet et non peribit, Deut. xxviii [66]: *Erit vita tua quasi pendens ante te.*

6 Spiritualiter simus angeli puritate conversationis, ascendentes emulatione perfectionis, signati caractere et signo dominice passionis. Hoc enim **signum habuit Christus, ut signet milites suos, qui prior signari voluit, ut alios precederet cum vexillo crucis. Io. vi [27]:** *Hunc Pater signavit Deus,* **cuius carni crux affixa fuit, que modo molli filo affigitur vestris vestibus. (7)** Et sicut sagittatores et balistarii contendunt ut signum figerant, ita Iudei unanimiter ut crucifigerent Christum, Trenis iii [12–15]: *Posuit me quasi signum ad sagittam, misit in renibus meis filias pharetre sue; factus sum in derisum omni populo, canticum eorum tota die replevit me amaritudinibus.*

7 Crux enim bene *signum* dicitur, quia se offert sensui et aliud representat intellectui. Est enim signum directivum, discretivum, rememorativum, remunerativum. Sic enim adhibentur signa quandoque in preliis, quandoque in biviis, quandoque in amicitiis, quandoque in premiis.

8 Signum directivum ponitur in biviis sicut cruces, ut viam rectam ostendant, et si erratum est ad crucem rectam viam resumant. **Ysa. xi [10]:** *Radix Iesse, qui stat in signum populorum; ipsum gentes deprecabuntur, et erit sepulchrum eius gloriosum.* Radix Iesse **Christus (7)**, qui de Iesse sumpsit originem secundum carnem et ex incendio amoris se in holocaustum exhibuit. Unde et Iesse interpretatur incendium vel 'insule holocaustum'. Ipse *stat in signum populorum*, **id est in cruce (7)**, quod est *signum populi* ad ostendendum viam rectam paradisi. Si enim rectum est secundum Philosophum inter terminos spatium brevissimum, certum est quod via assumendi crucem est via rectior ad salutem, quia quanto via brevior tanto rectior. Crux autem citissime facit crucesignatos devotos, immo

martires veros, pro causa Christi de terra ad celum evolare, unde Luc. [ix, 23]: *Qui vult venire post me, abneget semetipsum et tollat crucem suam et sequatur me.*

9 Et sequitur: *Et erit sepulcrum eius gloriosum.* Glorificatur enim Christi sepulcrum, quando ex amore et devotione crucem assumunt, ut videant illud et honorent ipsum. Et vere **magna** gloria est sequi Dominum, *indui vestibus regiis* [Est. vi, 8] et habere **aliquid** signum vel **panniculum de armis** suis, quod vulgariter dicimus **'penuncel'** (8).

10 Est etiam signum discretivum, quo signantur milites in preliis, Numeri ii [2]: *Singuli per turmas et signa atque vexilla castrametati sunt.* Hoc enim signo discernit Dominus suos [Ez. ix, 4, 6]: *Signa thau super frontes virorum gemen-tium, parvulum et mulieres interficite; omnem autem super quem videritis signum thau ne occidatis!* **Soli enim** *gementes et dolentes super abhominationibus, que fiunt in Ierusalem* (6) signo crucis muniti, quod signum pretendit, ista littera thau a demonibus liberantur. Pectus enim ferreum habet et non est dignus misericordia qui non dolet de obprobrio patris sui et de hereditate sua perdita, Tren. v [2]: *Hereditas nostra versa est ad alienos et domus nostra ad extraneos.*

11 Sed contigit aliquando milites formidolosos fugere, qui tamen, quando vident vexillum domini sui elevatum, revocantur ad pugnam et vincunt per Dei adiutorium et signum ostensum, Ysa. xi [12]: *Levabit Dominus signum in nationes et congregabit profugos Israel et dispersos Iuda colliget.* (7) Crux enim signum revocatorium est eorum scilicet, qui diu erraverunt per devia peccatorum, Ysa. xlix [22]: *Ecce, levabo ad gentes manum meam et exaltabo ad populos signum meum; manum meam* (6), que est destructiva scelerum, reformativa operum, ostensiva vulnerum, collativa munerum; *et exaltabo* inquit *signum meum,* quia sicut habita victoria ponitur super muros regium signum, ita crucesignati congrediuntur contra dyabolum et vincunt per signum.

12 ii Mac. viii [23–24]: *Dato signo adiutorii Dei* commiserunt Iudei *cum Nichanore et maiorem partem exercitus eius vulneribus debilem factam fugere compulerunt.* Nota ergo quod Iudeis in arcto constitutis apparuit signum de celo, quo viso sese recollegerunt et hostes vicerunt, sicut faciunt milites, quando vident signum regis: animantur et rege statuto in prelio et iusto existente bello fugere verentur. Bellum nunc iustum est, quia contra inimicos fidei, usurpatores nostri patrimonii, pro causa Dei, et fidei et nostre salutis res est. Stat rex noster in prelio vulneratus, ut viriliter dimicet Christianus et, si usque ad sanguinem sustineat, in vulnera sui regis aspicat et confidat.

13 Unde et tempore Constantini, cum deberet ingredi contra hostes suos iuxta Danubium, dicitur apparuisse signum crucis in celo et vox audita est: 'Constan-tine, in hoc vince!', quod et rei probavit eventus. Exo. xii [13]: *Erit sanguis vobis in signum, et videbunt sanguinem; nec erit in vobis plaga disperdens, quando percussio terram Egypti.* ii Mac. xv [35]: *Suspenderunt caput Nichanoris in summa arce, ut esset evidens et manifestum signum auxilii Dei.* Hoc autem est signum regis Ierusalem, ad litteram scilicet crux rubea in albo panno, Christi scilicet passio in corde mundo, non draco cupiditatis vel aquila ambitionis que sunt signa Romanorum, immo verius antichristi et bestie in Apo. [xiii], quibus signantur milites dyaboli.

14 Ergo, veri Christiani, Ysa. lxii [10]: *Preparate viam, planum facite iter, levate signum ad populos!* Hoc est dare aliis bonum exemplum: *Levate*, id est surgite, et sumite crucis signum. Quando homo fert baculum elevatum et erectum, tunc timet canis. Quando ponitur signum in prediis vel in vineis, tunc fugit avis. Quando vero homo baculum trahit per terram vel abscondit subtus capam, tunc canis mordet a posteriori. Sic crucis signum non est abscondendum sed aperte portandum et accipiendum contra canes infernales, qui multum timent baculum, quo gravissime verberati sunt et veri fideles consolati, Ps. [xxii, 4]: *Virga tua et baculus tuus ipsa me consolata sunt.* Ysa. xxx [31]: *A voce Domini pavebit Assur,* id est dyabolus, *virga percussus.*

15 Est etiam crux signum rememorativum sicut signum quod datur amicis in perpetuandis amicitiis, ut viso signo fiat amici absentis rememoratio. Hoc enim signum nobis relinquit Dominus ad Patrem per crucem recessurus, Can. viii [6]: *Pone me ut signaculum super cor tuum, ut signaculum super brachium tuum, quia fortis est ut mors dilectio.* Ponamus ergo crucem Christi *super cor*, hoc est in corde per affectum amoris, et *super brachium* per effectum operis. Et si vere Christum diligis, pro Christo mori paratus eris. Nulla enim carnis illecebra, nulla prosperitas, nulla dignitas, non robur corporis, non quilibet elegantia seculi, nec hominum gratia, nichil denique ex omnibus, que in mundo vel concupisci vel diligi possunt, morti prevalet iminenti.

16 *Ut signaculum* inquit. Signaculum ponitur ad notitiam sicut circulus in taberna, ad custodiam sicut sigillum in carta, ad gratiam et decorem sicut in auribus sponse et aliquarum mulierum in aliquibus regionibus murenule auree vermiculate argento. Et tu hoc signo signeris, quod arceat adversarios, teipsum custodiat, proximum edificet et Christum letificet. Hanc crucem Christi in corde habeas et eius stigmata in corpore tuo feras, ut intus offerens victimam holocausti etiam foris habeas pellem eius. Debet enim qui se dicit per internam dilectionem in Christo manere per apertam operum et passionum eius imitationem sicut ille ambulavit et ipse ambulare, Exo. xiii [9]: *Erit quasi signum in manu tua*, et quasi appensum quod ob recordationem *ante oculos tuos.*

17 Ergo, si amicus Dei es, recordare obprobriorum que fiunt Christo, quando inimici crucis Christi extenderunt manus sacrilegas in civitatem sanctam Ierusalem, ubi Christiani in Sarracenorum servitute sunt, ubi sacramenta Christi deficiunt, ubi nomen Christi blasphematur, ubi idolum abhominationis, Machometi scilicet nomen, iugiter exaltatur et honoratur, Iere. li [50]: *Nolite stare, recordamini procul Domini, et Ierusalem ascendat super cor vestrum.* <u>Poterat Dominus Ierusalem liberare, sed voluit amicos probare suos (26)</u>; sicut enim lapidem ponderosum solent proicere iuvenes ad probandas vires, ita Dominus per terram **illam probat, qui sunt animo fortes et qui pusillanimes**, Za. xii [3]: *Ponam Ierusalem lapidem oneris cunctis populis.*

18 Affligitur Dominus in sui patrimonii amissione et vult amicos suos probare, si sunt fideles vasalli eius. Qui enim a domino ligio tenet feodum, si desit ei dum impugnatur et hereditas sua illi aufertur, merito feodo privatur. Vos autem quicquid habetis a summo imperatore tenetis, qui vos hodie citari facit, ut ei succuratis; et licet iure feodi non teneremini, tamen tanta beneficia contulit vobis (20) et adhuc tanta offert stipendia, ut remissionem peccatorum

etc., quod ad istud signum adcurrere deberetis, ut veri testes fidei essetis sicut filii eterne hereditatis, Iere. xxxii [44]: *Imprimetur signum, et testis apparebit in terra Beniamin*, qui interpretatur 'filius dextere'.

19 Crux etiam est signum remunerativum in premiis. Sic enim pauperes in conviviis introducuntur cum signis, sicut Templarii libere sine pedagio procedunt, quando eorum vestimentis signum crucis ostendunt, sic vere crucesignati sine repulsa ingrediuntur ianuam paradisy, Ysa. ultimo [lxvi, 18–19]: *Venient et videbunt gloriam meam, et ponam in eis signum* (6) *et mittam ex eis, qui salvati fuerint, ad gentes.* Ieronimus in originali: 'Quo signo qui fuerit impressus manus percutientis effugiet,' sicut dicitur Eze. ix, 'et isto signo postes domorum in Egypto signabantur quando pereunte Egypto solus Israel mansit illesus,' sicut dicitur Exo. xii.

20 Et Iosue ii [17–18]: *Innoxii erimus a iuramento, quo adiurasti nos, si ingredientibus nobis terram signum* non *fuerit funiculus iste coccineus, et eum ligaveris in fenestra.* Crux enim Christi *funiculus* est *coccineus*, per quem peccatores de cavernis suis, peccatorum scilicet latibulis, educuntur, per quem liberata est Raab aliis pereuntibus [cf. Ios. ii, 6]. Et dum duri et obstinati pereunt (5), crucesignati fideles hoc funicolo ad Christum trahuntur et eis terra promissionis *in funiculo distributionis* [Ps. lxxvii, 54] datur, quia veri crucesignati, qui vere contriti et confessi ad servitium Dei accinguntur et in ipso moriuntur, veri martires reputantur, liberati a peccatis mortalibus et venalibus et ab omni penitentia sibi iniuncta, absoluti et a pena peccatorum in hoc seculo et a pena purgatorii in alio, a tormentis gehenne securi gloria (18) eterna per hoc signum investientur.

21 Sic enim consuetudo est nobilium, quod per cyrothecam vel aliam rem vilem vasallos suos investiunt feodis pretiosis; sic Dominus per crucem, que est ex modico filo, vasallos suos investit de celesti regno (46). Quando enim bonum forum est rerum venalium, tunc sapientes necessariis, ut non indigeant, muniunt hospitium suum contra caristiam superventuram, quam metuunt; modo Dominus de regno suo optimum facit forum (31), dum crucesignatis exponit pro peregrinatione modici temporis regnum celorum.

22 Non simus sicut symia, que nucem abicit, dum exterius amaritudinem in cortice sentit, et numquam ad dulcedinem nuclei pervenit, non sicut asinus, qui in molendino commoratur, et quia recedere non vult ab eo, quando molendinum incenditur et ipse cum eo; qui asinus est adeo piger, quod videns lupum venientem infigit caput suum dumeto vel spinis et permittit renes suos devorari a lupo usque ad pulmonem et, quia abscondit faciem suam, credit quod nullam sustineat lesionem.

23 Vos ergo, fratres, considerantes premia celestia non terreamini a laboribus itineris, quia omnes passus Dominus in libro suo scribit ad mercedem remunerationis, ut sicut *non peribit capillus de capite* [Lc. xxi, 18] nec momentum de tempore, ita nec passus de nostra peregrinatione.

24 Recitat magister Iacobus de Vitriaco, quod, cum semel **predicaret de cruce suscipienda, aderat ibi vir quidam religiosus, conversus Cysterciensis dictus**

frater Symon, divinis visionibus assuetus, qui rogavit Dominum cum lacrimis, ut ostenderet ei quale meritum collaturus erat crucesignatis. Qui statim in spiritu vidit Beatam Virginem filium suum tenentem et, secundum quod uniusquisque signum crucis corde contrito recepiebat, filium suum illi dabat. (21) Qui ergo ita signatus fuerit, sigillum regis secum portabit, nec dilationem introitus regni sustinebit.

25 Apoc. vii [2–3] vidit Iohannes *angelum habentem signum Dei vivi,* clamantem angelis percussoribus, ne nocerent signatis. Patet ergo, quomodo crux dicitur signum directivum, discretivum, rememorativum et remunerativum.

Ad crucesignatos et crucesignandos sermo secundus

1 *Vidi alterum angelum* etc., *habentem signum Dei vivi* (1) [Apc. vii, 2], crucem scilicet Christi, in qua invenitur vita, Prov. viii [35]: *Qui me invenerit, inveniet vitam et hauriet salutem a Domino, vitam* gratie, *salutem* glorie.

2 Signat autem dyabolus suos signo mortis, Christus autem suos signo vite. Signo mortis signantur duplices et proditores similes Iude, qui dedit Christo osculum in signum pacis et perficiebat opus proditionis, Mt. xxvi [48–9]: *Qui tradidit eum dedit eis signum dicens: Quemcumque osculatus fuero, ipse est; tenete eum,* et sequitur: *Accedens ad Ihesum dicit: Ave, rabi!, et osculatus est eum.* Sic multi in facie ungunt et a tergo pungunt, ore se Christianos dicunt et opere Christum crucifigunt.

3 Signo autem dyaboli signantur carnales et incontinentes, Sap. ii [8–9]: *Nullum pratum sit quod non pertranseat luxuria nostra* – nemo nostrum exsors sit luxurie nostre – *ubique relinquamus signa letitie.* Hec sunt signa mortis: Sicut, quando videntur ludere delfines in mari signa sunt proxime tempestatis, sed parvi pisces sub petris absconduntur et tempestatem evadunt nec cum fluctibus iactantur, sic amatoribus mundi multis turbinibus rerum secularium iactatis et ludentibus et pereuntibus in terra propria, crucesignati salvantur et quasi absconduntur in terra aliena et ignota. Sicut Abraham, cui facte sunt promissiones, postquam de terra sua et cognatione sua exivit, Gal. iii [16]: *Abrahe dicte sunt promissiones et semini eius,* id est eis qui de terra sua exeunt exemplo ipsius.

4 Signo etiam dyaboli signantur invidentes. Hoc est signum quod habuit Caym in capite, tremor scilicet et inquietudo capitis, ut dicunt Gn. iv [14–15]. Qui invidi sunt velut ursi semper inquieti; ursus enim ligatus ad stipitem numquam pene desinit vel in circuitum pergere vel pedibus suis caput suum modo in unam partem, modo in aliam iactare; ita invidia vix permittit cor aliquo momento requiescere. Et quia ex invidia detractio, ideo Dan. vii [5] dicitur illi *bestie,* que erat *similis urso: Surge, comede carnes plurimas!*
5 Invidi enim vitam suam preferunt, alienam rodunt, proximorum infirmitates delectabiliter carpunt. Ergo *carnes* comedunt, sicut ursus plantas suas lambendo suggit et *carnes* alienas devorat et comedit; et utinam ita *carnes* lacerarent, quod

ossibus parcerent! Hii sunt, qui detrahunt crucesignatis et crucem suscipere paratis et sicut canes mordent in baculo crucis; sed crucesignati quasi boni peregrini pertranseunt et non immorantur cuilibet cani oblatranti. Canis enim nequam iacet super fenum et manducare nequit nec cetera animalia, que manducare possent, manducare sinit, Prov. iii [27]: *Noli prohibere benefacere eum qui potest; si vales et ipse benefac* (39).

6 Propter hoc Luc. ii [34] dicitur: Christus *positus in signum, cui contradicetur.* Sapientes enim mundi huic signo et divites detrahunt verbo et contradicunt facto similes truncis veteribus, qui nichil aliud quam fumigare faciunt et accendi non possunt, quia Iere. vi [29]: *Frustra conflavit conflator,* id est Christus, qui sufflatorium fecit ex pelle carnis sue et ligno crucis et clavis, ut ignem sue caritatis accenderet in cordibus nostris, quo faciliter accenduntur pauperes quasi stupa, sed non hii trunci veteres pleni luto et aqua.

7 Signo etiam dyaboli signantur notorii peccatores, Eze. xvi [25]: *Ad omne caput vie educasti signum prostitutionis tue et abhominabilem fecisti decorem tuum. Ad omne caput vie* signum hoc ponitur, quando aperte peccatur, quando culpa publicatur; ergo, sicut publice peccasti, publice accipe signum Christi, ut sicut alios exemplo tuo corrupisti ita exemplo tuo invites alios ad opus meriti. Iustum est enim, ut qui se Deo abstulit et perdidit cum aliorum destructione seipsum cum multorum edificatione restituat. Cur confundimini aperte accipere crucem? Non accipiebatis consilium ab uxoribus, a parentibus eundi ad dyabolum? (38)

8 Cur ergo expectatis consilium eundi ad Deum? Impleatur in vobis quod dicit propheta [Ps. lxxxv, 17]: *Fac mecum signum in bono, ut videant qui oderunt me et confundantur, quoniam tu, Domine, adiuvisti me et consolatus es me. Ut videant qui oderunt me,* scilicet demones, *et confundantur* coram omnibus, sicut latro confunditur quando in furto comprehenditur et in medio foro in pallori ponitur (38). Impletur autem in peccatoribus notoriis illud Sap. v [13]: *Nullum quidem signum virtutis valuimus ostendere; in malignitate autem nostra consumpti sumus.*

Ad crucesignatos et crucesignandos sermo tertius

1 *Vidi alterum angelum habentem signum* etc. (1) [Apc. vii, 2]. Hoc signo crucis signat Dominus suos, unde electi in Apoc. vii dicuntur signati.

2 Est autem crux *signum* clementie quantum ad reos, victorie quantum ad dubios et formidolosos, iustitie quantum ad sanctos, glorie quantum ad perfectos.

3 De primo, Hester iiii [11]: *Cuncte noverunt provincie quod, si quis non vocatus atrium interius regis* assueti *intraverit, statim interficiatur, nisi forte rex auream virgam ad eum extenderit pro signo clementie atque ita possit vivere.* Non audet peccator accedere ad Deum videns se reum; porrigit ei *rex virgam,* crucem scilicet, per suam clementiam et sic impetrat veniam. Hec est virga de qua Levit. ultimo [xxvii, 32] dicitur, quod *quicquid sub pastoris virga transierit sanctificatum erit Domino.* Ad litteram enim, ut dicunt, pastor habebat virgam tinctam sanguine et *quicquid decimum* de grege transibat tangebat et sanguine signans Domino sanctificabat.

4 <u>Virga enim crucis et sanguine Christi sanctificamur et ab aliis signatis discernimur (12)</u>. Sed timeant rebelles et in peccatis suis perseverantes, ne signum clementie vertatur eis in signum iracundie, Numeri. xvii [10]: *Refer virgam Aaron in tabernaculum testimonii, ut servetur ibi in signum rebellium filiorum Israel,* ut tanto puniantur gravius, quanto potuerunt misericordiam invenire levius.

5 Quicquid enim sustinent crucesignati modicum est et quasi nichil <u>respectu premii interminabilis</u>: labor brevis, merces in ianuis, <u>Ro. viii [18]</u>: *Non sunt condigne passiones huius temporis ad futuram gloriam, que revelabitur in nobis (24)*. Ergo, ad hoc signum accedatis qui hactenus fuistis in <u>tenebris et peccatis, Ysa. xiii [2]</u>: *Super montem caliginosum levate signum (7)*, id est super cor tenebrosum crucis vexillum.

6 Est etiam crux signum clementie. Sicut enim Christus in cruce per dilectionem inexpressibilem, quam ad nos habuit, per quinque canales corporis quinque fluvios sanguinis patefecit sufficiens diluvium ad lotionem totius mundi, ita et nunc per viscera misericordie sue se totum crucesignatis diluendis exponit, quia Can. iiii [15] *fons* prius erat signatus, sed nunc *fons ille parvus crevit in fluvium* magnum *et in aquas plurimas redundavit*, Hest. x [6].

7 Est enim crux signum victorie. Per hoc enim signum homo vincit seipsum et omnem carnalem affectum, diabolum et mundum. Propter hoc Apoc. vii [9] dicitur de electis crucesignatis quod ipsi sunt *in conspectu agni, amicti stolis albis et palme in manibus eorum. Amicti stolis albis,* quia venerunt de tribulatione et laverunt stolas suas et dealbaverunt eas in sanguine *agni. Et palme in manibus eorum* in signum quod victores sunt effecti. Palma enim arbor est victorie. Hoc signo armavit se beatus Martinus, cum barbari minarentur obiciendum eum. 'Ergo, inquit, signo crucis non clipeo protectus aut galea hostium cuneos penetrabo securus.' Et in Tripartita Historia l[ib]. ix c[ap]. ix legitur, quod statuit Constantinus ut imprimeretur crux in monetis Christianis; et hoc signo signarentur arma militum suorum.

8 Hoc autem signo non tantum vincuntur hostes infernales vel materiales sed etiam affectus carnales. Unde legimus de quodam nobili milite, quod iturus ultra mare fecit adduci ad se filios parvulos, quos valde diligebat. Et cum eos diu aspiciens amplecteretur, dixerunt ei famuli eius: Dimitte pueros istos et recedatis, quia multi vos expectant, ut vos deducant. Quibus ille: Ideo coram me filios meos adduci feci, ut excitato affectu ad eos cum maiori angustia mentis reliquam eos pro Christo et ita magis merear apud Deum. Profecto enim patria, propria, parentes, uxor et filii vincula sunt retinentia.

9 Sed teste Ieronimi: 'Facile rumpit hec vincula amor Christi et timor gehenne,' pro cuius amore cum magno glaudio sancti labores sustinent et in laboribus delectantur, sicut ursus ictibus impinguatur, sicut aque Marath per immissionem ligni dulcorantur [cf. Ex. xv, 23], per farinam Helysei coloquintide agri, illa scilicet silvestria holuscula, de quibus clamabant filii prophetarum: *Mors in olla, vir Dei* [iv Rg. iv, 40], sua amaritudine privantur.

10 Hoc figuratum est in signo Ione, Mat. xii [39–41] et Ione i [15]: <u>Misso enim Iona in mari</u> *stetit mare a fervore suo,* <u>quia quod prius videbatur importabile exemplo Crucifixi fit leve, qui se</u> *exinanivit* <u>usque ad carnem, usque ad crucem, usque ad mortem</u> (12) [Phil. ii, 7–8]. <u>Sicut enim tigris rabido cursu insequitur</u>

venatorem et tanto affectu prosequitur fetum, ut se mittat in venatoris spiculum, ita Christus, ut nos eriperet de manu venatoris, id est dyaboli, in spiculum mortis se misit (13).

11 Et ideo teste Augustini, cum Christus per alia beneficia ad amorem suum nos incitaret, per mortis beneficium nos coegit (14). Huius victorie signum in figura eorum, qui nolunt crucem accipere: nolebat Achaz, rex impius, petere, quia nolebat Deum glorificare, Ysa. vii [11–12]: *Pete tibi signum a Domino Deo tuo; et dixit; Non petam et non temptabo Dominum*, alia littera est: non exaltabo Dominum. Sciebat enim rex impius quod si peteret accepturus esset et glorificaretur Dominus.

12 Crux etiam signum iustitie. Iustitia enim est, ut conformemur Christo, qui pro nobis tribulationem sustinuit a principio nativitatis sue usque ad finem vite, Luc. ii [12]: *Hoc vobis signum: Invenietis infantem pannis involutum et positum in presepio. Pannis involutum*, in quo paupertas; non enim erat ornatus sericis sed involutus panniculis. *Positus in presepio*, in quo vilitas. *Infantem* expositum scilicet frigori hyemis illo tempore in quo asperitas.

13 Que est iustitia ista vel satisfactio, ut per hiis tribus queras: divitias, delicias et honores? Christus in presepio, tu in palatio; Christus in vilibus pannis, tu in sericis et ornamentis; Christus in asino, tu in equis et phaleris; Christus in cruce, tu in balneis; Christus in sepulcro, tu in lectis eburneis et superstitiosis; Christus nudus in cruce, tu in mutatoriis que pendent in perticis; Christus confixus manus, tu in manicis consuticiis et cyrothecis et anulis; Christus confixus pedes, tu in calceis rostratis, laqueatis, lunulatis, perforatis; Christus in corona spinea, tu in discriminalibus mitris, vittis et collitergiis et sertis; Christus aceto potatus, tu vino inebriatus; Christus cucurrit ad clavos ferreos, tu ad gariophilos; Christus ligatus ad columpnam, tu dissolutus evagaris per camporum et platearum licentiam effrenatam; Christus perforatum habuit latus lancea et tu cinctum aurea zona vel argentea; Christus pretioso sanguine animam tuam redemit, tu illam vili pretio dyabolo vendis; semel crucifixus est a Iudeis, tu eum pluries crucifigis in membris et super dolorem vulnerum addis; conspuis eum in facie, dum bonis detrahis; acetum ei porrigis, dum malitia et rancoris corruptione in proximum exardescis.

14 Sed verum signum iustitie apparet in crucesignatis, qui corde, ore et opere se exercent in servitio Dei: corde per devotionem, ore per gratiarum actionem, corpore et opere per laboris satisfactionem. Et hee sunt tres sagitte quas iecit Ionatas, filius regis, in agro *quasi exercens se ad signum*, i Reg. xx [20].

15 Efficax enim satisfactio est labor peregrinationis, quia sicut omnibus membris homo peccavit, ita in cunctis membris laborando satisfacit. Et si peccavit nimio affectu ad uxorem et filios, satisfacit dimittendo eos; et licet hec satisfactio sit multum meritoria, magis tamen est consolatoria quam afflictiva : *Petra enim fundit rivos olei*, Iob xxix [6], quo unguntur contra asperitatem vie pedes peregrini. Si ergo in duro lecto iaceas, attende quod Christus tener et parvulus reclinatus est in duro presepio et duriorem lectum habuit in patibulo. Si dolent pedes ex itinere, cogita quod pedes Christi clavis confixi sunt pro tua liberatione. Si doles caput, quia forte pulvinar non habuisti, cogita quod Christus habuit durum cervical, quando spinis voluit coronari.

16 De hoc signo Iud. vi [37–40], quando expressus est ros de vellere et remansit vellus incorruptum; quia mittitur a Deo ros dulcedinis et gratia consolationis celestis in cor crucesignati, quod non est per impatientiam fractum sed celitus confortatum.

17 Crux etiam est signum glorie. Mt. xxiv: *Tunc apparebit signum Filii Hominis in celo*, tunc quando *sol obturabitur et luna non dabit lumen suum*; tunc *apparebit*, tunc radiabit et lucebit lumen crucis, unde Crisostomus, omelia prima de cruce et latrone. Sicut imperatorem regalis pompa precedit et militaris ordo preeundo vexilla humeris portare consueverunt et hiis eius declaratur adventus, sic Domino de celo veniente angelorum cetus et archangelorum multitudo illud signum humeris portant excelsis et regalem nobis adventum nunciant.

18 Patet ergo quod crux, que primitus fuit signum ignominie, signum est glorie, Ecc[us]. xxxvi [6–7]: *Innova signa et immuta mirabilia, glorifica manum et brachium dexterum, excita furorem et effunde iram.* Bene dicit *glorifica manum et brachium dextrum*, id est crucesignatum pro Christo pugnantem et in modum manus dextere ictus suscipientem et caput suum defendentem. *Excita furorem* et cetera, quantum ad eos, qui sunt cruci rebelles et Christum crucifigunt in membris suis. Propter hoc enim veniet Christus cum cruce, ut hii qui eum crucifixerunt sue sentiant damnationis cecitatem; et ideo impudientie eorum signum portat et tunc vulnera corporis demonstrabit.

19 Hoc est quod cantatur in ecclesia, hoc signum crucis erit in celo cum Dominus ad iudicandum venerit et illa claritas glorie radiabit in crucesignatis, Gn. ix [13]: *Arcum meum ponam in nubibus, et erit signum federis inter me et terram.* Quia sicut arcus creatur in nubibus ex solari radio penetrante nubes et fuit signum cessationis diluvii et serenitatis, ita in cordibus crucesignatorum et corporibus relucebit divina claritas et cessatio iracundie Dei et manifestatio eterne felicitatis. Ipsi enim fuerunt quasi nubes elevati ad celestia, discurrentes ad exequenda divina precepta, summi regis signiferi, domus eius clavigeri.

20 Crux enim clavis est celi, que portas paradisi (10) quinque milibus annorum clausas aperuit crucesignato et crucifixo bono latroni [cf. Lc. xxiii, 42–3]. Et eodem tempore duo beneficia immo tria Dominus exhibuit: nam paradisum patefecit, latronem primum ante omnes homines in ipsum introduxit et crucesignatis maximam spem dedit, quando cherubin custodientibus paradisum cum flammeo gladio latro paradysum intravit.

21 De hac clave Ysa. xxii [22]: *Ponam clavem domus David super humerum eius (10)*. Hinc est quod hodie aperitur thesaurus glorie celestis, et ipse dominus papa, qui sponsus est ecclesie, obligat bona sponse sue et ex plenitudine potestatis, quam habet sicut Christi vicarius, offert tam largas indulgentias accipientibus crucem et succurentibus Terre Sancte.

22 Dicitur quod bonum forum trahit argentum de bursa. Non ergo surdam aurem faciatis Domino clamanti et offerenti nobis paradisum. Ipse enim quasi ebrius et crapulatus a vino modo bonum forum facit et quasi pro nichilo dat regnum suum (31). Ps. [xxxv, 7]: Pro nichilo *salvos facies* illos, quia moriuntur et salvantur multi crucesignati, antequam tempus veniat peregrinandi. Multi hodie currunt et properant, dum modica pecunia offertur eis, et non currunt ad regnum

celorum, quod offertur eis. Et, ut vulgariter loquimur, multi accurrerent si clamaretur: 'Gaaigne maile, gaaigne denier!' Et nos clamamus: 'Hauot a paradis!', et accurrunt pauci (30). Et timent, Domine, *qui habitant terminos terrenorum a signis tuis* [Ps. lxiv, 9]!

BIBLIOGRAPHY

MANUSCRIPT SOURCES

Avignon, Bibliothèque Municipale, Musée Calvet 327 (= A).
Avranches, Bibliothèque Municipale, 132.
Barcelona, Archivo de la Corona de Aragon, Ripoll 187 (= B).
Cambridge, University Library, Peterhouse 200 (= C).
Douai, Bibliothèque Municipale, 503 (= D).
Florence, Biblioteca Medicea-Laurenziana, Plut. 33 sin. 1.
Frankfurt a. M., Stadt- und Universitätsbibliothek, Praed. 29 (= F).
Marseille, Bibliothèque Municipale, 392 (= M).
Naples, Biblioteca Nazionale, VIII.A.36 (= N).
Paris, Bibliothèque Mazarine, 1010 (= P1).
Paris, Bibliothèque Nationale de France, lat. 3284 (= P2).
Paris, Bibliothèque Nationale de France, lat. 15943 (= P3).
Paris, Bibliothèque Nationale de France, lat. 15947 (= P4).
Paris, Bibliothèque Nationale de France, lat. 15953 (= P5).
Paris, Bibliothèque Nationale de France, lat. 17509 (= P6).
Paris, Bibliothèque Nationale de France, nouv. ac. lat. 999.
Pisa, Biblioteca Cateriniana del Seminario, 21 (= Pa).
Reims, Bibliothèque Municipale, 612 (= Re).
Rome, Biblioteca Angelica, 157 (= R1).
Rome, Archivio Generale dell'Ordine dei Predicatori, XIV.35 (= R2).
Segovia, Catedral, Estanceria B 331 (= S).
Troyes, Bibliothèque Municipale, 228 (= T1).
Troyes, Bibliothèque Municipale, 1099.
Troyes, Bibliothèque Municipale, 2001 (= T2).
Vatican, Biblioteca Apostolica, Pal. lat. 452 (= V1).
Vatican, Biblioteca Apostolica, Archivio Capitolare di S. Pietro, G.48 (= V2).

PRINTED SOURCES

Ambrosius Mediolanensis, 'De Ioseph', CSEL, XXXII/2, 73–122.

'Expositio Evangelii Secundum Lucam', *CCSL*, XIV.

Analecta Novissima Spicilegii Solesmensis Altera Continuatio, ed. J. B. Pitra, 2 vols. ([Paris], 1885, 1888).

Augustinus, 'In Iohannis Evangelium Tractatus cxxiv', *PL*, XXXV, cols. 1579–976.

(Augustinus), 'Dialogus Quaestionum lxv', *PL*, XL, cols. 733–52.

Augustinus , 'Sermones Dubii', *PL*, XXXIX, cols. 1639–720.

Beda Venerabilis, 'In Lucae Euangelium Expositio', *CCSL*, CXX, 5–425.

[S.] Bernardi Opera, ed. J. Leclerq, C. H. Talbot and H. M. Rochais, 9 vols. (Rome, 1957–77).

Biblia Latina cum Glossa Ordinaria ed. A. Rusch, 4 vols. [reprint] (Turnhout, 1992).

Biblia Sacra Iuxta Vulatam Versionem, ed. R. Weber, 2 vols. (Stuttgart, 1969).

Cassiodorus, 'Historia Ecclesiastica Tripartita', *CSEL*, LXXI.

Catherina Scota, *Ars Optima Editionis*, ed. G. R. Atia (Ad Viam Lotharingiae, 1995–8).

Chartularium Universitatis Parisiensis, ed. H. Denifle and A. Châtelain, 4 vols. (Paris, 1889–97).

Conciliorum Oecumenicorum Decreta, ed. J. Alberigo, P.-P. Ioannou, C. Leonardi et al. (Basle, 1962).

Corpus Antiphonalium Officii, ed. R.-J. Hesbert, 6 vols. (Rerum Ecclesiasticarum Documenta, series maior 7–12; Rome, 1963–79).

[The] Exempla or Illustrative Stories from the Sermones Vulgares of Jacques de Vitry, ed. T. F. Crane (London, 1890).

Gregorius Magnus, *Dialogues II*, ed. A. de Vogüé (Sources Chrétiennes 260; Paris, 1979).

'Liber Responsalis', *PL*, LXXVIII, cols. 725–850.

'Moralia in Iob Libri i-x', *CCSL*, CXLIII.

Guibertus Tornacensis, *Tractatus de pace*, ed. E. Longpré (Bibliotheca franciscana ascetica medii aevi 6; Ad Claras Aquas [Quarracchi], 1925).

Hieronymus, 'Commentariorum in Esaiam Libri xii-xviii', *CCSL*, LXXIII A.

'Commentariorum in Hiezechielem Libri xiv', *CCSL*, LXXV, 3–743.

'Commentariorum in Matthaeum Libri iv', *CCSL*, LXXVII.

'Epistulae I', *CSEL*, LIV.

'Epistulae III', *CSEL*, LVI.

Hieronymus, 'Liber Interpretationis Hebraicarum Nominum', *CCSL*, LXXII, 59–161.

Humbertus de Romanis, *De Predicatione Sancte crucis* ([Nürnberg], 1495).

'Opus Tripartitrum', *Appendix ad Fasciculum Rerum Expetendarum et Fugiendum*, ed. E. Brown (London, 1690), 185–229.

Iacobus de Vitriaco, *Historia Occidentalis*, ed. J. F. Hinnebusch (Spicilegium Friburgense 17; Fribourg, 1972).

Iohannes Chrysostomus, 'De Cruce et Latrone Homilia I', *PG*, XLIX, cols. 399–408.

Isidorus Hispalensis, *Etymologiae Liber xii*, ed. J. André (Paris, 1986).

Petrus Abaelardus, *Carmen ad Astralabium*, ed. J. M. A. Rubingh-Bosscher (Groningen, 1987).

[P.] Ovidi Nasonis Amores, Medicamina facei feminae, Ars Amatoria, Remedia Amoris, ed. E. J. Kenney (Oxford, 1961).
[P.] Ovidi Nasonis Tristium Libri Quinque, Ibis, Ex Ponto Libri Quattuor, Halieutica, Fragmenta, ed. S. G. Owen (Oxford, 1915).
Proverbia, Sententiaeque Latinitatis Medii Aevi, ed. H. Walther, 9 vols. (Carmina medii aevi posterioris Latina 2; Göttingen, 1963–86).
Salimbene de Adam, 'Cronica', *MGHS*, XXXII.
Septuaginta, ed. A. Rahlfs, 2 vols. (Stuttgart, 1935).
Sulpicius Severus, *Vita S. Martini*, ed. J. Fontaine (Sources Chrétiennes 133; Paris, 1967).
Thomas de Chobham, 'Sermones', *CCCM*, LXXXII A.
'Summa de arte praedicandi', *CCCM*, LXXXII.

SECONDARY WORKS

Baldwin, J. W., *Masters, Princes and Merchants. The Social Views of Peter the Chanter and his Circle*, 2 vols. (Princeton, 1970).
Bataillon, L.-J., 'Les instruments de travail des prédicateurs au XIIIe siècle', *Culture et travail intellectuel dans l'Occident médiévale* (Paris, 1981), 197–209.
'Intermédiaires entres les traités de morale pratique et les sermons: les *distinctiones* bibliques alphabétiques', *Les genres littéraires dans les sources théologique et philosophiques médiévales. Actes du Colloque internationale de Louvain-la-Neuve, 25–27 mai 1981* (Louvain-la-Neuve, 1982), 213–26.
'*Similitudines* et *exempla* dans les sermons du XIIIe siècle', *The Bible in the Medieval World. Essays in Memory of Beryl Smalley*, ed. K. Walsh and D. Wood (Studies in Church History, Subsidia 4; Oxford, 1985), 191–205.
'Sermons rédigés, sermons reportés (XIIIe siècle)', *Medioevo e Rinascimento*, 3 (1989), 69–86.
'Early Scholastic and Mendicant Preaching as Exegesis of Scripture', *Ad Litteram. Authoritative Texts and their Medieval Readers*, ed. M. D. Jordan and K. Emery, Jr. (Notre Dame Conferences in Medieval Studies 3; Notre Dame, 1992), 165–98.
Baudry, L., 'Wibert de Tournai', *Revue d'histoire franciscaine*, 5 (1928), 29–61.
Berg, D., *Armut und Wissenschaft. Beiträge zur Geschichte des Studienwesens der Bettelorden im 13. Jahrhundert* (Bochumer Historische Studien 15; Düsseldorf, 1977).
Bériou, N., 'La reportation des sermons parisiens à la fin du XIIIe siècle', *Medioevo e Rinascimento*, 3 (1989), 87–124.
'De la lecture aux épousailles. Le rôle des images dans la communication de la Parole de Dieu au XIIIe siècle', *Cristianesimo nella storia*, 14 (1993), 535–68.
'La prédication de croisade de Philippe le Chancelier et d'Eudes de Châteauroux en 1226', *La prédication en Pays d'Oc (XIIe-début XVe siècle)* (Cahiers de Fanjeaux 32; Toulouse 1997), 85–109.
L'avènement des maîtres de la parole. La prédication à Paris au XIIIe siècle, 2 vols. (Paris, 1998).

Bériou, N. and Touati, F.-O., *Voluntate Dei Leprosus. Les lépreux entre conver-sion et exclusion aux XIIème et XIIIème siècles* (Testi, Studi, Strumenti 4; Spoleto, 1991).

Brett, E. T., *Humbert of Romans. His Life and Views of Thirteenth-Century Society* (Studies and Texts 67; Toronto, 1984).

Briscoe, M. G. and B. H. Jaye, *Artes Praedicandi, Artes Orandi* (Typologie des sources du moyen âge occidental 64; Turnhout, 1992).

Brundage, J. A., *Medieval Canon Law and the Crusader* (Madison, 1969).

Boyle, L.E., 'Robert Grosseteste and the Pastoral Care', *Proceedings of the Southeastern Institute of Medieval and Renaissance Studies, Summer 1976*, ed. D. B. J. Randall (Medieval and Renaissance Series 8; Durham, N.C., 1979), 3–51.

——— 'The Inter-Conciliar Period 1179–1215 and the Beginnings of Pastoral Manuals', *Miscellanea Rolando Bandinelli Papa Alessandro III*, ed. F. Liotta (Siena, 1986), 43–56.

Cardini, F., 'Gilberto di Tournai. Un francescano predicatore della crociata', *Studi Francescani*, 72 (1975), 31–48.

Catalogue général des manuscrits des bibliothèques publiques de France (B. Départements) [in progress] (Paris, 1886ff).

Catalogue général des manuscrits latins [in progress] (Paris, 1939ff).

Cenci, C., *Manoscritti Francescani della Biblioteca Nazionale di Napoli*, 2 vols. (Spicilegium Bonaventurianum 7, 8; Grottaferrata, 1971).

Charansonnet, A., 'L'évolution de la prédication du Cardinal Eudes de Châ-teauroux (1190?-1273): une approche statistique', *De l'homélie au sermon. Histoire de la prédication médiévale*, ed. J. Hamesse and X. Hermand (Publications de l'Institut d'Etudes Médiévales. Textes, Etudes, Congrès 14; Louvain, 1993), 103–42.

——— 'La tradition manuscrite des collections de sermons du Cardinal Eudes de Châteauroux (1190?-1273): étude et application', *Revue d'histoire des textes* [forthcoming].

——— 'Du Berry en Curie: la carrière du Cardinal Eudes de Châteauroux (1190?-1273) et son reflet dans sa prédication', *Territoires et spiritualité dans le bas-Berry au Moyen Age* (Châteauroux, 1999) [forthcoming].

Cole, P. J., *The Preaching of the Crusades to the Holy Land, 1095–1270* (Medieval Academy Books 98; Cambridge, Mass., 1991).

Cole, P. [J.], D. L. d'Avray and J. [S. C.] Riley-Smith, 'Application of Theology to Current Affairs: Memorial Sermons for the Dead of Mansurah and on Innocent IV', *Historical Research*, 63 (1990), 227–47.

Constable, G., *Three Studies in Medieval Religious and Social Thought. The Interpretation of Mary and Martha; The Ideal of the Imitation of Christ; The Orders of Society* (Cambridge, 1995).

Cramer, V., 'Kreuzzugspredigt und Kreuzzugsgedanken von Bernhard von Clairvaux bis Humbert von Romans', *Das Heilige Land in Vergangenheit und Gegenwart*, 1 (1939) [= *Palästinahefte des Deutschen Vereins vom Heiligen Land*, 17], 43–204.

D'Amsterdam, B., 'Guibert de Tournai', *Dictionnaire de spiritualité*, VI, cols. 1139–46.

D'Avray, D. L., *The Preaching of the Friars. Sermons Diffused from Paris before 1300* (Oxford, 1985).

Death and the Prince. Memorial Preaching before 1350 (Oxford, 1994).

D'Avray, D. [L.] and M. Tausche, 'Marriage Sermons in *ad status* Collections of the Central Middle Ages', *Archives d'histoire doctrinale et littéraire du moyen âge*, 55 (1981), 71–119.

Delisle, L., *Inventaire des manuscrits de la Sorbonne* (Paris, 1870).

Inventaire des manuscrits latin de N. Dame et d'autres fonds conservés à la Bibliothèque Nationale sous les no. 16719–18163 (Paris, 1871).

Le cabinet des manuscrits de la Bibliothèque Nationale, vol. II (Paris, 1874).

Dictionnaire de spiritualité, 17 vols. (Paris, 1937–95).

Dictionnaire d'histoire et de géographie écclesiastiques [in progress] (Paris, 1912ff).

Forni, A., 'La "nouvelle prédication" des disciples de Foulques de Neuilly: intentions, techniques et réactions', *Faire croire: modalités de la diffusion et de la réception des messages religieux du XIIᵉ au XVᵉ siècle* (Collection de l'Ecole Française de Rome 51; Rome, 1981), 19–37.

Gauchat, P., *Cardinal Bertrand de Turre. His Participation in the Theological Controversy concerning the Poverty of Christ and the Apostles under Pope John XXII* (Rome, 1930).

Gilson, E., 'Michel Menot et la technique du sermon médiéval', *Revue d'histoire franciscaine*, 2 (1925), 299–350 [repr. in E. Gilson, *Les idées et les lettres* (Paris, 1932), 93–154].

Golubovich, G., *Biblioteca Bio-bibliographica della Terra Santa e dell'Oriente Francescano*, 16 vols. (Ad Claras Aquas [Quarracchi], 1906–27).

Goyens, J., 'Bertrand de la Tour', *Dictionnaire d'histoire et de géographie écclesiastiques*, VIII, col. 1084.

Hamesse, J., 'La méthode de travail des reportateurs', *Medioevo e Rinascimento*, 3 (1989), 51–61.

Iozzelli, F., *Odo da Châteauroux. Politica e religione nei sermoni inediti* (Studi e Testi 14; Padua, 1994).

James, M. R., *A Descriptive Catalogue of the Manuscripts of the Library of Peterhouse* (Cambridge, 1899).

Kaeppeli, T., *Scriptores Ordinis Praedicatorum Medii Aevi* [in progress] (Rome, 1970ff).

Ladner, G. B. '*Homo Viator*: Mediaeval Ideas on Alienation and Order', *Speculum*, 42 (1967), 233–59.

Lebreton, M.-M., 'Eudes de Châteauroux', *Dictionnaire de Spiritualité*, IV, cols. 1675–8.

Lecoy de la Marche, A. 'La prédication de la croisade au treizième siècle', *Revue des questions historiques*, 48 (1890), 5–28.

Longère, J., *Oeuvres oratoires des maitres parisiens au XIIᵉ siècle*, 2 vols. (Paris, 1975).

La prédication médiévale (Paris, 1983).

'Quatres sermons *ad religiosas* de Jacques de Vitry', *Les religieuses en France au XIIIᵉ siècle*, ed. M. Parisse (Nancy, 1985), 215–300.

'La prédication et l'instruction des fidèles selon les conciles et les status synodaux depuis l'antiquité tardive et jusqu'au Concile de Trente', *Colloque sur l'histoire de la Sécurité Sociale. Actes du 109ᵉ Congrès Nationale des Sociétés Savantes, Dijon 1984*, vol. I (Paris, 1985), 390–418.

'Un sermon inédit de Jacques de Vitry: *Si annis multis uixerit homo*', *L'Eglise et la mémoire des morts dans la France médiévale*, ed. J.-L. Lemaitre (Paris, 1986), 31–51.

'Guibert de Tournai (d. 1284). Sermon aux chanoines réguliers: *Considerate lilia agri quomodo crescunt (Mat. VI, 28)*', *Revue Mabillon*, n. s. 3 (1992), 103–15.

Maier, C. T., *Preaching the Crusades. Mendicant Friars and the Cross in the Thirteenth Century* (Cambridge Studies in Medieval Life and Thought 28; Cambridge, 1994 and 1998).

'Crusade and Rhetoric against the Muslim Colony of Lucera: Eudes of Châteauroux's *Sermones de Rebellione Sarracenorum Lucherie in Apulia*', *Journal of Medieval History*, 21 (1995), 343–85.

'Crisis, Liturgy and the Crusade in the Twelfth and Thirteenth Centuries', *Journal of Ecclesiastical History*, 48 (1997), 628–57.

'Mass, the Eucharist and the Cross: Innocent III and the Relocation of the Crusade', *Pope Innocent III and his World*, ed. J. C. Moore (Aldershot, 1999), 351–60.

'Kirche, Kreuz und Ritual: Eine Kreuzzugspredigt in Basel im Jahr 1200', *Deutsches Archiv für Erforschung des Mittelalters*, 55 (1999), 95–115.

Markowski, M., '*Crucesignatus*: Its Origins and Early Usage', *Journal of Medieval History*, 10 (1984), 157–65.

Molinier, A., *Catalogue des manuscrits de la Bibliothèque Mazarine*, 4 vols. (Paris, 1885–92).

Moorman, J. H. R., *A History of the Franciscan Order from its Origins to the Year 1517* (Oxford, 1968).

Morenzoni, F., *Des écoles aux paroisses. Thomas de Chobham et la promotion de la prédication au début du XIIIᵉ siècle* (Collection des Etudes Augustiniennes. Série moyen-âge et temps modernes 30; Paris, 1995).

Murray, A., 'Archbishop and Mendicants in Thirteenth-Century Pisa', *Stellung und Wirksamkeit der Bettelorden in der städtischen Gesellschaft*, ed. K. Elm (Berliner Historische Studien 3, Ordensstudien 2; Berlin, 1981), 19–75.

Narducci, H., *Catalogus codicum manuscriptorum praeter graecos et orientales in Bibliotheca Angelica olim Coenobii Sancti Augustini de Urbe*, vol. I (Rome, 1893).

Paravicini-Bagliani, A., *Cardinali di Curia e 'familiae' cardinalizie dal 1227 al 1254*, 2 vols. (Italia Sacra 18, 19; Padua, 1972).

Poschmann, B., *Penance and Anointing of the Sick*, trans. and revised by F. Courtney (Freiburg i.Br. and London, 1964).

Powitz, G., *Die Handschriften des Dominikanerklosters und des Leonhardsstifts in Frankfurt a. M.* (Die Kataloge der Stadt- und Universitätsbibliothek Frankfurt a. M. 2; Frankfurt a. M., 1968).

[Dal] pulpito alla navata. La predicazione medievale nella sua recenzione da part

degli ascultatori (secc. XIII-XIV). *Convegno internazionale di Storia Reli-giosa in memoria di Zelina Zafarena*, ed. G. C. Garfagnini (= *Medioevo e Rinascimento* 3; Florence, 1989).

Renard, J.-P., *La formation et la désignation des Predicateurs au début de l'ordre de Prêcheurs 1215-1237* (Fribourg, 1977).

Riley-Smith, J. [S. C.], 'Crusading as an Act of Love', *History*, 65 (1980), 177-92.

— *The First Crusade and the Idea of Crusading* (London, 1986).

— *The Crusades. A Short History* (London, 1987).

Röhricht, R., 'Die Kreuzpredigten gegen den Islam. Ein Beitrag zur Geschichte der christlichen Predigt im 12. und 13. Jahrhundert', *Zeitschrift für Kirchen-geschichte*, 6 (1884), 550-72.

Rubin, M., *Corpus Christi. The Eucharist in Late Medieval Culture* (Cambridge, 1991).

— 'What did the Eucharist Mean to Thirteenth-Century Villagers?', *Thirteenth Century England IV: Proceedings of the Newcastle Upon Tyne Conference. 1991*, ed. P. R. Coss and S. Lloyd (Woodbridge, 1992), 47-55.

Rusconi, R., 'De la prédication à la confession: transmission et contrôle de modèles de comportement au XIIIe siècle', *Faire croire: modalités de la diffusion et de la réception des messages religieux du XIIe au XVe siècle* (Collection de l'Ecole Française de Rome 51; Rome, 1981), 67-85.

Schneyer, J. B., 'Das Predigtwerk des Erzbischofs Friedrich Visconti von Pisa (1254-77) auf Grund der Rubriken des Cod. Florenz, Laur. Plut. 33 sin. 1', *Recherches de théologie ancienne et médiévale*, 32 (1965), 307-32.

— *Repertorium der lateinischen Sermones des Mittelalters für die Zeit von 1150-1350*, 11 vols. (Beiträge zur Geschichte der Philosophie und Theologie des Mittelalters 43; Munich, 1969-90).

Siberry, E., *Criticism of Crusading 1095-1274* (Oxford, 1985).

Smalley, B., *English Friars and Antiquity in the Early Fourteenth Century* (Oxford, 1960).

Steier, G., 'Bettelorden-Predigt als Massenmedium', *Literarische Interessensbil-dung im Mittelalter. DFG-Symposion 1991*, ed. J. Heinzle (Germanistische-Symposien-Berichtsbände 14; Stuttgart, 1993), 314-36.

Stroick, A., 'Verfasser und Quellen der Collectio de Scandalis Ecclesiae (Re-formschrift des Fr. Gilbert von Tournay, O.F.M., zum II. Konzil von Lyon, 1274)', *Archivum Franciscanum Historicum*, 23 (1930), 3-41, 273-99, 433-66.

Tangl, G., *Studien zum Register Innocenz' III.* (Weimar, 1929).

Tubach, F. C., *Index Exemplorum. A Handbook of Medieval Religious Tales* (FF Communications 204; Helsinki, 1969).

Tugwell, S., 'Humbert of Romans's Material for Preachers', *De Ore Domini. Preacher and Word in the Middle Ages*, ed. T. L. Amos, E. A. Green and B. M. Kienzle (Studies in Medieval Culture 27; Kalamazoo, 1989), 105-17.

— 'De Huiusmodi Sermonibus Texitur Omnis Recta Predicatio: Changing Atti-tudes towards the Word of God', *De l'homélie au sermon. Histoire de la prédication médiévale*, ed. J. Hamesse and X. Hermand (Publications de l'Institut d'Etudes Médiévales. Textes, Etudes, Congrès 14; Louvain, 1993), 159-68.

Tyerman, C. [J.], *The Invention of the Crusades* (London, 1998).

Vicaire, M.-H., 'Humbert de Romans', *Dictionnaire de spiritualité*, VII, cols. 1108–16.

Wolfram, G., 'Kreuzpredigt und Kreuzlied', *Zeitschrift für deutsches Altertum*, 30 (1886), 89–132.

INDEX OF BIBLICAL CITATIONS

I use the abbreviations from the Stuttgart edition of the Vulgate by Weber (see bibliography)

Gn.
i: James II, 15
ii: James II, 15
ii, 17: James II, 16
iii, 4: James II, 16
iv, 14: Gilbert II, 4
iv, 15: Gilbert II, 4
vi: James II, 16, 24
vii: James II, 16, 24
viii: James II, 16, 24
ix, 13: Gilbert III, 19
xi: Eudes I, 18
xii, 1: Eudes I, 17, 18
xxviii, 12: James II, 12
xxix, 20: James II, 24
xxix, 31: Eudes III, 2
xxix, 32: Eudes III, 2
xxix, 33: Eudes III, 2
xxix, 34: Eudes III, 2
xxix, 35: Eudes III, 2
xxx, 6: Eudes III, 2
xxx, 7: Eudes III, 2
xxx, 8: Eudes III, 2, 3
xxxii, 10: James II, 10
xxxv: Eudes III, 2
xxxvi: Eudes III, 2
xli, 43: Eudes V, 7
xlix, 8: Eudes II, 7

xlix, 9: Eudes II, 7
xlix, 10: Eudes II, 7
xlix, 11: Eudes II, 7
xlix, 21: Eudes III, 1, 4, 8, 10, 11

Ex.
v, 1: James II, 16
xii: Gilbert I, 19
xii, 13: Gilbert I, 13
xii, 23: Eudes V, 10
xiii, 9: Gilbert I, 16
xv, 23: Eudes IV, 12. Gilbert III, 9
xxii, 18: Humbert III, 11
xxxiii, 15: Eudes II, 12

Lv.
xx, 27: Humbert III, 11
xxi, 23: James II, 3
xxiv, 16: Humbert III, 11
xxvii, 32: James II, 12. Gilbert III, 3

Nm.
ii, 2: Gilbert I, 10
ix, 9: Gilbert I, 5
xiv, 42: Eudes II, 12
xvii, 10: Gilbert III, 4
xxi, 8: Gilbert I, 5
xxv: James I, 17

272

xxix, 6: Gilbert III, 15
xxxvi, 6: Eudes I, 26
xli, 12: Eudes I, 10

Ps.
v, 6: Humbert III, 15
v, 7: Humbert III, 15
viii, 8: Eudes II, 3
xxi, 15: Eudes I, 7
xxii, 4: Gilbert I, 14
xxv, 5: Humbert III, 15
xxxv, 7: Gilbert III, 22
xxxviii, 4: Eudes I, 9
xxxviii, 13: Humbert I, 1
xliv, 4: Eudes II, 9
xlvi, 3: Eudes II, 3
xlvii, 9: James II, 9
lv, 8: James II, 22
lxiv, 9: Gilbert III, 22
lxviii, 10: James I, 17
lxxiii, 3: Bertrand III, 2
lxxiii, 12: James I, 8, 15
lxxiv, 9: James I, 12
lxxvi, 20: Eudes I, 22
lxxvii, 54: James II, 5. Gilbert I, 20
lxxxv, 17: Gilbert II, 8
lxxxviii, 19: Bertrand II, 3
xc, 13: Eudes V, 9
xcvii, 1: James II, 25. Eudes III, 11
ciii, 4: Eudes I, 13. Gilbert I, 3
cvi, 2: James II, 15
cvi, 3: James II, 15
cxii, 4: Eudes II, 3
cviii, 32: Eudes III, 4
cxviii, 54: Humbert I, 6
cxxvi, 2: James II, 25
cxxvi, 3: James II, 25
cxxxi, 4: James I, 2
cxxxi, 5: James I, 2
cxxxvi, 5: James I, 8
cxxxvii, 5: Humbert I, 6
cxl, 2: James II, 6

Prv.
i, 24: James II, 32
i, 25: James II, 32
i, 26: James II, 32

iii, 18: Eudes IV, 14
iii, 27: James II, 39. Gilbert II, 5
iii, 28: James II, 39
viii, 35: Gilbert II, 1
xvii, 17: James I, 20
xx, 17: James I, 11
xxi, 13: James II, 32

Ecl.
i, 17: Eudes IV, 4
i, 18: Eudes IV, 4
iv, 9: Eudes IV, 5
vii, 27: Eudes IV, 3
ix, 1: Eudes IV, 8

Ct.
ii, 12: Eudes III, 8
ii, 15: James I, 15
vii, 8: Eudes IV, 15
viii, 5: James II, 15
viii, 6: Eudes III, 9. Gilbert I, 15, 16

Sap.
i, 1: James II, 29
ii, 8: Gilbert II, 3
ii, 9: Gilbert II, 3
iv, 7: James II, 28
iv, 13: James II, 28
iv, 19: Bertrand I, 3
v, 13: Gilbert II, 8
vi, 6: James I, 6
x, 17: James II, 27

Sir. (= Ecclesiasticus)
ii, 16: Humbert I, 6
iv, 34: James II, 8
vi, 20: James II, 25
xii, 8: James I, 20
xx, 12: James II, 28
xxiii, 22: James I, 12
xxiv, 22: James II, 12
xxxvi, 6: Gilbert III, 18
xxxvi, 7: Gilbert III, 18
xxxviii, 4: James II, 12
xxxviii, 5: James II, 12. Eudes IV, 1, 10
xl, 1: Eudes I, 27
xlviii, 1: Eudes I, 11

GENERAL INDEX

The names of the five authors of the sermons presented in this book are not included in the index.

278